Bible Studies
Hebrews to Jude

Second Edition

James Malm

ISBN: 978-1-7753510-1-6

Copyright © 2019 James Malm
All Rights Reserved

Dedication

This work is dedicated to the Great God whose house is eternity; the Father and Sovereign of all that exists and the sum of all Truth, Wisdom, Love, Justice and Mercy.

May God's house be filled with children whose chief joy is to be like Him!

Visit Our Website

theshininglight.info

Table of Contents

Hebrews 7

    Introduction 8

    Hebrews 1 21

    Hebrews 2 24

    Hebrews 3 30

    Hebrews 4 34

    Hebrews 5 38

    Hebrews 6 43

    Hebrews 7 51

    Hebrews 8 60

    Hebrews 9 66

    Hebrews 10 73

    Hebrews 11 80

    Hebrews 12 90

    Hebrews 13 98

    The New Covenant Priesthood of Zadok 105

    Physical Sacrifices in the New Covenant 112

James 119

    James 1 120

    James 2 126

    James 3 130

    James 4 134

    James 5 140

First Peter 147

    1 Peter 1 148

    1 Peter 2 157

    1 Peter 3 162

    1 Peter 4 166

    1 Peter 5 170

Second Peter 177

    2 Peter 1 178

2 Peter 2	183
2 Peter 3	190
First John	**203**
Love and the Law of God	204
1 John 1	208
1 John 2	211
1 John 3	219
1 John 4	227
1 John 5	233
Second John	**241**
2 John 1	242
Third John	**249**
3 John 1	250
Jude	**259**
Jude 1	260

Hebrews

Introduction

What is a high priest?

A high priest is a person chosen and appointed by God to mediate between God and the people. We read how Israel at Sinai said, "You go and speak for us Moses. Don't let God speak to us lest we die." So God made Moses the mediator of the Mosaic Covenant.

Likewise, it is Jesus Christ, the very Creator who is the Mediator of this New Covenant between the brethren and God the Father: Which New Covenant is a spiritual covenant because it involves complete reconciliation to God the Father; and ultimately a change from the flesh into spirit.

Under the Mosaic Covenant, various animals were sacrificed which were typical of what Jesus Christ would later do. They served to keep men at peace with God physically within the Mosaic Covenant where there were NO spiritual promises, only promises of physical blessings.

However those animals could not atone spiritually for the sins of even one man. All the animals ever sacrificed could never atone spiritually for the sins of one man; simply because man made in the image of God, man made "after our likeness and in our image," as it is written; is greater than all the animals. Man is of the God kind and animals are of a lesser kind, and therefore all of them together do not amount to a man.

The sacrifice and the killing of animals could not spiritually atone for sin, could not pay for sin. Only the killing of a man can pay the penalty for his sins.

That is, every man must die for his own sin, as it is written (2 Chron 25:4). Nevertheless, the Creator of man could die for His creation which is what the sacrifice of Jesus Christ was all about. And Jesus Christ became our intercessor with God the Father because He went to the Father being a better sacrifice than all the animals slain during the covenant of Moses or the Mosaic Covenant; or before that from Abel.

Jesus Christ brought Himself as our Creator, to be killed and die for the sincerely repented sins of humanity, and in so doing He became our intermediary, our intercessor: He became our High Priest! He stands between us and God the Father. Jesus Christ is the High Priest of the spiritual New Covenant!

1 Peter 1:9 But ye are a chosen generation, [to become] **a royal priesthood, an holy nation**, a peculiar [special] people; that ye should shew forth the praises [in words and deeds of faith] of him who hath called you out of darkness into his marvellous light; **1:10** Which in time past were not a people, but are now the people of God: which had not obtained mercy, but now have obtained mercy.

Today's leaders and ministers are not some kind of Mosaic Levites over God's called out. The Mosaic priests and Levites were only an instructional allegory of the New Covenant priesthood of Melchizedek [Jesus Christ].

The WHOLE BODY of the called out, has been called out to become priests of the High Priesthood of Jesus Christ (Rev 1:6, 5:10).

Elders are merely elder brothers whose job is to help each one of the brethren to develop and overcome, and to learn to become priests and kings. Elders are not to be leading the brethren to follow after themselves and they do not have any authority to bind or loose any part of the Word of God.

In your family do the elder brothers have the right to disannul the words of your father? Of course not; and neither do mere mortal men have the authority to change the teachings of God the Father or any part of the Word of God.

Elders are to be examples of zeal for learning and keeping the whole Word of God and are to be focusing the brethren on the Head of the universe God the Father, and on the High Priest of the New Covenant Jesus Christ!

Jesus Christ the High Priest of the New Covenant enters into the presence of God the Father as a perfect sacrifice and a High Priest able to intercede for sinful humanity and pay for PAST sins sincerely repented of. Christ serves God the Father and He serves man. He intercedes between man and God and establishes harmony between God the Father and man. He brings about peace between God and man because He removes the one thing that separates man from God. And that one thing is sin; it is law breaking.

Isaiah 59:1 Behold, the Lord's hand is not shortened, that it cannot save; neither his ear heavy, that it cannot hear: **59:2** But **your iniquities have separated between you and your God, and your sins have hid his face from you**, that he will not hear.

Christ's sacrifice pays for that law breaking and if we turn away from that law breaking and sincerely repent of all PAST sin and are sorry enough to commit to stop breaking God's Word in future, then Jesus Christ will go to God the Father on our behalf and present the Father with His perfect sacrifice, paying the penalty which we deserved: And we shall be cleansed and we shall be brought into a peaceful, perfect, harmonious relationship with God the Father.

This is the function of a high priest, to intercede between God and man: And that is the function of Jesus Christ who has become our High Priest.

Under any high priest there are other priests to assist him in his ministry.

The priests of the New Covenant are to teach the people what sin is; they are to teach the people to turn away from sin, to stop sinning, to stop breaking the Word of God.

Being priests of the spiritual High Priest Jesus Christ is the job that every the New Covenant called out person is in training for; to bring the whole earth to sincere repentance and to teach all humanity the way to godliness under the High Priesthood of Jesus Christ when he comes!

The priests; the priesthood, are teachers to turn all people toward God the Father, to teach them to repent of their sins and cause them to turn away from their commandment breaking, to cause them to turn toward and embrace God the Father with a whole heart, with passionate zeal and enthusiasm. Teaching all men to love, honor, respect, and obey, to live by every Word of God the Father.

Jesus Christ as High Priest of the New Covenant atones for our sin and then he builds a priesthood, which is now and especially after the resurrection to spirit to help teach ALL people to turn away from sin and stop sinning.

This is what Jesus said when He told His disciples:

Matthew 28:19, Go ye therefore, and teach all nations [Teach them what? Teach them to live by every Word of God!], baptizing them in the name of the Father, and of the Son, and of the Holy Spirit. Teaching them **to observe all things, whatsoever I have commanded you.** [What did He command? He commanded us to live by every Word of God (Mat 4:4). He said, "go and sin no more" and He told the young man, keep the commandments.] **And, lo, I am with you always, even unto the end of the world.**

The whole body of the New Covenant called out is being trained to teach all nations to live by every Word of God.

That is the Gospel, the Good News, that if people stop rejecting God's Word, if they embrace God with a whole heart; and if they are then baptized into God the Father, which is symbolically washing away past sins repented of and destroying those past sins to rise up a new spiritual person, making a commitment to God; to love Him and to live by every Word of God. Then our sins will be forgiven and the sacrifice of our High Priest, Jesus Christ will be applied to us as he enters into the throne room of God the Father and makes intercession for us applying His sacrifice to us.

That is the Gospel. That is the Good News of Salvation

For what is a kingdom without citizens? And the Kingdom of God will have godly citizens who have turned from their rebellion, turned to embrace God the Father with all their hearts; and they will become good citizens; law abiding citizens which is what a kingdom is all about.

As Jesus said to Peter, **"Feed my sheep."** He repeated this a second time, **"Feed my sheep."** Then he repeated it a third time. **"feed my sheep."** And He was not just talking to Peter. He was talking specifically to Peter because Peter had denied him three times therefore He was emphasizing to Peter "You must feed my sheep." But the same commandment is true of all the disciples, all of the New Covenant called out are in training to feed God's sheep.

Parents are to diligently teach their children and are to discuss the scriptures and sharpen one another in the faith, always thinking and speaking of God and his Ways.

Deuteronomy 6:5 And **thou shalt love the Lord thy God with all thine heart, and with all thy soul, and with all thy might.**

6:6 And these words, which I command thee this day, shall be in thine heart:

6:7 And **thou shalt teach them diligently unto thy children, and shalt talk of them when thou sittest in thine house, and when thou walkest by the way, and when thou liest down, and when thou risest up.**

6:8 And thou shalt bind them for a sign upon thine hand [keep them in your deeds] , and they shall be as frontlets between thine eyes [always in our minds].

NO man has the authority to loose any part of the whole Word of God; which loosing is rebellion against the Word of Almighty God!

Malachi 3:16 Then **they that feared the LORD spake often one to another: and the LORD hearkened, and heard it, and a book of remembrance was written before him for them that feared the LORD, and that thought upon his name.**

3:17 And they shall be mine, saith the LORD of hosts, in that day when I make up my jewels; and I will spare them, as a man spareth his own son that serveth him.

3:18 Then shall ye return, and **discern between the righteous and the wicked, between him that serveth God and him that serveth him not.**

The Gospel is not just preaching about a coming kingdom. The Gospel is much bigger than that: It is far bigger than that. The Gospel is about eternal salvation through internalizing the very nature of God through living by every Word of God!

It is about providing loyal, law abiding citizens for that kingdom; the Gospel is about salvation for humanity!

The true gospel is about the sincere repentance of humanity: And even before the repentance of all humanity, comes the repentance of those called out to be first fruits. We need to be fed the unleavened bread of life, which is every Word of God the Father. We need to be taught how to please God, how to serve God.

We all need to be fed the very Bread of Life which is every Word of God Jesus Christ in print; and to internalize God's nature through a diligent faithful loving passionate zeal to live by every Word of God the Father!

And then after the resurrection of first fruits, the changed to spirit chosen will become full priests of the High Priesthood of Jesus Christ, teaching ALL humanity to do likewise and to live by every Word of God.

It is Jesus Christ who is the spirit High Priest of the New Covenant and is our HEAD, and it is God the Father who is the HEAD of Christ! We are NEVER to depart from any part of the whole Word of God!

1 Corinthians 11:3 But I would have you know, that **the head of every man is Christ**; and the head of the woman is the man; and **the head of Christ is God**.

The Gospel is the gospel of sincere repentance, of turning away from sin: And if we turn away from sin we will have a place in the Kingdom of God, in the family of God!

To recap, while in the flesh ALL of the called out are in training to be changed to spirit and become priests of the Priesthood of Melchizedek, the resurrected Jesus Christ.

A high priest is an intermediary, an intercessor between the people and God the Father, and the priesthood under the High Priest, are those people who have been called to help the High Priest to teach all the people to serve God, to turn from sin, and to embrace God and to live by every Word of God.

In other words, the high priest reconciles the people to God the Father by the application of a sacrifice. While, the lower level priests reconcile the people to God the Father by teaching them to turn away from sin and to turn towards God the Father to embrace Him and live by every Word of God.

Why are we commanded to preach repentance when only those that the Father calls can respond positively?

Brethren: We are in "on the job" training!

By preaching the gospel of sincere repentance NOW; we are learning how to preach it when all the people are humbled and WILL respond positively in the Kingdom of God!

We are being taught now as trainees; so that we will be prepared to be resurrected to spirit and then to teach all of humanity as priests and kings UNDER our High Priest, Jesus Christ!

Right now we are miserable failures at preaching the Gospel watering it down out of fear to offend, compromising to try and avoid paying the price for that Wonderful Pearl of the Kingdom; and struggling for the pre-eminence over our brethren instead of just trusting God and going forward teaching sincere repentance and faithful obedience to every Word of Almighty God.

Today we are being allowed to make our mistakes, being allowed to learn through experience: So that we can learn the right Gospel and become prepared and qualified to teach all men as priests of the Most High in the changed to spirit priesthood of Jesus Christ!

All is not lost! God has allowed us to make our mistakes now, so that we will never repeat those mistakes when the chosen are fully inducted into his priesthood. The best teacher is experience, and we are learning the hard way so that we will remember our lessons for all eternity!

The Master Builder is hard at work training and perfecting his priesthood!

The Priesthood of Aaron Restored back to Melchisedec

Jesus Christ becoming a High Priest forever, brings forward a very important question. How could Jesus, being a Jew, a man born of Judah; be a high priest when God through Moses declared that the priesthood belongs to Aaron and Aaron's sons which were of Levi? Jesus Christ was not of Levi, He was of Judah. How could He, Jesus Christ, become a high priest when the high priesthood was given to Aaron?

This is a very important question, very important for the Jews and the Levites because it disenfranchise or ends the Levitical priesthood. If suddenly Levites or the sons of Aaron are no longer the priesthood and there is now a new priesthood, a different priesthood, a priesthood of Judah, then the Levites have lost their position. They have lost the right of the priesthood. So, this is a very, very important question. This question is the reason why the apostle Paul writes his letter to the Hebrews.

Before beginning in Hebrews, I would like to discuss this matter of Melchizedek.

Melchizedek was called a High Priest, or a priest of the Most High God; without beginning of days or end of years, without father or mother. There is more to this Melchizedek than just that. He was a High Priest of the Eternal Father during the days of Abraham. And it is Abraham who paid tithes or a tenth of his wealth to this Melchizedek.

The first thing we need to understand is that the very word Melchizedek means, "He who has the right to rule, he who rules by absolute right." And that applies to Jesus Christ as our Creator. As our Creator Father, the one who gave up his God-hood to become flesh and then die for the people, he has absolute authority and an absolute right to rule over humanity.

The next thing is that Melchizedek was a priest in the days of Abraham [actually since Adam first sinned]. This means that he was a priest of God long before Levi even existed, before Levi's father even existed. Levi was not yet born, Aaron was not born and Moses was not born.

The Mosaic Covenant had not begun and the covenant of the priesthood of Levi had not begun. Yet Melchizedek was already a priest of the Most High God which means that the priesthood of Melchizedek PREDATES the Levitical priesthood and it predates the Mosaic Covenant. The priesthood of Melchizedek came first. It was the original priesthood.

Now, when the Mosaic Covenant ended; and remember the Mosaic Covenant was a marriage covenant between God the Creator who became Jesus Christ and the physical nation of Israel. This was a theocratic marriage covenant as Jesus said, I am your husband and you are rebellious and adulterous wife, and later on, He said, I have put away Israel from out of my sight because of their whoredoms and their adulteries and their rebellions.

Jesus Christ will put away all those who go a whoring after idols of men and false traditions and false teachings today as well! Jesus Christ will cast His Ekklesia into great tribulation (Rev 3:15) for our refusal of any zeal to keep the whole Word of God today?

These men who teach that they should be followed as the deciders because they have the authority of God; will shake uncontrollably and stammer before Christ when he comes!

Matthew 7:21 Not every one that saith unto me, Lord, Lord, shall enter into the kingdom of heaven; but **he that doeth the will of my Father which is in heaven.**

7:22 Many will say to me in that day, Lord, Lord, have we not prophesied in thy name? and in thy name have cast out devils? and in thy name done many wonderful works? **7:23** And then will I profess unto them, I never knew you: depart from me, ye that work iniquity.

7:24 Therefore whosoever heareth these sayings of mine, **and doeth them,** I will liken him unto a wise man, which built his house upon a rock:

Are we to be built on the false traditions of men, or are we to be built on the whole Word of God?

Ephesians 2:20 And are built upon the foundation of the **apostles and prophets, Jesus Christ himself being the chief corner stone**;

At Sinai, the people had entered into a covenant with him by saying, "All that the Eternal has spoken, we will do." And what did the Eternal speak? What did he say? He said, Keep my commandments and live by my Word and I will bless you. I will love you and take care of you. I will watch over you and protect you and provide you with all manner of blessings and lead you into a good land. I will defend you from your enemies and give you all manner of blessings if, this is very important now: If you live by my Word turning neither to the left or the right (Deu 28-31).

The book of Deuteronomy which we read through every seventh year at the Feast of Tabernacles is a farewell message from Moses.

Moses warned the people and reminded them that we must keep God's commandments if we want to receive God's blessing: And if we do not live by every Word of God He will eventually get tired of fighting with us and He will reject us for being a rebellious, faithless, adulterous wife.

God worked with Israel; and He forgave and forgave and forgave until they left Him following their own false traditions instead of being zealous to live by every Word of God and they would not come back and finally even murdered their Husband.

During the past six thousand years those called to Christ in the spiritual New Covenant were not married to him but in a state of testing; the marriage of the Lamb takes place at the resurrection of the chosen in the next few years.

Yet Jesus Christ remained a Husband to physical Israel, even though she was separated from God because of her sins: Until the day, the hour, the moment, came: when He the Husband, Jesus Christ died; and at the second He died the Mosaic Covenant relationship was finally, completely, totally ended because the death of one of the parties to a marriage ends the marriage.

The covenant called the Mosaic Covenant between God and Israel, ended with the death of one of covenanters who was God made flesh. He was her Husband and He was killed. He was dead and that ended the Mosaic Covenant; every part of the Mosaic Covenant ended with the death of the Husband, including that part called the Levitical priesthood and including that part called the high priesthood of Aaron.

With the ending of the covenant, there was no more Aaronic intercession between the people of the Mosaic Covenant and God. There was nothing for them to intercede for; because there was no longer any Mosaic Covenant.

The Mosaic Covenant was over: It ended and the Aaronic intercessor's job was ended; the priesthood of Aaron was over and finished and the priesthood of Levi, that is the priesthood under the high priesthood of Aaron, also ended with the death of Jesus Christ.

The end of the Mosaic Covenant meant the END OF THE PRIESTHOOD OF AARON.

The priesthood then reverted back to Melchizedek [Jesus Christ]; **the very spirit high priest who walked and talked with Adam, Noah and Abraham!**

The whole book of Deuteronomy is a warning from Moses, for the nation to keep its covenant with God and a warning that that COVENANT WOULD END if the people refused to keep its provisions and obey their husband.

Later on Jeremiah was inspired to prophecy that the Mosaic Covenant would end to make way for a new and better covenant.

Jeremiah 31:31 Behold, the days come, saith the LORD, that I will make a new covenant with the house of Israel, and with the house of Judah: **31:32** Not according to the covenant that I made with their fathers in the day that I took them by the hand to bring them out of the land of Egypt; which my covenant they brake, although I was an husband unto them, saith the LORD: **31:33 But this shall be the covenant that I will make with the house of Israel; After those days, saith the LORD, I will put my law in their inward parts, and write it in their hearts; and will be their God, and they shall be my people.**

Jeremiah then goes on to quote God (Christ) as saying:

Jeremiah 31:34: And they shall teach no more every man his neighbour, and every man his brother, saying, Know the LORD: for **they shall all know me, from the least of them unto the greatest of them, saith the LORD; for I will forgive their iniquity, and I will remember their sin no more**. **31:35** Thus saith the LORD, which giveth the sun for a light by day, and the ordinances of the moon and of the stars for a light by night, which divideth the sea when the waves thereof roar; The LORD of hosts is his name: **31:36** If those ordinances depart from before me, saith the LORD, then the seed of Israel also shall cease from being a nation before me for ever. **31:37** Thus saith the LORD; If heaven above can be measured, and the foundations of the earth searched out beneath, I will also cast off all the seed of Israel for all that they have done, saith the LORD.

In saying this, God declared that the Old Mosaic Covenant; must pass away to make room for a New Covenant that would be an ETERNAL AND PERMANENT COVENANT.

This New Covenant is a BETTER COVENANT with better promises and the gift of the ABILITY to keep this New Covenant through the Holy Spirit.

The people who failed to keep the Mosaic Covenant will ultimately be called into a New Covenant and will be given the enabling power of God's Spirit to allow them to keep the New Covenant!

A New Covenant spiritual Israel, a spiritual Judah, made up of people called out of every race into a New Covenant; is being created by God and empowered to live by every Word of God through the Spirit of God.

The priesthood of Levi, of Aaron, the priesthood of the Mosaic Covenant ended with the end of the Mosaic Covenant: And the priesthood therefore reverted back to the priesthood of Melchizedek, who was the Father's intermediary with man from Adam to Sinai.

Jesus Christ [Melchizedek] was a high priest by the exclusive right of being the Creator and later giving up his godhood to die for humanity. He had the right to be the priest of God before Aaron existed, and Jesus Christ has the right to be the New Covenant high priest of God.

He has the right to be the High Priest of God because he made mankind and later He brought unto God the Father His own self as a perfect sacrifice; having overcome all evil and given Himself for His creation.

Therefore He can enter unto God the Father's throne room to make intercession for humanity. In so doing, He performs the function of a high priest; and because He has an absolute right to do this, He fulfils the function of Melchizedek.

That is, Melchizedek had the right, the absolute right, the unchallengeable right to his office as the Father's first and original High Priest the very Creator; and later the risen Jesus Christ has the same absolute right to the New Covenant High Priesthood because he lived a perfect life without any sins and then gave his life for his creation to be resurrected back to the position that he had previously given up to Aaron.

Even during the priesthood of Aaron Jesus Christ was still the spirit High Priest of God, because the Aaronic priesthood was only a physical shadow of the spirit priesthood to teach us about the spiritual priesthood!

Melchizedek's priesthood the High Priesthood of Jesus Christ, existed before the Aaronic priesthood, and God only established a physical priesthood of Aaron as an object lesson to teach us about the spiritual High Priesthood of Jesus Christ. The Aaronic priesthood was only an instructive allegory of the spiritual priesthood of the New Covenant of the true spirit High Priest Jesus Christ!

And it was only natural that when the allegorical Levitical priesthood ended; that the previous true spiritual priesthood of Melchizedek [Jesus Christ] be renewed.

We are ready to begin studying the book of Hebrews.

We are promised that we shall become kings and priests of God and rule on the earth for a thousand years.

But that is only the beginning, a thousand years later the great harvest of mankind will begin and all the masses of humanity who have ever lived and died never having known anything of God, and they will have to be taught during that seven thousand year period called the Feast of Tabernacles; and there will be a priesthood then as well.

Priests and kings, the resurrected saints will be there to teach and rule these people, teaching them to live by every Word of God. It is very important if we want to fulfill our calling as kings and priests that we prepare ourselves, that we think about these things and that we meditate day and night on the Word of God.

David was prepared to be a king over Israel and part of his preparation was a study of the law, a study of the Word of God. Just like David a very large part of our preparation is a very careful study of and a deep meditation on the whole Word of God and on the duties and functions of the priesthood and of being a king.

We need to start preparing ourselves. We need to get ready because the day is soon coming and if we are not ready, if we are not over-comers, and if we are not properly prepared; we may have been called, but we will not be chosen for that responsibility.

To be a king or a priest is an incredibly responsible position and it requires people who are knowledgeable and responsible and who have the character of God and an understanding of the laws of the kingdom.

If we don't study those things, we are not properly preparing ourselves.

It is the job of the ministry to help prepare the people and quite honestly, today's ministry has not done their job.

It is up to us to prepare ourselves; starting by putting God first, putting His Word first, thoroughly studying God's Word and continually meditating upon the things of God and a continual request for the gift of God's Spirit and the gift of wisdom and understanding as we diligently study and work to live by every Word of God.

We need to prepare ourselves. This is not some kind of a game. This is not some sort of a daydream, like a little two-year old dreaming of being a doctor and figuring all he has to do is pick up a stethoscope. There is preparation involved. There is hard work and effort involved.

If we want an office of responsibility, we must be willing to pay our dues and work at preparing ourselves.

Hebrews 1

Hebrews 1:1 "God, who at sundry times and in diverse manners spake in time past unto the fathers by the prophets, **1:2** Hath in these last days spoken unto us by his Son, whom he hath appointed heir of all things, **by whom also he made the worlds.**"

God the Father made not just the earth but all the worlds, by and through the Son. The Son was the Implementing Creator of all things and He did His creating by the Executive Authority of God the Father.

1:3 Who [the one who became Jesus Christ: Hebrew Yeshua] being the [Jesus (Melchizedek) had a bright glory with the Father, and gave the glory of his godhood up to give himself for humanity and then be resurrected back to his original glory.] brightness of his glory, and the express image of his person [being in full unity with God the Father], and upholding all things by the word of his power, when he has himself purged our sins, **sat down on the right hand of the Majesty on high.**

The Son purged all sincerely repented sins by his faithful sinless life and atoning sacrifice, and having been resurrected now sits at the right hand of God the Father in heaven as our High Priest. The Son was the express image [being one in full unity with God] of God the Father, being like the

Father, as He said at His last Passover, If you have seen me, you have seen the Father.

1:4 Being made so much better than the angels, as he hath by inheritance obtained a more excellent name than they,

By his faithful obedience and service to God the Father, Jesus was worthy to be resurrected back to spirit and obtained a more excellent reputation or a more excellent family name, than the angels.

1:5 "For unto which of the angels said he, that is the Father, at any time, You are my Son, this day have I begotten thee? **1:6** And again, I will be to him a Father, and he shall be to me a Son. And again, when he bringeth in the first-begotten into the world, he saith, And let all the angels of God worship him. **1:7** And of the angels he says, Who makes his angels spirits, and his ministers a flame of fire. **1:8** But **unto the Son he says, Thy throne, O God** [The resurrected Jesus Christ would again be called God, after was resurrected back to his former position as a part of the YHVH [the eternal spirit] family that he had given up to be made flesh.], **is for ever** and ever: a scepter of righteousness is the scepter of thy kingdom."

1:9 Thou hast loved righteousness [righteousness is the whole Word of God], and hated iniquity [hated any departure from any part of the whole Word of God]; therefore God, even thy God, hath anointed thee with the oil of gladness above thy fellows. **1:10** And, **Thou, Lord, in the beginning hast laid the foundation of the earth; and the heavens are the works of thine hands.**

This is a direct statement that: You Lord, that is Jesus Christ; in the beginning laid the foundation of the earth; and the heavens are the work of Your hands. Whose hands? The hands of the Lord Jesus Christ. Yes, he did pre-exist His human birth: Yes, he did exist before he gave up his godhood to be made flesh and dwell among men.

Anyone who says that Jesus was a creation of God the Father at the time of His conception is ignorant of the writings of the apostle Paul.

1:11 They shall perish; but thou remainest; and they all shall wax old as doth a garment; **1:12** And as a vesture shalt thou fold them up, and they shall be changed: but thou art the same, and thy years shall not fail.

1:13 But to which of the angels said he at any time, Sit on my right hand, until I make thine enemies thy footstool? **1:14** Are they not all ministering spirits, sent forth to minister for them who shall be heirs of salvation?

No, Jesus Christ was not created at the moment of his conception. He was in fact the Creator of all things. And no, he was not the angel Michael before his human birth as some would claim.

He was God the Implementing Creator [under God the Father, the Executive Creator] who gave up his godhood to be made flesh and being the Creator God, his sacrifice could then atone for all of humanity.

Hebrews 2

God's judgment on unrepentant sinners is certain.

Hebrews 2:1 Therefore we ought to give the more earnest heed to the things which we have heard [in the Holy Scriptures], lest at any time we should let them slip. **2:2** For if the word spoken by angels [God's messengers] was steadfast, [was certain] and every transgression and disobedience received a just recompense of reward.

Every act of disobedience to the Word of God will be reckoned with, will be judged; and every one of those who rebel against any part of the whole Word of God will be corrected if they do not sincerely repent. Unrepentant sinners cannot escape if we sin and follow idols of men, rejecting any zeal to live by every Word of God, which is the Word of our Salvation.

2:3 How shall we escape, if we neglect so great salvation; which at the first began to be spoken by the Lord, and was confirmed unto us by them that heard him;

The Creator gave up his God-hood and came down to the earth being made flesh, to give his life for us and to teach us sincere repentance. His Messiah-ship was evidenced by many miracles from God, and after He had left the earth those who had heard Him proceeded to witness to these things and to tell others about His words and about the way to salvation.

2:4 God also bearing them witness, both with signs and wonders, and with divers miracles, and gifts of the Holy Ghost, according to his own will? **2:5** For **unto the angels hath he not put in subjection the world to come,** whereof we speak

The chosen overcomers and not the angels will rule in the coming age, the coming Kingdom of God; which will ultimately fill the universe and last for all eternity.

2:6 But one in a certain place testified, saying, What is man, that thou art mindful of him? or the son of man that thou visitest him? **2:7** Thou madest him a little lower than the angels; thou crownedst him with glory and honour, and didst set him over the works of thy hands: **2:8 Thou hast put all things in subjection under his feet. For in that he put all in subjection under him, he left nothing that is not put under him. But now we see not yet all things put under him.**

At this time Jesus waits at the right hand of God the Father, until all things [except God the Father himself] are ultimately placed under the authority of Jesus Christ, under God the Father.

Jesus Christ is not only a high priest but will be a ruler holding all things in subjection under Himself under God the Father when the Father sends him to establish his Kingdom. Right now Christ awaits his inheritance of the earth which is not yet put under him fully.

2:9 But we see Jesus, who was made a little lower than the angels for the suffering of death, crowned with glory and honour; that he by the grace of God should taste death for every man. **2:10** For **it became him, for whom are all things, and by whom are all things**, in bringing many sons unto glory, to make the captain of their salvation perfect through sufferings.

Because this Jesus Christ was the Creator of all men, He could die for all men.

It was appropriate and desirable that Jesus Christ lead the way by being the first to be resurrected to spirit; and that He be the one to give His life to then be resurrected into a new body of spirit; so that He can demonstrate and show man that this is possible.

Jesus was without sin, but there were still things that He learned through the things that He suffered: And having learned those things, having learned about the weaknesses of the flesh, learned about temptation, learned about the struggles of the flesh, He could then be a high priest who had empathy for the people.

2:11 For both he that sanctifieth and they who are sanctified are **all of one**: for which cause he is not ashamed to call them brethren, **2:12** Saying, I will declare thy name unto my brethren, in the midst of the church [The "church" is all godly faithful individuals, it is not a corporate entity.] will I sing praise unto thee.

Christ sanctified the sincerely repentant through His sacrifice and He did this to bring us into a relationship with Himself and with God the Father, so that we could all become one in complete unity with God and so that we can all be part of one family: And He is not ashamed to call us His brothers and sisters, His brethren.

2:13 And again, I will put my trust in him. And again, Behold I and the children which God hath given me.

Because we are flesh and blood, Christ became flesh and blood to be like us.

2:14 Forasmuch then as the children are partakers of flesh and blood, he also himself likewise took part of the same [He gave up his godhood and became flesh and blood.]; that through death he might destroy him that had the power of death, that is, the devil; **2:15** And **deliver them who through fear of death were all their lifetime subject to bondage.**

Sinners are subject to the fear of certain death. We all know from the moment that we can think and understand, that we are going to die; and Jesus Christ came to save us from the bondage to sin and death.

2:16 For verily [truly] he took not himself the nature of angels; but he took on him the seed of Abraham.

Christ gave up his godhood and was made a fleshly man, to experience life in the flesh so he could better serve God the Father and his creation

2:17 Wherefore in all things it behoved him to be made like unto his brethren, **that he might be a merciful and faithful high priest in things pertaining to God, to make reconciliation for the sins of the people. 2:18** For in that he himself hath suffered being tempted, he is able to succor or comfort them that are tempted.

The High Priest of the spiritual New Covenant is Jesus Christ. Christ was our Creator made flesh, who gave his life for us and was raised up as our Wave Offering and spirit High Priest.

The Creator God was made flesh and dwelt among men to experience the weakness of the flesh and the temptations of this world and to overcome them; so that He could become a spirit high priest bringing in the best sacrifice of all, the sacrifice of the very Creator God for His creation and so affect a reconciliation of sincerely repentant mankind with God the Father.

By successfully overcoming; He become our Redeemer, our High Priest, our Mediator, our Intercessor, our resurrected living Sacrifice. He is a High Priest, who is able to comfort us; to relieve us from the distress of death and to deliver us from the bondage of sin. He qualified to do this, having experienced life; and experiencing the weaknesses of the flesh and understanding temptation he could have a better empathy and understanding for God's people.

This is about Jesus Christ who became our resurrected Melchizedek High Priest; not Aaron nor any other man or woman.

The New Covenant called out are spiritual priests in training after the order of Melchizedek; and our High Priest Jesus Christ is a priest forever after the order of Melchizedek. Therefore we, each and every one of the called out; are all called out to be kings and priests; called to become priests of the Most High God after the order of Melchizedek.

> **Revelation 5:10** And hast made us unto our God kings and priests: and we shall reign on the earth.

Right now we are only IN TRAINING for the potential of becoming priests and kings; if we overcome and if we are chosen at the resurrection we will become full kings and priests in the resurrection to spirit.

We need to understand that! We need to understand that every single individual is called to be a priest in the first general resurrection to spirit, and we must all learn to live like a priest of God the Almighty Father, under our Melchizedek High Priest, Jesus Christ!

We must learn to keep the commandments of God, learn to set an example of godliness and we must learn to live and teach others to live by every Word of God.

Teaching our families and proclaiming the Gospel of Repentance and the keeping of the whole Word of God today is the training course that the Master Builder has laid out for us, so that we may learn by doing what God will require us to do in his Kingdom!

All of us, every single one of us; from the youngest convert to the most elderly person, from the widow to the macho man are called to become a resurrected spirit priest, if you are called of God.

If we overcome, if we learn to live by every Word of God and turn away from sin and embrace God the Father with a whole heart, then the sacrifice of Christ will be applied to us bringing forgiveness for sincerely repented sin and there is reconciliation with God the Father.

We can enter into a relationship with God if we are called to God; and if we overcome we shall be chosen and we will have a part in the resurrection to spirit.

Just remember that the priesthood has to set a higher standard as a Shining Example of godliness for the people.

Eventually the whole world, everyone; will be following the standard set by Jesus Christ: And we as resurrected priests must also follow the standard set by Jesus Christ and to lead the way by example, even as Jesus Christ led the way by His example.

We need to set the example of avoiding even the appearance of sin. If we go to a restaurant and buy food on the Sabbath or the Holy Days and then try to justify it in our own minds: We are sinning! We are absolutely forbidden to cause others to sin by encouraging them to work on the Sabbath; and we are absolutely forbidden to participate in the sins of others. And we are to avoid even the very appearance of sin.

1 Thessalonians 5:22 Abstain from all appearance of evil.

We are to set AN EXAMPLE OF RIGHTEOUSNESS; AND WE ARE NOT TO PARTICIPATE IN THE SINS OF OTHERS!

If not repented of, if not stopped, any departure from any part of the Word of God will keep us from being chosen to be a priest after the order of Melchizedek, after the High Priesthood of and within the priesthood of Jesus Christ.

We are to be examples of righteousness and teachers of righteousness: Which is living by every Word of Almighty God! We are to preach the Gospel of repentance and the keeping of all of God's Word NOW, to prepare us to do the same thing as resurrected priests of the Most High in the Kingdom of God!

Brethren, the Gospel we preach and our example in zealous faithful living by every Word of God, is so very, very important!

Remember that organizational unity is a counterfeit of the complete unity with God to which we were called! Do not seek unity with men at the cost of unity with God!

Many today are making a god out of organizational unity and declaring that a call to unity with Almighty God is causing divisions in their idol of organizational unity!

God is not the author of division between himself and the faithful brethren; however he is absolutely the author of dividing the wheat from the chaff, the sheep from the goats, the holy from the profane!

If calling to zealously live by every Word of God and complete unity with God is causing organizational divisions; then the teachings of that organization are dividing the brethren from God!

Hebrews 3

Hebrews 3:1 Wherefore, holy [truly godly] brethren, partakers of the heavenly calling, consider the **Apostle** [Messenger] **and High Priest of our profession, Christ Jesus**; **3:2** Who was faithful to Him that appointed Him [Jesus Christ was faithful to God the Father right up to and including dying; consider that his faith was in the fact that the Father would actually raise him up.]. As also Moses was faithful in all his house, [Moses was faithful with all his family, his household]. **3:3** For this man was counted worthy of more glory than Moses [Jesus Christ was given a greater glory than Moses, because Jesus was the Creator, the Builder of the creation and gave his life for his creation; while Moses was the creation of Christ.] Inasmuch as he who hath builded the house hath more honor than the house.

Jesus Christ was the Creator of all flesh.

The Being that gave up his God-hood to become flesh as Jesus Christ was the God that Moses met at the burning bush and the God that Moses knew throughout the period in the wilderness.

Moses knew Jesus Christ. As it is written in another place,

> **1 Corinthians 10:4** And did all drink the same spiritual drink: for they drank of that spiritual Rock that followed them: and **that Rock was Christ**.

Jesus Christ is the Creator God who became the Husband of Israel through a covenant which was mediated by Moses.

Hebrews 3:4 For every house is builded by some man; but **he that built all things is God**.

The one who gave up his God-hood to become flesh as Jesus Christ, was the Implementing Creator who built all of creation.

3:5 And Moses verily was faithful in all his house, as a servant, for a testimony [an example] of those things which were to be spoken after; **3:6** But Christ as a son over his own house; **whose house** [we are the spiritual Temple of God by the indwelling Holy Spirit of God the Father and Jesus Christ] **are we, if we hold fast the confidence and the rejoicing of the hope firm unto the end.**

We become the house of God through sincere repentance, the application of the redeeming sacrifice of Christ and the indwelling of the Spirit of God.

The house of God [the temple] is the place where God dwells. He dwells in His house, His temple, and we become the temple of God if we persevere and overcome and turn to God with a whole heart and if He then comes through the power of His Spirit to dwell within us.

> **1 Corinthians 3:16 Know ye not that ye are the temple of God, and that the Spirit of God dwelleth in you? 3:17 If any man defile the temple of God, him shall God destroy; for the temple of God is holy, which temple ye are.**

WHY will we defile ourselves, the temple of God; by following idols of men and false traditions contrary to the Word of God? When such defilement only brings our destruction?

Hebrews 3:7 Wherefore (as the Holy Ghost saith, To day if ye will hear his voice,

We are commanded not to harden our hearts against a zeal to follow and live by every Word of God; turning away from our Mighty Deliverer like Israel did in the wilderness when they set up false men to take them back into the bondage of sin.

Today most folks follow idols of men and false traditions away from God, as was done in ancient Israel. All those things were recorded for our instruction so that we would not make the same errors; and yet even with having God's Spirit we still commit the same sins on a spiritual level.

3:8 [Brethren] Harden not your hearts, as in the provocation, in the day of temptation in the wilderness: **3:9** When your fathers tempted me [Christ], proved me [Christ], and saw my [Christ's miracles] works forty years. **3:10** Wherefore I [the one who became Jesus Christ] was grieved with that generation, and said, They do alway err in their heart; and they have not known my ways. **3:11** So I sware in my wrath, They shall not enter into my rest.)

Just as those people who covenanted with God at Sinai did not follow, know, and keep the ways of God: We who have covenanted with God the Father and Jesus Christ at baptism, have also strayed very far from the God of Our Salvation. If we do not quickly and sincerely repent we will not be among the CHOSEN in the first general resurrection to spirit.

We are to take heed to be zealously faithful to the whole Word of God lest we should be deceived into departing from God to follow idols of men and their false teachings

3:12 Take heed, brethren, lest there be in any of you an evil heart of unbelief, in departing from the living God. 3:13 But exhort one another daily, while it is called To day; lest any of you be hardened through the deceitfulness of sin.

We are godly ONLY as long as we follow and are totally faithful to God the Father and Jesus Christ; therefore we MUST prove all things by the whole Word of God and hold fast to the Word of God ONLY!

3:14 For **we are made partakers of Christ, if we hold the beginning of our confidence stedfast unto the end**; **3:15** While it is said, To day if ye will hear his voice [listen to, follow and live by every Word of God] , harden not your hearts, as in the provocation.

3:16 For some, when they had heard, did provoke: howbeit not all that came out of Egypt by Moses.

Not everyone that was called out of Egypt sinned in refusing to follow Christ and seeking to return to their bondage to sin; but those who did were destroyed in the wilderness and did not enter the physical promised land.

Many were called out of Egypt and many were destroyed while others [their children] entered into that physical promised land.

It is the same with the spiritual New Covenant called out; those who do not have the works of faith [which is to follow and live by every Word of God without any hint of compromise], those who turn aside from zeal for God to follow idols of men and false teachings away from God: Will not enter that spiritual Promised Land of eternal life in the first general resurrection to spirit.

ONLY the passionately faithful who keep the whole Word of God and follow the Lamb whithersoever he goeth, will be raised up in the first main resurrection to spirit and the Marriage of the Lamb!

God the Father and Jesus Christ are the deciders, the leaders, the HEADS of the faithful brethren; NOT ANY MAN or ORGANIZATION OF MEN!

3:17 But with whom was he grieved forty years? was it not **with them that had sinned**, whose carcases fell in the wilderness? **3:18** And to whom sware he that they should not enter into his rest, but to **them that believed not**? **3:19** So we see that they could not enter in because of unbelief.

We also see that this unbelief had as its fruit, sin and rebellion against God.

God said, "Go into the land." They said, "No, we will not go in." They rebelled against God because they feared and they did not believe God's promises.

This was written for our instruction; for we still do not believe and obey the whole Word of God to this day. We fear to be zealous for learning and keeping the whole Word of God in the same manner that these men feared to enter the land.

In that case and in our case the same issue was lack of faith; like those who could not enter the physical promised land through lack of faith, many of us will not enter the spiritual Land of Promise [eternal life] if we lack the faith to be DOERS of the whole Word of God.

Hebrews 4

Hebrews 4:1 Let us therefore fear, lest, a promise being left us of entering into his rest [the promise of a resurrection to eternal life], any of you should seem to come short of it. **4:2** For unto us was the gospel preached, as well as unto them: but **the word preached did not profit them, not being mixed with faith in them that heard it.**

The gospel was also preached to Israel by Moses and what was that gospel? Even within the Mosaic Covenant it was, REPENT and OBEY God.

The book of Deuteronomy is a farewell message from Moses; and in that book, Moses states over and over, Keep the commandments of God. Keep your covenant with God: which Covenant is that they would obey God and do all that He says, living by every Word of God.

That Gospel did not save those who did not have the works of faith, to believe and obey God; and today the Gospel will not profit anyone who does not have the works of faith to believe God and to live by every Word of God!

If you want to enter into God's rest; that is, to receive His blessing of the resurrection to eternal life, including the blessing of eternal prosperity and peace, we must keep the New Covenant and live by every Word of God.

4:3 For we which have believed [and obeyed] do enter into rest [rest from bondage to sin and death], as he said, As I have sworn in my wrath, if they shall enter into my rest: although the works were finished from the foundation of the world.

4:4 For he spake in a certain place of the seventh day on this wise, And God did rest the seventh day from all his works. **4:5** And in this place again, If they shall enter into my rest.

4:6 Seeing therefore it remaineth that some must enter therein, and they to whom it was first preached entered not in because of unbelief

Only those who have the works of faith to keep the whole Word of God will enter into the resurrection to spirit and that spiritual rest of which the Sabbath is a type; ONLY those who in faith BELIEVE God and his promises and become DOERS of his Word will be resurrected to eternal life.

Those who do not believe and do not have the works of faith to live by every Word of God: Will NOT enter into that rest.

4:7 Again, he limiteth a certain day, saying in David, To day, after so long a time; as it is said, To day if ye will hear his voice, harden not your hearts. **4:8** For if Jesus had given them rest, then would he not afterward have spoken of another day.

Because they remained in sin, they were not given rest through Christ [the promise of a resurrection to spirit].

4:9 There remaineth therefore a rest to the people of God. [or as the margin says:] **a keeping of a Sabbath for the people of God.**

4:10 For he that is entered into his rest, he also hath ceased from his own works, as God did from his.

To cease from all our own labors on the Sabbath and spend time with our Maker, in FAITH; is an allegory of abandoning our own sinful works to be filled with the spiritual things of God.

4:11 Let us labour therefore to enter into that rest, lest any man fall after the same example of unbelief.

The Word of God reveals all our sins, which sins are living contrary to any part of the whole Word of God: We all must work very hard to destroy all sin in ourselves and to internalize every Word of God.

4:12 For the word of God is quick, and powerful, and sharper than any twoedged sword, piercing even to the dividing asunder of soul and spirit, and of the joints and marrow, and is a discerner of the thoughts and intents of the heart.

4:13 Neither is there any creature that is not manifest [nothing is unknown to God] in his sight: but **all things are naked and opened unto the eyes of him with whom we have to do.**

Jesus Christ knows us; He knows our minds and he knows the intents of our hearts. He knows whether we are faithful to him or not and he knows whether we are faithful to God the Father or not.

He knows whether we are filled with passionate love and Christ-like zeal for God the Father's Word, or if we are only going through the motions in a pathetic attempt to try and reap that rest [the reward] without paying the price of FAITHFUL obedience and passionate zeal. God the Father and Jesus Christ know whether we are faithful to the New Covenant of faithfully living by every Word of God to which we are called.

ONLY if we persevere and endure to the end and overcome; will we enter into a rest in the spiritual Promised Land in the resurrection to spirit and eternal life.

4:14 Seeing then that **we have a great high priest, that is passed into the heavens, Jesus the Son of God, let us hold fast our profession.**

Paul reveals that Jesus Christ has now become our spirit High Priest and that Jesus has passed up into the heavens after his resurrection to work in interceding for us with the Father. Therefore, let us hold fast our profession, our belief, our faith and our works of faith.

4:15 For we have not an high priest which cannot be touched with the feeling of our infirmities; but was in all points tempted like as we are, yet without sin. **4:16** Let us therefore come boldly unto the throne of grace, that we may obtain mercy, and find grace to help in time of need.

Yes, we have a High Priest, who gave up his God-hood to be made flesh and who was tempted in the flesh and experienced the weaknesses of the flesh and suffered in the flesh. Therefore, He has empathy for us and He understands the things we have to endure and the things we go through and the problems we have.

God the Father and Jesus Christ will support and succor the faithful who believe and live by every Word of God; and he will reject the faithless who will not keep all of God's Word with righteous zeal.

Jesus Christ is not going to justify our rebellion and our sins and our faults, if we do not sincerely repent of them and STOP sinning.

> **Romans 2:13** (for not the hearers of the law are just before God, but the doers of the law shall be justified [by the application of the redeeming sacrifice of Christ].

Only if we are repentant and sincerely trying to live by every Word of God can we go to God the Father through our High Priest Jesus Christ, asking for forgiveness and for help, asking for the power to overcome, and God will give us that power through God's Holy Spirit.

We can endure, we can overcome, we can beat sin and we can beat Satan through the power of God and through the power of God's Spirit and the Spirit of Jesus Christ DWELLING IN US. But we have to ask for that Spirit. We have to diligently seek it and we have to allow it to dwell within us. Then we have to follow where it leads and we have to do what it guides us to do.

Paul writes in Romans 7:12, that the law is holy and just and good. And we know that God's Spirit is holy, therefore it will do nothing against the Scripture, it will do nothing against any part of the Word of God. It will empower us to live by every Word of God!

Any man or spirit who says, " We keep the commandment because we want to, not because we must" or "this is only physical," or "this is insignificant and not important," or "God will understand my need to do this sin and will overlook it;" is a LIAR and does not have the Holy Spirit of God!

This is a spirit of Antichrist and of Satan! Because, regardless of what we want; the whole Word of God is binding forever and ever!

God's Spirit will always point you to God, because it is God's Spirit! It is the Spirit of God and is not divided from God, being always absolutely consistent with every Word of God!

Hebrews 5

Hebrews 5:1 For every high priest taken from among men is **ordained for men in things pertaining to God, that he may offer both gifts and sacrifices for sins:**

The job of a high priest is to offer sacrifices for sins and to bring us into harmony with God by offering atonement for our sins; and to intercede with God for the people as a mediator between mankind and God the Father.

5:2 Who can have compassion, [a high priest should have compassion] on the ignorant, and on them that are out of the way; for that he himself also is compassed with infirmity.

Because a human high priest is subject to the same things as all the people, he understands the human condition. Because the human high priest also has temptations and sins he must offer sacrifices for his own sins as well as the sins of the people.

5:3 And by reason hereof [because he has sinned, a physical high priest must also offer for his own sins] he ought, as for the people, **so also for himself, to offer for sins.**

5:4 And no man taketh this honour unto himself, but **he that is called of God** [every high priest and true servant of God is personally called by

God], as was Aaron. **5:5** So also Christ glorified not himself to be made an high priest; but he that said unto him, Thou art my Son, to day have I begotten thee.

A high priest is called by God and appointed by God to make offerings for sins on behalf of the people: And because a high priest taken from among men is himself subject to sin, he must also offer atonement for his own sins.

Jesus Christ being without sin had no need to offer any atonement for his own sins, but offered HIMSELF as a perfect sinless offering for the people!

The very Implementing Creator gave up his God-hood to be made flesh as Jesus Christ and gave his life for the people in obedience to God the Father; and because his life had been perfect and without sin he was raised up by God the Father back to the glory which he had had before as a spirit with eternal life; and became a spirit High Priest forever, restoring the order of Melchizedek which existed before Aaron.

5:6 As he saith also in another place, Thou art a priest for ever after the order of Melchisedec. **5:7** Who in the days of his [Christ's] flesh, when he had offered up prayers and supplications with strong crying and tears unto him that was able to save him from death, and was heard in that he feared.

The Being who became the Son respected and obeyed God the Father right up to and including dying for the people, according to God the Father's will.

The prayers of Jesus Christ were heard by God the Father because Jesus Christ obeyed God the Father.

Because the One who became the Son had obeyed God the Father to the death; Jesus Christ was resurrected and raised up to eternal life to return to his previous glory as a spirit High Priest [Melchizedek] to intercede with God the Father for the sincerely repentant.

> **1 John 3:22** And whatsoever we ask, we receive of him, **because we keep his commandments, and do those things that are pleasing in his sight.**

The called out have also been called to become priests of God the Father [under our High Priest Jesus Christ] and it behooves us to be faithful to God the Father just as Jesus Christ was absolutely faithful, pure and without any sin!

Therefore once the sacrifice of the Lamb of God has been applied to us after our sincere repentance and our commitment to "Sin No More," we are to fight with the power of the ultimate overcomer, Jesus Christ; to overcome all sin and to grow towards the purity and holiness of God.

That does not mean that Jesus overlooks our sin as some say! It means that if we seek out his deliverance, he will grant us the Holy Spirit of power to overcome our sin!

Hebrews 5:8 Though he were a Son [Jesus Christ] he learned obedience by the things which he suffered; **5:9** And being made perfect, he became the author of **eternal salvation unto all them that obey him**; **5:10** Called of God an high priest after the order of Melchisedec

Yes, Christ feared, He respected, He trusted, He obeyed God the Father!

He lived by every Word of God Father and we must also obey God the Father and Jesus Christ, who commanded us to live by every Word of God (Mat 4:4).

5:11 Of whom [Melchisedec] we have many things to say, and hard to be uttered, seeing ye are dull of hearing.

Most of today's church leaders and elders are full of pride and will not listen to anyone; yet they know very little as they ought to know it, and are not even able to bear the skim milk of the Word.

5:12 For when for the time ye ought to be teachers, **ye have need that one teach you again which be the first principles of the oracles of God**; and are become such **as have need** [lacking even the milk of the Word]**of milk**, and not of strong meat.

Most of today's church leaders and elders have no understanding of the strong meat of sound doctrine and reject even the milk, in favor of following the false traditions of their idols of men.

We see this in their many false teachings and their refusal to stop falsely teaching that the Rabbinic Calendar was used by Christ for the Biblical Festivals, when it was not even finalized with its postponements until 1178 A.D. They reject the sanctity of the Sabbaths and truth, to cling to lies.

5:13 For **every one that useth milk is unskilful in the word of righteousness: for he is a babe. 5:14** But strong meat belongeth to them that are of full age, even those who by reason of use have their senses exercised to discern both good and evil.

People who are full of God's Spirit, who are mature in the faith and in the things of God, should be able to discern between the Holy and the profane, between good and evil, between truth and falsehood, between right and wrong.

That is the purpose of God's Spirit; which is to lead us to God and to show us what is right and what is wrong as defined by the Word of God.

What WE think is right or wrong is meaningless because we lack the wisdom of God; whatever God says is right, is truly right; and whatever God says is wrong, is truly wrong.

God has the experience and the wisdom to know the difference: And we, by using that Spirit and diligently keeping the whole Word of God will begin to acquire the wisdom of godliness.

The Spirit of God is the Spirit of Truth. It leads us into all truth. The Spirit will guide us into all truth and therefore it will lead us into the wisdom of God.

> **John 16:13** Howbeit when he, **the Spirit of truth, is come, he will guide you into all truth**: for he shall not speak of himself; but whatsoever he shall hear, that shall he speak: and he will shew you things to come.

How then do we know which spirit is of God and which spirit is not of God?

The spirit or person that admits that Jesus Christ is dwelling in us, and that in us Jesus Christ will be doing what he has always done, living by every Word of God and empowering us to also keep the whole Word of God is the Holy Spirit of God.

Any spirit that says that Jesus understands and will overlook our sins, or teaches that God gives grace [mercy] to those who do not STOP sinning, or who compromise with any part of the whole Word of God to follow idols of men and cleave to false traditions: is of Satan the Devil!

> **1 John 4:1** Beloved, believe not every spirit, but try the spirits whether they are of God: because many false prophets are gone out into the world. **4:2** Hereby know ye the Spirit of God: Every spirit that confesseth that Jesus Christ is come in the [to dwell in our flesh by the Holy Spirit] flesh is of God:

We are very young and God has had billions and trillions of years to acquire His wisdom, so we are not going to get it all in a day or in a human lifetime, but we can get a start on it.

If we do what we think is right, that is self-righteousness.

Self-righteousness means being righteous in our own eyes; it means doing what we think is right, or being filled with personal pride, as most of today's Ekklesia leaders are, rejecting truth in order to cling to error!

True, godly righteousness is doing what God says is right: It is living by every Word of God in a godly humility.

Hebrews 6

Hebrews 6:1 Therefore leaving the principles [advancing forward from the basics] of the doctrine of Christ, let us go on [let us grow towards perfection in godliness] unto perfection;

We are to go forward in spiritual growth from the foundation of sincere repentance, baptism, the application of the sacrifice of Christ and God's gift of his Holy Spirit: Growing day by day towards the perfection of true godliness!

. . . not [not continuing in willful sin and having to repent again] laying again the foundation of repentance from dead works, and of faith toward God, **6:2** Of the doctrine of baptisms, and of laying on of hands, and of resurrection of the dead, and of eternal judgment. **6:3** And this will we do, if God permit.

If we go to God and repent and seek His ways and commit ourselves to Him; and then we turn around and try to justify a lack of zeal to keep the whole Word of God, thinking that we are in a "state of grace" after baptism; then when we go back to God for forgiveness, God will say to us:

"No. You have not stopped rebelling against God's Word. I have no time for you until you wake up and STOP sinning, until you wake up and turn from your wickedness and embrace My ways with deeds of faith and not just lip-service."

In truth those who have truly been enlightened and have willfully and deliberately turned their backs on any part of the whole Word of God, have made a mockery of Christ's sacrifice and will not repent until God has mercy on them and thoroughly corrects them and calls them to sincere repentance again.

That is, they cannot be forgiven until they have learned their lesson.

This is not referring to someone whose foot **unintentionally** slips and who is truly trying to live by every Word of God. This is referring to deliberate and willful self-justifying rejection of any part of the whole Word of God as is done in most of today's spiritual Ekklesia.

6:4 For it is impossible for those who were once enlightened, and have tasted of the heavenly gift, and were made partakers of the Holy Ghost, 6:5 And have tasted the good word of God, and the powers of the world to come, 6:6 If they shall fall away, to renew them again unto repentance; seeing they crucify to themselves the Son of God afresh, and put him to an open shame.

Today very many leaders and elders in the Ekklesia are not zealous to keep the whole Word of God, but instead reject God's Word and truth to cling to idols of men and false teachings.

Satan has sowed not only tares but thorns and briers among the leadership who have then led the Ekklesia astray. Yet there is hope for the truly called of God who have been sincerely deceived by these evil men who have crept in unawares (Jude 1), deceiving the called out.

It is through our spiritual laxity that Satan has found his "in" and has sowed his evil ones to divert us from the true path.

There is hope because they have been sincerely deceived, even though they have allowed themselves to be deceived by not being faithful to prove all things by God's Word and to cleave to the Mighty One of Jacob.

Brethren, the hope of today's Laodicean, deceived, lax Ekklesia; is in the severe correction of the great tribulation; so that the called out who are sincerely deceived might find humility before God in their correction, and that they will sincerely repent of following idols of men contrary to following the whole Word of God.

That is the purpose of the tribulation, so that when their fears fall upon them, they will remember that God did not leave them without a warning; and they will quickly sincerely repent and seek Him out with a whole heart!

Then the genuinely called out will be delivered from the thorns and briers of false teachers who today dominate today's spiritual Ekklesia; and the brethren will be delivered from their deceivers into the fertile soil of God's Word and the rain of the Holy Spirit of God will bring forth much fruit!

6:7 For the earth which drinketh in the rain that cometh oft upon it, and bringeth forth herbs meet for them by whom it is dressed, receiveth blessing from God:

Then the thorns and briers of false teachers will be destroyed in the fiery correction of a righteous God, so that the temporarily deceived might be saved out of their hand!

6:8 But that which beareth thorns and briers is rejected, and is nigh unto cursing; whose end is to be burned.

> **John 15:6 If a man abide not in me, he is cast forth as a branch, and is withered; and men gather them, and cast them into the fire, and they are burned.**

If anyone does not abide in Christ, and does not do what Christ commanded, which is to live by every Word of God the Father; they will be cut off and thrown into the fire.

Most of the Ekklesia today are very close to the unpardonable sin of refusing to repent and justifying our own ways, not living by God's ways.

We are in need of very strong correction to torment the flesh so that the spirit may be saved.

This is the condition of the majority of the Ekklesia today; we are always right in our own eyes and we will not turn back to the Eternal with zeal to live by every Word of God. Jesus Christ stands at the door knocking and is ignored by most, because people are consumed with zeal for their own ways and reject any zeal to live by every Word of God (Rev 3:14-22).

We either keep God's Word; which is there to protect all of His children from being abused by one another and to give them the foundation of knowledge and wisdom which will lead to peace, harmony, happiness, prosperity and eternal life; or we are going to be taken and cast out of Christ's assembly of the faithful to God and into the fire of correction.

Paul then addresses the faithful pillars who stand firmly on the foundation of the whole Word of God and who are passionately, zealously diligent; to learn it and to keep it.

Hebrews 6:9 But, beloved, we are persuaded better things of you, and things that accompany salvation, though we thus speak.

God is a rewarder of those who love him enough to learn and to keep his Word and Will! God will reward his faithful with entry into the spiritual Promised Land of eternal life

6:10 For God is not unrighteous to forget your work and labour of love [the love of God is to serve God and to live by every Word of God], which ye have shewed toward his name, in that ye have ministered to the saints, and do minister.

6:11 And we desire that every one of you do shew the same diligence [to be diligent for the godliness of living by every Word of God] to the full assurance of hope unto the end:

Let us not be spiritually lazy and slothful in the Word of God as many have been, being deceived by false teachers who with clever words have deceived many who are not grounded on the sound doctrine of the whole Word of God.

Let us be diligently faithful to learn and to keep the whole Word of God, and to follow men only as they are proved out by the whole Word of God.

6:12 That ye be not slothful, but followers of them who through faith and patience inherit the promises

There is none greater than God the Father, the Head of Jesus Christ and King of the universe; and besides God the Father there in none greater than our espoused Husband and High Priest, Jesus Christ! Therefore follow men ONLY as they follow our Head Jesus Christ, and His Head, God the Father!

6:13 For when God made promise to Abraham, because he could swear by no greater, he sware by himself, **6:14** Saying, Surely blessing I will bless thee, and multiplying I will multiply thee.

Jesus Christ, by patiently enduring and remaining without sin obtained the promise of the resurrection to spirit and eternal life! Let us each and every person also put away all sin and every hint of wickedness to follow the example of our LORD, so that we may also inherit eternal life with him!

6:15 And so, after he had patiently endured, he obtained the promise.

God swore by himself because there is no greater than God; therefore God is the one which we should exalt above all else in our lives; and we should exalt the whole Word of God above the words of any man!

6:16 For men verily swear by the greater: and an oath for confirmation is to them an end of all strife.

God swore to Abraham and to the patriarchs and to the prophets about the coming of Messiah, the Christ to die for the sins of the world and to become our High Priest.

Paul was presenting to the Hebrews and demonstrating to them from the Scriptures that it was prophesied and it was meant to be that the priesthood, the high priesthood of the Mosaic Covenant would pass away; and a better high priesthood with a better sacrifice and better promises would be restored.

We now have a High Priest who can enter into the most holy place, hidden behind the veil, the holy throne of God the Father in heaven, with a perfect sacrifice and present that sacrifice before the Father and say, "I have atoned for this man's sins. He has repented. He is sorry. He has stopped doing these things and I have paid the price which he has earned. Now, he can be reconciled to you.

The sincerely repentant can then be brought into a close harmonious relationship with God the Almighty Father: And we can then enter into the most holy place into the presence of God the Father, because we have repented of our sins and our sins have been atoned for and we have stopped rebelling against God and His Word.

Sincere repentance and the application of the sacrifice of Christ gives us access to the King of the universe, and we may come before Him and seek Him boldly through the mediation of Jesus Christ.

It is Christ's sacrifice coupled with our repentance and our turning away from sin, which provides us with the opportunity for access to God the Father and we can then boldly go to God and ask Him for His Spirit. We can ask Him to empower us to overcome sin, and empower us to go and sin no more.

Sin is the breaking of the Word of God, as it is written: **"sin is the transgression of the law"** (1 John 3:4). And God will empower us and strengthen us with His Spirit so that we can live by every Word of God.

He who overcomes to the end shall be saved. Many are called, few are chosen (Mat 22:14). Those who are chosen will be those who overcome all sin throughout their lives to the very end.

What is overcoming? It is stopping sin and internalizing the very nature of God through the indwelling of Jesus Christ by the Spirit of God. It means overcoming the breaking of any part of God's Word.

This is not a hopeless task. Quite the contrary, it is a task full of hope because Jesus Christ overcame all. He said, "I have overcome the world (John 16:33)." With the help of His Spirit and the Spirit of God the Father; we can also overcome the world like Christ did.

For someone to say that the flesh is weak and in this life we cannot overcome in the flesh **on our own**, is correct; we cannot overcome ON OUR OWN but we CAN overcome by Jesus Christ dwelling within us!

Do not make our weakness of the flesh an excuse to continue sinning. Rather seek and use the power that God gives to us and work hard to overcome all sin.

Yes, the flesh is weak, it is very weak, and the flesh cannot overcome on its own; but God is very strong; and if we sincerely repent, we have access to God and we have access to His strength through the application of the sacrifice and the intercession of our High Priest Jesus Christ.

We need only fully commit ourselves to obey Him and keep every Word that proceeds out of the mouth of the Living God. We need only ask for the application of Christ's sacrifice and then we need only go to God the Father and seek Him diligently, seek His Spirit, seek His wisdom, ask for understanding; and ask for the strength and power of a sound mind to control our actions.

When we do these things, we can overcome. It will take hard effort, but eventually we will overcome the world, if we keep fighting and giving out the effort. Not by our own self nor by our own strength and not by the power of our flesh; but by the power of Jesus Christ through the Spirit of God dwelling in us!

6:17 Wherein God, willing more abundantly to shew unto the heirs of promise the immutability [surety] of his counsel, confirmed it by an oath: **6:18** That by two immutable things, in which it was impossible for God to lie, we [We must be reconciled to God the Father and we may enter in to the Most Holy Place of God the Father only through Jesus Christ our High

Priest who has entered in before us.] might have a strong consolation, who have fled for refuge [we are to flee from the spiritual Egypt of bondage of sin, running to God] to lay hold upon the hope [of salvation by Jesus Christ] set before us:

6:19 Which hope we have as an anchor of the soul [pneuma, spirit], both sure and stedfast, and which entereth into that [God the Father] within the veil; **6:20** Whither [where Christ the forerunner has already entered] the forerunner is for us entered, even Jesus, made an high priest for ever after the order of Melchisedec.

Jesus Christ is our High Priest of the New Covenant. We have a high priesthood of the Creator God, our Maker, and not a human intercessor who was made by that Creator.

Do you see what this means?

All priesthoods of men have been ended and the only priesthood of the New Covenant is the restored priesthood of Melchizedek [Jesus Christ]!

Today, No man and No ministry is to stand BETWEEN the called out and God the Father except Jesus Christ! NO!

It is the proven and faithful Jesus Christ who is now our High Priest, and we must follow God the Father and our High Priest Jesus Christ directly and personally: We are to follow men ONLY as they follow God the Father and Jesus Christ the High Priest to whom we were called by God the Father!

Indeed when the Mosaic priesthood of Aaron went astray in the past, were the people to follow them astray from God? NO! Absolutely NOT! The people were to remain faithful to God even if the human priests of Levi went astray; which was a lesson for us that we should do likewise in regards to today's ministry!

> The priesthood of Aaron ended with the ending of the Mosaic Covenant; and the New Covenant priesthood of Jesus Christ was restored with the Wave Offering presentation to God the Father.
>
> Why then does it say in Isaiah 66 that God will yet take the descendants of Aaron for Levites and priests to serve in the Ezekiel Temple?
>
> Because when Christ comes the Levitical descendants of Zadok will be converted to the New Covenant and they will then serve the New

Covenant High Priest Jesus Christ, in the physical aspects of the Ezekiel Temple!

Hebrews 7

Genesis 14:18 And Melchizedek king of Salem brought forth bread and wine: and he was the priest of the most high God [God the Father].

Melchizedek blessed Abram by God the Father; showing that Melchizedek was not the Father in heaven and was the High Priest and Intercessor between man and God the Father in heaven.

> **Genesis 14:19** And he blessed him, and said, Blessed be Abram of the most high God, possessor of heaven and earth: **14:20** And blessed be the most high God [El Elyon, God Most High; God the Father], which hath delivered thine enemies into thy hand. And he [Abram] **gave him tithes of all.**

Notice that Abram recognizes this Being and immediately acknowledges his authority over Abram by giving him a tithe of all. There was no: "Who are you?" or "Why should I give to you what came to me at the risk of life?" No, there was only an immediate recognition of authority and an immediate submission to that authority. From this it is clear that Abram had experience with and KNEW this Being from previous encounters.

We know that the Implementing Creator Melchizedek [who later gave up his godhood to become flesh as Jesus Christ] became the Intercessor between man and God the Father after man sinned and the Creator walked with and taught Adam, Abel and Cain and was likely the Being seen by Noah and many others.

The Implementing Creator who later gave up his Godhood to become flesh as Jesus Christ, visited Abram several times manifesting himself as Melchizedek and Abram had no surprise at seeing him. That was because the Creator probably appeared to Abram as Melchizedek on multiple occasions and was well known to Abram.

This is the first place that tithes are mentioned in the Bible, and here Abram gives this Melchizedek tithes of the spoil of battle; showing that while Israel was later specifically commanded to tithe on agriculture [because they were an agricultural people] produce: God's servants are entitled to a tithe of ALL increase.

Who made you and the earth you stand on? Who made the air you breath? Who gave you the wisdom and skill to make clothes or cars? Who provided the metals and minerals you utilize?

To claim that God only requires tithes in payment for the land used agriculturally; and then ignore that God is the maker, and overseer, and owner of ALL things is myopic and self-delusional.

Shall we say then, that the potter, the tailor, or the inn keeper need not go up to the Feast's of God because they have no tithe on their labours? Shall we say that God is not equitable; taking only from one endeavor and not from others?

Israel was at that time an agrarian society so God commanded them in agrarian terms; but the principle that we are to acknowledge the gifts of God to us, is not limited to agricultural things at all!

Abram gave a tenth of the spoil to acknowledge that God had given him victory with safety, and had delivered his nephew will all the captives!

The law plainly says that the laborer is worthy of his wages, no matter what his job; and that those who serve in the gospel should have a reasonable living from their work.

Tithing on all our net increase acknowledges God the Father [and the Being who became the Son] as ALL in all; the fountain of all knowledge and wisdom, and all of creation!

> **Genesis 14:18** And Melchizedek king of Salem brought forth bread and wine: and he was the priest of the most high God [The Most High God; who is God the Father.].

The name Melchizedek means: "king of righteousness" consisting of two words, Melek-King, Zedek-Righteousness; which is the interpretation of this name. This person was also known as the King of Salem meaning king of peace.

The whole Word of God is the righteousness of God defined; and the Word and Righteousness of God brings peace; first between man and God and then between godly people.

Therefore this Melchizedek as king of peace and the king of righteousness was the spirit High Priest interceding between God and humanity before the physical priesthood of Aaron!

Melchizedek is spelled with a "Z" from the Hebrew; and with an "S" when translated from the Greek.

Hebrews 7:1 For this Melchisedec, king of Salem [peace], priest of the most high God, who met Abraham returning from the slaughter of the kings, and blessed him; **7:2** To whom also Abraham gave a tenth part of all; first **being by interpretation King of righteousness, and after that also King of Salem, which is, King of peace**;

Paul identifies this Melchizedek further, saying that he was without beginning or end; which is the definition of the God [Elohim] family itself; for even the angels had a beginning. Paul clearly identifies Melchizedek as a member of the God family: And this Melchizedek was the "priest of the most high God [God the Father in heaven]."

Paul clearly writes that Melchizedek the Implementing Creator, who later gave up his godhood and became flesh as Jesus Christ, was the High Priest between God the Father in Heaven and those called out from Abel.

The Implementing Creator who gave up his godhood to be made flesh as Jesus Christ was the true spirit High Priest between God the Father and the spiritually Called Out from Abel to the present.

The exception to this was the time during which he gave up his office to be made flesh as Jesus Christ

7:3 Without father, without mother, without descent, having neither beginning of days, nor end of life; but made [was] **like unto the Son of God;** abideth a priest continually.

The word Melchisedec means ruler or king or high priest by divine right; having an absolute authority and an absolute right to that office.

Melchisedec is here referred to as the king of Salem, the word Salem meaning peace, referring to him as God the Father's High Priest bringing reconciliation and peace between mankind and God the Father.

Melchisedec was King of Righteousness and King of Peace; and both of those titles fit and apply to Jesus Christ.

7:4 Now consider how great this man was, unto whom even **the patriarch Abraham gave the tenth of the spoils** [to Melchizedek]. **7:5** And verily they that are of **the sons of Levi, who receive the office of the priesthood, have a commandment to take tithes of the people according to the** [Mosaic] **law**, that is, [to take tithes of Israel] of their brethren, though they come out of the loins of Abraham:

7:6 But he whose descent is not counted from [Melchisedec who became flesh as Jesus Christ was not descended from Levi, yet he took tithes from Abraham BEFORE Levi existed.] them received tithes of Abraham, and blessed him [Melchizedek blessed Abraham and his descendants including Levi.] that had the promises. **7:7** And without all contradiction the less is blessed of the better.

Therefore although he was not a descendant of Levi, Jesus Christ who was Melchisedec before he gave up his godhood to be made flesh, received tithes before Levi existed.

Levi received tithes of Israel; but before Levi was ever born, Jesus Christ in the form of Melchisedec received tithes of Abraham Levi's progenitor.

Therefore Levi payed tithes to Christ [Melchisedec] through his ancestor Abraham; which means that we are to tithe to the New Covenant priesthood of Melchisedec [Jesus Christ] today just as Abraham did!

7:8 And here men that die receive tithes; but there he receiveth them, of whom it is witnessed that he liveth. **7:9** And as I may so say, **Levi also, who receiveth tithes, payed tithes in Abraham. 7:10 For he was yet in the loins of his father** [Abraham], **when Melchisedec met him** [received tithes of Abraham].

7:11 If therefore perfection were by the Levitical priesthood, (for under it the people received the law,) what further need was there that another priest should rise after the order of Melchisedec, and not be called after the order of Aaron?

The law concerning the priesthood of Aaron was annulled by the end of the Mosaic Covenant [with the death of the Husband of that Covenant], and **the pre-existing priesthood of Melchisedec** [Jesus Christ] **was restored.**

7:12 For the priesthood being changed, there is made of necessity a change also of the law.

The Mosaic Covenant placed a descendant of Levi as High Priest and when the Mosaic Covenant ended by the death of the Husband; a new spiritual Covenant was offered to the called out of all nations to become a spiritual Israel with a new High Priest; not of Aaron, but of Melchisedec [the resurrected Jesus Christ]; the Melchisedec High Priesthood being restored after the end of the temporary physical Aaronic high priesthood.

Jesus Christ [Melchisedec] was the God Being who gave up his God-hood to be made flesh and placed in the womb of Mary his surrogate mother to be born into Judah.

7:13 For he of whom these things are spoken pertaineth to another tribe [Judah], of which no man gave attendance at the altar. 7:14 For it is evident that our Lord sprang out of Juda; of which tribe Moses spake nothing concerning priesthood.

7:15 And it is yet **far more evident: for that after the similitude of Melchisedec there ariseth another priest, 7:6 Who is made, not after the law of a carnal commandment, but after the power of an endless life. 7:17** For he testifieth, **Thou art a priest for ever after the order of Melchisedec.**

The priesthood of Aaron could only mediate the Mosaic Covenant which had no spiritual promises and no promise of eternal life. Therefore there was a need for a better spiritual High Priest to mediate a spiritual New Covenant with better promises.

7:18 For **there is verily a disannulling of the commandment going before** [the Mosaic Covenant] **for the weakness and unprofitableness thereof.**

The spiritual New Covenant gives humanity a better hope [of eternal life as spirit] and therefore a better [a spirit] High Priest to reconcile us to God the Father, bringing the gift of the Holy Spirit and eternal life to all who would live by every Word of God.

A better New Covenant with a better sacrifice than animals, with better promises and with the empowerment of the Holy Spirit to enable us to

KEEP that New Covenant; is now overseen by a New Covenant spiritual and eternal High Priesthood of Melchizedek [Jesus Christ].

The Mosaic Covenant and the priesthood of Aaron was an instructional allegory of the New Covenant and the spiritual priesthood of Melchisedec [Jesus Christ], which reconciles the sincerely repentant with God the Father.

7:19 For the law made nothing perfect, but **the bringing in of a better hope did; by the which we draw nigh** [are reconciled to God the Father] **unto God.**

The New Covenant makes one perfect through sincere repentance, the application of the atoning sacrifice of the Lamb of God and the indwelling of God's Spirit, married to a dedicated zeal to become like God our Father in heaven.

Future law keeping makes nothing perfect, because doing so in future does not atone for PAST sin.

The physical sacrifices of the Mosaic Covenant were an allegorical type of the spiritual New Covenant, but could not reconcile anyone spiritually to God the Father since the life of a person is worth more that the life of animals.

Only the sacrifice of the Creator himself could reconcile the sincerely repentant to God the Father; for the wages of sin [which is death] must be paid.

7:20 And inasmuch as not without an oath he [Jesus Christ] was made [High] priest: **7:21** (For those priests [of Levi] were made without an oath; but this with an oath by him that said unto him, The Lord sware and will not repent, Thou art a priest for ever after the order of Melchisedec:) **7:22** By so much was Jesus made a surety of a better testament [Being restored as the spirit High Priest of God the Father and becoming the High Priest of the New Covenant].

Because the men of Levi died in their generations, there was a continual change of high priests; but the High Priesthood of Jesus Christ is eternal, existing from Adam as Melchisedec, right to the present; except for the period when Christ gave up his position to be made flesh.

Indeed the physical Mosaic high priest and priesthood served the spirit High Priesthood of Melchisedec [except when Christ was in the flesh], and Melchisedec [Jesus Christ] was the spiritual Husband (Jer 31:32) of Israel that Levi served!

7:23 And they truly were many priests, because they were not suffered to continue by reason of death: **7:24** But this man, because he continueth ever, hath an unchangeable priesthood. **7:25** Wherefore he is able also to save them to the uttermost that come unto God by him, seeing he ever liveth to make intercession for them.

7:26 For such an [spiritual] high priest [was suitable as an eternal High Priest] became us, **who is holy, harmless** [blameless]**, undefiled, separate from sinners** [without sin and set apart from all sinners]**, and made higher than the heavens;**

Jesus Christ the eternal High Priest offered up himself as the Creator of Humanity, who being worth more that all humanity and being without any sin; was a perfect sacrifice and needed to be offered only once to atone for all the sins of all humanity: While the physical sacrifices of animals only served to keep people in the physical Mosaic Covenant and had NO spiritual promises and animals needed to be killed on a continual basis.

7:27 Who needeth not daily, as those high priests, to offer up sacrifice, first for his own sins, and then for the people's: for this he did once [being the perfect sinless sacrifice of the Creator himself], when he offered up himself.

7:28 For the law maketh men high priests which have infirmity; but the word of the oath, which was since the law, maketh the Son, who is consecrated [an eternal spirit High Priest] for evermore.

Our High Priest, Jesus Christ, now lives forever and is able to make continual intercession for us for all eternity: And His sacrifice being perfect, no longer needs to be made again and again. He doesn't have to be killed day after day, year after year. No!

However, every time someone repents, that perfect sacrifice needs to be RE-APPLIED to the repentant sinner.

The difference is in the actual dying as opposed to the actual applying of the sacrifice. They are two different things.

Christ died, regardless of whether any man ever repents or not. He was dead and he was resurrected. That has nothing to do with whether people repent, or turn from sin or not. However, when people do sincerely repent, the sacrifice is now available to be applied to them.

The priesthood of Aaron has been superseded by the high priesthood of Jesus Christ, who is the High Priest forever after the order of Melchisedec. That is, Jesus Christ is the King of Peace between man and God the Father and the eternal High Priest of the eternal New Covenant.

He is our High Priest of the New Covenant for all eternity. He has superseded the priesthood of Aaron; and in doing this, he has fulfilled the promises that God made to the patriarchs and the prophets (Jeremiah 31:31-37).

When we see the words "forever" and "without beginning or end" and we begin to take a deep prayerful think on Hebrews 7 we end up with some remarkable understanding.

Jesus Christ was the Implementing Creator and he began conversing with man as soon as man was created, for on the seventh day the Creator and Adam and Eve spent the day together.

Then we have the record of some of the various conversations of the Creator with Adam and Eve, Cain, Abel, the ancients including Noah, right up to Abraham, Isaac, Jacob and beyond.

In all these things the Being Melchizedek who later became flesh as Jesus Christ, was speaking with human beings in place of [as a High Priest of] God the Father.

In the time of Abraham the Creator Jesus Christ was known by the name of Melchisedec, and when he presented himself to Moses he revealed himself as The Great "I Am" which means the same thing as Melchisedec: "the forever existing one." Without beginning or end, without father or mother!

We can see that Melchisedec [the Creator who later became flesh as Jesus Christ] was the spirit High Priest [appearing in human form] between God the Father and all humanity from Adam, appearing in the form of a man.

It was when he revealed himself in a part of his glory on Mt Sinai that the people demanded a human high priest or mediator; and the priesthood of Aaron was given to Israel to be an allegory of the High Priesthood of the Creator Melchisedec, who gave up his God-hood to become fully flesh as Jesus Christ.

The lesson in this is that the Creator Melchisedec who became Jesus Christ was a spiritual High Priest coming between humanity and God the Father: from the very beginning of Creation!

The physical priesthood of Aaron was only a temporary expedient for the Mosaic Covenant; and even in **the Mosaic Covenant: the priesthood of Aaron was really serving the spirit High Priest, the Creator Melchisedec, who was the Husband of Israel and later became flesh as Jesus Christ.**

Both the Mosaic Covenant and the Aaronic priesthood were instructional allegories of the spiritual New Covenant and its spiritual High Priest, who was/is the Implementing Creator; and in the Mosaic Covenant and the priesthood of Aaron the people actually served [whenever they were faithful] Jesus Christ as their Husband.

The physical high priest acted out the function of mediator between man and God which is the role of Jesus Christ as the ONLY true Mediator and Intercessor between man and God.

> **1 Timothy 2:5** For **there is one God, and one mediator between God and men, the man** [while in the flesh] **Christ Jesus;**

Melchisedec had given up his Godhood to be made flesh as Jesus Christ; and then died for the sins of the world and was later resurrected back to his former glorious Godhood, replacing the Aaronic priesthood and restoring the priesthood of Melchizedek!

Every one of God's called out, are called out to become priests of the high priesthood of Jesus Christ [Melchizedek]; and we are all in training to become priests under our spiritual High Priest Jesus Christ; to support Him, to assist Him and to become laborers to help him bring in the harvest of humanity after being chosen for that office in the resurrection to spirit!

Hebrews 8

Hebrews 8:1 Now of the things which we have spoken **this is the sum**: We have such an high priest, who is set on the right hand of the throne of the Majesty in the heavens; **8:2** A minister of the sanctuary, and of the true tabernacle, which the Lord pitched, and not man.

The called out to the New Covenant have an eternal High Priest who sits at the right hand of God the Father in heaven; Our High Priest [and priesthood] is not of Aaron, He is the Creator/Melchisedec; the risen Christ!

8:3 For every high priest is ordained to offer gifts and sacrifices: wherefore it is of necessity that this man have somewhat also to offer.

If Jesus Christ were still a man in the flesh he would not be a priest because he was not a son of Aaron, but because he lived a perfect sinless life and gave his life as an atoning sacrifice for his creation.

Jesus Christ was raised up from death in the flesh and RESTORED to the glory that he had before giving up his godhood to be made flesh, RESTORING the eternal High Priest of Melchizedek; while the Mosaic Covenant and its Aaronic priesthood ended because of the death of the Mosaic Covenant Husband of Israel.

John 17:5 And now, O Father, glorify thou me [together] with thine own self **with the glory which I had with thee before the world was.**

Hebrews 8:4 For if he were on earth [still in the flesh], he should not be a priest, seeing that there are priests that offer gifts according to the law [the Mosaic Covenant]:

The law called the Law of Moses which is really the Law of God, said that sacrifices should be offered and that the physical offerings should be administered by the physical priests who are the descendants of Aaron.

Once that Mosaic Covenant and Aaronic priesthood was ended by the death of the Husband of Israel, Jesus Christ, who was not a descendant of Aaron; this Jesus Christ was resurrected to spirit and returned to his former glory as Melchizedek the eternal spirit High Priest.

8:5 Who [The Aaronic priesthood and the physical tabernacle/temple service were an allegory of the heavenly High Priesthood of the Creator, Melchisedec [Jesus Christ] ; who became flesh and gave himself for his creation.] **serve unto the** [as an] **example and shadow of heavenly things**, as Moses was admonished of God when he was about to make the tabernacle: for, See, saith he, that thou make all things according to the pattern shewed to thee in the mount.

8:6 But now hath he [the physical Jesus Christ] obtained a more excellent ministry [a better priesthood than Aaron], by how much also he is the mediator [the resurrected Jesus Christ has become the High Priest (Mediator) of the New Covenant] of a better covenant, which was established upon better promises.

The Mosaic Covenant was only physical and had only physical promises, but the New Covenant is spiritual and offers the promise of true effectual atonement to all sincerely repentant persons, reconciliation with God the Father and the gift of God's Holy Spirit and eternal life.

If the Mosaic Covenant had been perfect and could bring reconciliation between God the Father and the people, and give the gift of God's Spirit and eternal life; it would not need to have been superseded by a New Covenant which accomplishes those things.

8:7 For if that first covenant had been faultless, then should no place have been sought for the second.

Jeremiah 31:31: Behold, the days come, saith the Lord, that I will make a new covenant with the house of Israel, and with the house of Judah:

31:32 Not according to the covenant that I made with their fathers in the day that I took them by the hand to bring them out of the land of Egypt; which my covenant they brake, although I was an husband unto them, saith the Lord:

31:33 But this shall be the covenant that I will make with the house of Israel; After those days, saith the Lord, I will put my law in their inward parts, and write it in their hearts; and will be their God, and they shall be my people.

Hebrews 8:8 For finding fault with them, he saith, Behold, the days come, saith the Lord, when I will make a new covenant with the house of Israel and with the house of Judah: **8:9** Not according to the covenant that I made with their fathers in the day when I took them by the hand to lead them out of the land of Egypt; because they continued not in my covenant, and I regarded them not, saith the Lord.

How is it that every person shall know the Eternal?

> The answer is in **Joel 2:28,** And it shall come to pass afterward [after Christ's coming], that I will pour out my spirit upon all flesh;

> Some have been called out and given God's Spirit since Abel; and on Pentecost 31 A.D. there was an official small foretaste and precursor of a soon coming future Pentecost when God's Spirit will be poured out on ALL flesh!

> And after the day of the Lord has come, **Joel 2:32** It shall come to pass that whosoever shall call upon the name of the Eternal shall be delivered.

Hebrews 8:10 For **this is the covenant** that I will make with the house of Israel after those days, saith the Lord; **I will put my laws into their mind, and write them in their hearts: and I will be to them a God, and they shall be to me a people**: **8:11** And they shall not teach every man his neighbour, and every man his brother, saying, Know the Lord: for all shall know me, from the least to the greatest.

God's Word and Law will be written on the hearts and in the minds of people through the power of the Holy Spirit which is given to those who obey God.

Acts 5:32 And we are his witnesses of these things; and so is also **the Holy Ghost, whom God hath given to them that obey him**.

The New Covenant is that the law of God will be written on the hearts and minds of sincerely repentant people who commit themselves to "sin no more" (John 8:11). They will be reconciled to God the Father through sincere repentance, a commitment to "sin no more" and the application of the sacrifice of Christ; and then they will be empowered to obey and live by every Word of God through the gift of the Holy Spirit of God.

Anyone who teaches that after baptism we are filled with some kind of sentimental emotional feel good that they mistakenly call "love" and come into a state of grace where our future sins are overlooked; is ignorant and a false teacher.

The difference between the Mosaic Covenant and the New Covenant is that under the New Covenant, there is a real, genuine sacrifice for sincere repentance from sin, a real genuine reconciliation and relationship with God the Father, and a real empowerment to overcome and "sin no more" through the power of the Holy Spirit of God: resulting in a real spiritual conversion to become of the same mind and Spirit as God the Father and Jesus Christ: Which brings the gift of the resurrection to eternal life.

Hebrews 8:12 For I will be merciful to their unrighteousness, and their sins and their iniquities will I remember no more. **8:13 In that he saith, A new covenant, he hath made the first old.** Now that which decayeth and waxeth old is ready to vanish away.

The Old Covenant, the Mosaic Covenant, including the priesthood of Aaron; has vanished away; it ended with the death of one of the parties to that marriage covenant.

To recap:

As soon as sin entered in, the Implementing Creator Jesus Christ [Melchisedec] stood between the called out and God the Father as their Mediator [High Priest]; looking forward to his later physical life, sacrifice and resurrection.

The Creator, Melchisedec who became flesh as Jesus Christ, became and was the Husband of Israel from Sinai to the death of Christ in the flesh, and during that period Israel was given the Mosaic Covenant and the physical Aaronic priesthood to teach us about the spiritual High Priesthood of Melchisedec [Jesus Christ].

The priesthood of Aaron was a temporary physical instructional allegory to teach us about the spiritual High Priesthood of Jesus Christ; and even the priesthood of Aaron served [when faithful] the Husband of Israel [the Creator who became flesh as Jesus Christ].

When it became time for the Creator to be made flesh and be sacrificed for sins, the Mosaic Marriage ended with the death of the Husband of Israel, and the temporary physical instructional allegory of the Aaronic priesthood also ended; opening the way for the restoration of the resurrected to spirit High Priesthood of Melchisedec the Creator [Jesus Christ].

The Mosaic Covenant was mediated by Moses and a priesthood of Aaron; and that covenant was wholly physical with physical promises of physical blessings only, as an allegory of the spiritual priesthood of Jesus Christ in the spiritual New Covenant with the spiritual promise of a resurrection to eternal life as a spirit being.

The Mosaic Covenant ended with the death of one of the covenanters which was the Husband, Jesus Christ [Melchisedec in the flesh]. The end of the Mosaic Covenant being prophesied long before by Jeremiah (Jer 31), because that particular covenant could not provide the spiritual promise of eternal life.

There were physical blessings and promises under that Mosaic Covenant, but there was nothing spiritual involved. There was no real atonement for sin to reconcile people with God the Father. The blood of goats and lambs and bullocks could only atone for the physical acts of breaking the physical Mosaic Covenant; such physical sacrifices could NOT reconcile people to God the Father on a spiritual level.

Therefore, it was necessary and it was planned from the very beginning that Melchisedec would give up his godhood and be made flesh as Jesus Christ; and the very Creator would be sacrificed for the sins of mankind, reconciling the sincerely repentant to God the Father establishing a New Covenant which would supersede the Mosaic Covenant.

This New Covenant would have a different High Priest and a different priesthood than Aaron, restoring the priesthood of Melchisedec; as well as the fact that God's laws would be written in the hearts and minds of men through the gift of the Holy Spirit; and a new and better sacrifice that would reconcile men to God on a spiritual level, enabling them to enter a New SPIRITUAL Covenant with God.

The sacrifice of the very Creator would completely, totally; atone for the sincerely repented sins of humanity and reconcile the sincerely repentant to God the Father.

The Creator God gave up his God-hood to be made flesh, and once the Creator / Melchisedec became "God made flesh" as Jesus Christ [Hebrew: Yeshua Mashiach] completed his mission to live a perfect life and be sacrificed for those who had or would sincerely repent: He was resurrected by God the Father and returned to his previous glory!

Then he ascended to God the Father as our Wave Offering to become our High Priest, spiritual Mediator and Intercessor for us with God the Father for all eternity!

Today the physical Mosaic Covenant and its Aaronic priesthood is passed away; and the High Priesthood of Melchisedec [Jesus Christ] is re-established!

ALL of the called out not just elders, have been called into the Priesthood of Melchisedec [Jesus Christ] to become priests after the order of Melchisedec [Jesus Christ] forever; IF we overcome and are chosen!

Brethren the eternal Priesthood of Melchisedec [Jesus Christ] is the heritage, the birthright and the calling, of ALL the spiritual Ekklesia if we are faithful to our High Priest Melchisedec [Jesus Christ] and to God the Father!

With such a birthright of calling from God Almighty, why would anyone stray to follow idols of men [false teachers] contrary to any part of the whole Word of God?

> **1 Thessalonians 5:21 Prove all things; hold fast that which is good.**

Only the whole Word of God is good!

Hebrews 9

The physical tabernacle was built according to the pattern that God showed Moses, which pattern was a movable type of the heavenly Temple. The structural design as well as the furnishings were typical of the heavenly Temple of God the Father and were highly symbolic.

Hebrews 9:1 Then verily the first covenant had also ordinances of divine service, and a worldly sanctuary. **9:2** For there was a tabernacle made; the first, wherein was the candlestick [The oil burning in the seven branched lamp represents the oil of the Holy Spirit shining brightly in godly persons, producing the light of a godly example.], and the table and the [unleavened] showbread [The Bread of Presence represents the presence of the sinless Christ, the Bread of Life.]; which is called the sanctuary.

Behind the veil which represents sin dividing the people from the presence of God the Father was the Most Holy Place, picturing the throne room of God the Father.

9:3 And after the second veil, the tabernacle which is called the Holiest of all; **9:4** Which had the golden censer, and the ark of the covenant [the throne of God the Father] overlaid round about with gold, wherein was the golden pot that had manna, and Aaron's rod that budded, and the tables of the covenant; **9:5** And over it the cherubims of glory shadowing the mercyseat; of which we cannot now speak particularly.

After the tabernacle and later the physical Jerusalem temple were dedicated, the physical Mosaic priests went in to the first part of the structure but could not go into the Most Holy Place of God the Father; being cut off by the drapery symbolizing the sin which separates us from God the Father (Is 59:1-3).

9:6 Now when these things were thus ordained, the priests went always into the first tabernacle, accomplishing the service of God.

The high priest alone went into the Most Holy Place with sacrifices for himself and the people each year, ONLY on the Fast Day of Atonement.

9:7 But into the second went the high priest **alone once every year**, not without blood, which he offered for himself, and for the errors of the people:

The exclusion of the Mosaic priesthood and people from passing into the presence of God the Father, revealed that their sins were not atoned for by the blood of sheep, cattle and goats; which physical sacrifices were mere instructional examples of the need for a better sacrifice that could truly atone for sin.

This exclusion from God the Father revealed that the Mosaic Covenant could not atone for sin and reconcile people to God the Father; and that a New Covenant with better promises and a better sacrifice was needed.

9:8 The Holy Ghost this signifying, that the way into the holiest of all was not yet made manifest, while as the first tabernacle was yet standing:

The tabernacle and later temple with their various sacrifices and services were figures of the Mosaic Covenant and the Aaronic priesthood with its service, which were only temporary; lasting only until the Melchisedec [Jesus Christ] was made flesh and lived a perfect life, giving his own life as our atoning sacrifice and was then resurrected back to his former glory as a spiritual High Priest forever.

9:9 Which was a figure for the time then present, in which were offered both gifts and sacrifices, **that could not make him that did the service perfect** [could not atone for sin], as pertaining to the conscience; **9:10** Which stood only in meats [offerings] and drinks [offerings], and divers washings, and carnal ordinances, imposed on them **until the time of reformation** [until the restoration of the priesthood of Melchizedek].

In the Mosaic Covenant the people did not have access to the inner sanctuary, they did not have access to God the Father, and they did not have access to the Most Holy Place the throne room of the Eternal Father, King of the Universe.

Then Melchisedec, the Implementing Creator was made flesh as Jesus Christ and in the flesh successfully completed his mission, dying for the sincerely repented sins of humanity and was then resurrected to spirit and raised up to eternal life, becoming an eternal High Priest: Restoring the High Priesthood of the Creator [Melchisedec].

When sin entered the world, God the Father left this world in the hands of the Implementing Creator Jesus Christ to fulfill the plan and reconcile humanity with God the Father! Which work of reconciliation is the function of the spiritual High Priest, Melchisedec [Jesus Christ].

9:11 But Christ being come an high priest of good things to come, by a greater and more perfect tabernacle, not made with hands, that is to say, not of this building; **9:12** Neither by the blood of goats and calves, but **by his own blood he entered in once into the holy place, having obtained eternal redemption for us.**

The sacrifice of Jesus Christ the Lamb of God was found acceptable to God the Father and could now be applied to all sincerely repentant and faithful called out: and eventually all of humanity will be called out to God the Father through Jesus Christ the living resurrected sacrifice and High Priest of our Salvation.

9:13 For if the blood of bulls and of goats, and the ashes of an heifer sprinkling the unclean, sanctifieth to the purifying of the flesh: **9:14** How much more shall the blood of Christ, who through the eternal Spirit offered himself without spot to God, purge your conscience from dead works to serve the living God?

Jesus Christ lived a sinless life and was the Implementing Creator of all things and gave himself to die for humanity, being the perfect complete sacrifice his perfect life and obedience to the will of God the Father to the death atoned for all sincerely repented sin.

Then upon his resurrection and change to spirit, his former glory being restored Jesus Christ ascended to God the Father as our Wave Offering; to be presented "for us" as a complete and perfect propitiation for all sincerely repented sin. Then after offering the perfect gift of his own life for the repented sins of the world, he became the High Priest and Mediator of the New Covenant reconciling repentant humanity with God the Father!

9:15 And **for this cause he is the mediator of the new testament, that by means of death, for the redemption of the transgressions** that were under the first testament, **they which are called might receive the promise of eternal inheritance.**

Yes, many were called over the past six thousand years from Abel, but they were called in faith that Jesus Christ would successfully complete his mission of a perfect sinless life and die for his creation. It was only after Jesus Christ completed his mission and ascended to God the Father, that the faith of their calling was confirmed and made sure.

9:16 For where a testament is, there must also of necessity be the death of the testator. **9:17** For a testament is of force after men are dead: otherwise it is of no strength at all while the testator liveth.

The Mosaic Covenant was dedicated with a sacrifice, and the New Covenant was dedicated with a much better sacrifice.

9:18 Whereupon neither the first testament was dedicated without blood. **9:19** For when Moses had spoken every precept to all the people according to the law, he took the blood of calves and of goats, with water, and scarlet wool, and hyssop, and sprinkled both the book, and all the people, **9:20** Saying, This is the blood of the testament which God hath enjoined unto you. **9:21** Moreover he sprinkled with blood both the tabernacle, and all the vessels of the ministry.

The sprinkling of blood to ratify the Mosaic Covenant was a representation that the blood of the sacrifice of Christ purifies the sincerely repentant of the New Covenant; who then become the spiritual Temple of God when God through the Holy Spirit takes up residence to dwell in his faithful.

9:22 And almost all things are by the law purged with blood; and **without shedding of blood is no remission** [no atonement for sin].

The physical Mosaic tabernacle / temple was sanctified by the sprinkling of the sacrificial blood of certain specified clean animals as an allegory that the spiritual New Covenant is sanctified by the blood of the very Implementing Creator God made flesh

9:23 It was therefore necessary that the patterns of things in the heavens should be purified with these; but the heavenly [spiritual New Covenant] things themselves with better sacrifices than these.

The Being who created all things and then gave up his God-hood to be made flesh as Jesus Christ, overcame all temptations and sin to live a perfect life and obey the will of God the Father giving up his life for his creation; he was raised up from the dead back to his former glory as an eternal spirit and ascended to God the Father to be accepted as our perfect holy sacrifice and High Priest, to Mediate with God the Father for us!

9:24 For **Christ is not entered into the holy places made with hands, which are the figures of the true; but into heaven itself, now to appear in the presence of God for us**: **9:25** Nor yet that he should offer himself often, as the [physical Mosaic] high priest entereth into the holy place every year with blood of others; **9:26** For then must he often have suffered since the foundation of the world: but now once in the end of the world hath he appeared to put away sin by the sacrifice of himself.

Jesus Christ died ONCE, since his sacrifice was perfect and can atone for ALL the repented sins ever committed; yet if we should slip and UNINTENTIONALLY sin after our sincere repentance from our PAST sins, that unintentional sin needs to be sincerely repented of and the sacrifice needs to be reapplied!

When we are baptized we do not enter a "state of grace" where sin is overlooked; we must sincerely repent and STOP sinning.

The sacrifice of Christ will never be applied to the willful intentional sinner; it is only applied to the sincerely repentant who dedicate themselves to "go and sin no more!"

> **Romans 2:13** (For not the hearers of the law are just before God, but the doers of the law shall be justified [by the application of Christ's sacrifice].

Jesus Christ [Melchizedek] the High Priest of the New Covenant will come again to this earth and will resurrect and induct into his priesthood all those who seek God through him and are zealous to learn and to live by every Word of God, all those who through the power of God have internalized the very nature of God to become holy as God is holy, and become without sin as God is without sin.

> **Revelation 1:6** And hath made us **kings and priests unto God and his Father**; to him be glory and dominion for ever and ever. Amen.

When Christ returns he will resurrect and change to eternal spirit God's chosen and they will be made kings and priests (Rev 1:6, 5:10) of the High

Priesthood of Melchisedec [Jesus Christ]; being inducted into that priesthood by God the Father in heaven. After which they will return to work to bring all humanity to God the Father!

> **Revelation 19:1** And after these things I heard a great voice of **much people in heaven**, saying, Alleluia; Salvation, and glory, and honour, and power, unto the Lord our God:

Hebrews 9:27 And as it is appointed unto men once to die, but after this the judgment: **9:28** So Christ was once [died only once] offered to bear the sins of many; and unto them that look for him shall he appear the second time without sin unto salvation.

Goats, doves, sheep and bullocks could keep one in the Mosaic Covenant but they could not reconcile people to God the Father because the Mosaic Covenant had no spiritual promises and its sacrifices were not effectual on a spiritual level: Therefore because these animals were of less value than a human being and further the people could not obey God in the entire spirit and intent of the law; a New Covenant (Jer 31:31) with a better sacrifice and better promises was required.

The physical tabernacle could be purified by physical sacrifices, but spiritual or heavenly things must be purified with the better spiritual sacrifice of the true spiritual Lamb of God.

These physical sacrifices were only representative of a better sacrifice; which was the sacrifice of Jesus Christ, the true Lamb of God: And with His sacrifice, we can be purged from sin and reconciled with God the Father.

The wages of sin is death and those wages must be paid.

> **Romans 6:23** For the wages of sin is death; but the gift of God is eternal life through Jesus Christ our Lord.

Therefore, it was necessary that Christ died for our sins and pay that penalty for us. Otherwise, we would die and remain dead forever; having to pay for our own sins, because the blood of bulls and lambs cannot pay for our sin.

Simply put, a man is of much more value than these things and a lamb cannot atone for the sin of a man. Only the atoning sacrifice of the very Creator God could pay the indictment [list] of our sins.

The earthly tabernacle and the temple were copies or representations of a heavenly temple, and the administrations of the priesthood of Aaron were simply shadows or instructional allegories of spiritual things.

The priests of Aaron offered sacrifices as an acting out or allegory of the perfect sacrifice of Jesus Christ, Christ offered a better sacrifice, a more perfect sacrifice, a sacrifice which could fully atone for sin and save the spirit, which the physical sacrifices could not do.

Therefore, the physical Mosaic Covenant was an instructional allegory of the spiritual New Covenant: And the reality of the spiritual New Covenant with its perfect sacrifice and promises of eternal life is much better than the physical Mosaic Covenant allegory.

The spiritual is more holy, more complete and more effective, it is better in every way; because it brings forgiveness from repented sin on a spiritual heavenly level and completely reconciles the sincerely repentant with God the Father; because God the Father will write His Word and Law in the hearts and minds of people through the power of His Holy Spirit.

The New Covenant also containing the promise of eternal life for all who sincerely repent and overcome sin with the power of God's Spirit, internalizing the very nature of God!

Hebrews 10

The Mosaic sacrificial law which allowed the physical high priest access to the Most Holy Place only once a year and only with physical sacrifices, maintained the Mosaic Covenant; but it could not reconcile the people with God the Father on a spiritual level.

The Mosaic Covenant could not bring a resurrection to spirit and eternal life, neither of which were part of the Mosaic Covenant. Therefore a New Covenant with a better sacrifice than animals, containing the better promises of the enabling gift of the Holy Spirit, a resurrection to spirit and eternal life and reconciliation to God the Father was needed.

Hebrews 10:1 For the law having a shadow of good things to come, and not the very image of the things, can never with those sacrifices which they offered year by year continually make the comers thereunto perfect. **10:2** For then would they not have ceased to be offered? because that the worshippers once purged should have had no more conscience of sins.

The physical sacrifices were ordained to remind people of sins and to instruct us of the need for the perfect sacrifice of the Creator which would be brought into God the Father by the High Priest of the New Covenant of

Jeremiah 31:31. Every aspect of the Mosaic sacrificial system reflects some aspect of the sacrifice of Jesus Christ the Lamb of God.

10:3 But in those sacrifices there is a remembrance again made of sins every year. **10:4** For it is not possible that the blood of bulls and of goats should take away sins.

Because the blood of sacrificial animals could not truly reconcile humanity with God, the animals not being equal to the life of a person, God willed that an effectual perfect New Covenant and a perfect spiritual sacrifice of the very Implementing Creator be made.

Atonement for sin can come only through the application of the ultimate sacrifice of the Creator; reconciling the people to God the Father after sincere repentance, and a commitment to sin no more through the power of the Holy Spirit.

10:5 Wherefore when he cometh into the world, he saith, Sacrifice and offering thou wouldest not, but a body hast thou prepared me: **10:6** In burnt offerings and sacrifices for sin thou hast had no pleasure.

Therefore the Creator gave up his God-hood to be made flesh and to die to remove the sins of the sincerely repentant according to the will of God the Father; who willed that a New Covenant be established with a perfect sacrifice, doing away with sincerely repented sin and reconciling the sincerely repentant of humanity to himself.

10:7 Then said I, **Lo, I come** (in the volume of the book it is written of me,) **to do thy will, O God.**

Jesus Christ [Melchizedek] came to atone for all sincerely repented sin, and to reconcile the repentant to God the Father, thereby establishing the New Covenant promised in Jeremiah 31:31; which required a perfect sacrifice and the gift of God's Holy Spirit to write the law [the whole Word of God] on the hearts and in the minds of the sincerely repentant.

10:8 Above when he said, Sacrifice and offering and burnt offerings and offering for sin thou wouldest not, neither hadst pleasure therein; which are offered by the law:

God the Father accepts the better sacrifice which can indeed atone for sincerely repented PAST sins.

10:9 Then said he [Jesus Christ], **Lo, I come to do thy will, O God. He taketh away the first** [The Mosaic Covenant ended with the death of the

Husband Melchisedec [Jesus Christ], enabling the establishment of the New Covenant.], **that he may establish the second.**

10:10 By the which will [by God the Father's will] we are sanctified through the offering of the body of Jesus Christ once for all.

Because the sacrifice of Christ was perfect and complete [because the life of the Creator is worth more that all that he has created]; Christ needed to die only once to atone for all sin; although his sacrifice needs to be reapplied to the repentant if they should inadvertently slip.

10:11 And every priest standeth daily ministering and **offering oftentimes the same sacrifices, which can never take away sins: 10:12** But this man, after he had offered one sacrifice for sins for ever, sat down on the right hand of God; **10:13** From henceforth expecting till his enemies be made his footstool.

10:14 For by one offering [one perfect sacrificial death of himself] he hath perfected for ever them that are sanctified.

Melchisedec made flesh as Jesus Christ, has atoned for the sins of all who sincerely repent and commit to sin no more, and sets them apart [sanctifies] to reconciliation with God the Father.

Then on our sincere repentance the whole Word of God is written on our hearts and in our minds through the agency of God's Holy Spirit, the very nature of God being given to dwell in us (Jer 31, Joel 2:28).

10:15 Whereof the Holy Ghost also is a witness to us: for after that he had said before, **10:16 This is the covenant that I will make with them after those days, saith the Lord, I will put my laws into their hearts, and in their minds will I write them; 10:17** And their sins and iniquities will I remember no more.

Once we have sincerely repented and committed to sin no more with a baptismal commitment; the atoning sacrifice of Jesus Christ is applied to us and we may receive the Holy Spirit, which if we follow it, will lead us into the truth [John 16:13, John 17:17; God's Word is Truth] and empower us to learn and grow in godliness and to overcome sin.

10:18 Now where remission [remission of sin comes by sincere repentance and the application of the New Covenant sacrifice of Christ] of these is, there is no more [If a sacrifice is effectual to cover all sin there is no more need for further sacrifices [repeated deaths] of Christ, but that sacrifice must be reapplied if sin comes and is repented of in future.] offering for sin.

After sincere repentance and a baptismal commitment to sin no more, we are reconciled to God the Father by the application of the sacrifice of Christ and may enter into God the Father's presence beyond the [now removed] veil of sin that had previously separated us from Him. That veil being removed by the sacrifice of the fleshly body of Jesus Christ the Creator.

10:19 Having therefore, brethren, boldness to enter into the holiest by the blood of Jesus, **10:20** By a new and living way [the New Covenant], which he hath consecrated for us, through the veil, that is to say, his flesh; **10:21** And having an high priest over the house of God; **10:22** Let us draw near [near to God the Father in all things, forsaking all sin] with a true [faithful and pure] heart in full assurance of faith, having our hearts sprinkled [by the sacrificial blood of Christ] from an evil conscience, and our bodies washed with pure water [washed clean by the Spirit and the keeping of every Word of God].

> **Ephesians 5:25** . . . even as Christ also loved the church, and **gave himself for it; 5:26 That he might sanctify and cleanse it with the washing of water by the word,**

We are to hold fast to our baptismal commitment to sin no more, and we are to cleave with all our minds and spirit and body to a passionate Christ-like zeal to learn and live by every Word of God!

Hebrews 10:23 Let us hold fast the profession of our faith without wavering; (for he is faithful that promised;) **10:24** And let us consider one another to provoke unto love and to good works: **10:25** Not forsaking the assembling of ourselves together [Not assembling with just anyone, but assembling with those who are truly faithful to the whole Word of God.], as the manner of some is; but exhorting one another: and **so much the more, as ye see the day approaching**.

If we lose our zeal to keep the whole Word of God and become spiritually lazy, following men or temptation away from our Mighty Deliverer; and if we begin to justify our sins instead of immediately repenting from any sin we find in ourselves; we are searing our conscience, we are quenching God's Holy Spirit and we are in danger of the judgment of eternal death.

10:26 For if we sin wilfully after that we have received the knowledge of the truth, there remaineth no more sacrifice for sins, **10:27** But a certain fearful looking for of judgment and fiery indignation, which shall devour the adversaries.

10:28 He that despised Moses' law died without mercy under **two or three witnesses: 10:29 Of how much sorer punishment, suppose ye, shall he be thought worthy, who hath trodden under foot the Son of God, and hath counted the blood of the** [New] **covenant** [the sacrifice of Christ], **wherewith he** [we were first forgiven and Set Apart from sin] **was sanctified, an unholy thing, and hath done despite unto the Spirit of grace?**

Brethren, those who teach that upon baptism we enter a state of grace where we need not be zealous to keep the whole Word of God; are IGNORANT or LYING! Baptism is a commitment to "go and sin no more" not a license to situation ethics and continued willful self-justified sin.

10:30 For we know him that hath said, Vengeance belongeth unto me, I will recompense, saith the Lord. And again, **The Lord shall judge his people**.

10:31 It is a fearful thing to fall into the hands of the living God [because of wilful self-justified sin].

Brethren, let us remember our great joy in God's Word when our minds were first opened to His Light! Let us return to our first zeal to search out and accept all things of God exalting godliness above all else! Let us seek to regain our love of the Truth and our zeal to root out all error and sin!

Dear Brethren; Where has the love of the truth gone when our leaders are unwilling to even look at the truth of the Biblical Calendar, and if they do look they tell open lies about the subject to maintain their now obviously false traditions?

Where is our love of the truth when we reject or spin whole sections of scripture so that we can call the Sabbath holy as we pollute it by doing our own pleasures on God's time, or say that a High Day is on some other date than the day which God has commanded [which we do in regards to the Annual Sabbaths]?

Let us return to a passionate zeal to learn and to live by every Word of God; resisting all deceptions and temptations and enduring all trials dedicatedly seeking the holiness of God the Father, ruler of the universe.

Where are the Daniel's and his three friends today; who would endure all things for the whole Word of God?

> **Daniel 3:16** Shadrach, Meshach, and Abednego, answered and said to the king, O Nebuchadnezzar, we are not careful [afraid] to answer thee in this matter.
>
> **3:17** If it be so, our God whom we serve is able to deliver us from the burning fiery furnace, and he will deliver us out of thine hand, O king.
>
> **3:18 But if not, be it known unto thee, O king, that we will not serve thy gods, nor worship the golden image which thou hast set up.**

Today we worship the golden calves of idols of man, obeying the words of men and having no zeal to search and hold fast to the whole Word of God!

We are full of love and zeal for men and organizations of men; yet there is almost no zeal to keep the whole Word of God above the words of men! Truly it is written that in the last days the love of many [for the whole Word of God] shall wax cold.

Hebrews 10:32 But call to remembrance the former days, in which, after ye were [when our minds were first opened to the Light of God's Word] illuminated, ye endured a great fight of afflictions; **10:33** Partly, whilst ye were made a gazingstock both by reproaches and afflictions; and partly, whilst ye became companions of them that were so used.

In the beginning the newly converted loved the truth that Paul taught, even when he was imprisoned, and they gave joyfully to help him in his mission.

In our own personal beginning we also loved every Word of God, but we have lost our first love and now love idols of men in place of loving our Mighty One and His Holy Word!

10:34 For ye had compassion of me in my bonds, and took joyfully the spoiling of your goods, knowing in yourselves that ye have in heaven a better and an enduring substance. **10:35** Cast not away therefore your confidence [faith in God's promises], which hath great recompence of reward.

Let us learn and keep the whole Word of God with zealous patience and take pleasure in godliness!

10:36 For ye have need of patience, that, after ye have done the will of God, ye might receive the promise.

Our Lord is coming very soon now, in the sense that any one of us could die this very day. Therefore be always ready and full of enthusiasm to live by every Word of God.

10:37 For yet a little while, and he that shall come will come, and will not tarry.

10:38 Now the just shall live by faith [the works of faith]: but if any man draw back [from the works of faith and a zeal for learning and keeping the whole Word of God], my soul shall have no pleasure in him.

God will not take pleasure in anyone who turns aside from the works of faith to live by every Word of God; such a person will receive the same judgment from God as those who had wanted to turn back into Egypt.

Those who turn aside from zeal for the whole Word of God to follow idols of men, or who succumb to trials and temptations; are consigned to judgment if they do not sincerely repent.

Those who believe the promises of God and are full of faith and the works of faith, which is the zealous keeping of every Word of God and following our LORD with passionate loyalty; will be saved from sin and they will receive the reward of entry into the Promised Land of eternal life.

Our High Priest and God our loving Father speak to us saying: Be strong my son, be strong and persevere!

10:39 But we are not of them who draw back unto perdition; but of them that believe to the saving of the soul.

Hebrews 11

The Epistle to the Hebrews at Jerusalem was to explain the transition from the Mosaic Covenant to the New Covenant and the necessity of a transition of the priesthood from the priesthood of Aaron to the New Covenant Priesthood of Jesus Christ.

In Hebrews 10 Paul turns to the subject of faith in the New Covenant, its High Priest and its promises.

In Hebrews 11 Paul speaks of those who have demonstrated their faith by their works of faith throughout history.

Remember that these chapter divisions were established by men for convenience in searching the scriptures and are not always appropriately placed.

In ALL these cases one point stands out above all else: Every one of these people had the WORKS of FAITH.

These powerful examples of godliness never said that to believe is enough! They believed and obeyed and stood boldly on their faith doing the WORKS of FAITH! These people of God set a Shining Example for all people; that only the Eternal is to be exalted, obeyed and worshiped!

They ALL had faith and the WORKS of FAITH, which are zealous obedience to live by EVERY WORD of God! (Mat 4:4, Mat 4:10)! For faith without the works of faith is dead and useless!

Faith and the Works of Faith

> **James 2:14** What doth it profit, my brethren, though a man say he hath faith, and have not works? Can faith save him? **2:5** If a brother or sister be naked, and destitute of daily food, **2:16** and one of you say unto them, Depart in peace, be ye warmed and filled; notwithstanding ye give them not those things which are needful to the body, what doth it profit?
>
> **2:17** Even so **faith, if it hath not works, is dead, being alone. 2:18** Yea, a man may say, You hast faith, and I have works. **Show me thy faith without thy works, and I will show thee my faith by my works. 2:19** Thou believest that there is one God; thou doest well: the devils also believe, and tremble [Yet the demons will not obey God's Word, therefore their belief brings them nothing but the sure knowledge of their coming judgment.]. **2:20** But wilt thou know, O vain man, that **faith without works is dead**?
>
> **2:21** Was not Abraham our father justified [by his deeds] by works when he [obeyed God] had offered Isaac his son upon the altar? **2:22** Seest thou how faith wrought [brought the works of faith] with his works and by works was faith made perfect? **2:23** And the scripture was fulfilled which saith, Abraham believed God, and it was imputed unto him for righteousness: and he was called the Friend of God.
>
> **2:24** Ye see then how that by works a man is justified, and not by faith only. **2:25** Likewise also was not Rehab the harlot justified by works, when she had received the messengers, and had sent them out another way? **2:26** For **as the body without the spirit is dead, so faith without works is dead.**

There is a spirit in our body, a spirit of man; and without the body it cannot function; it cannot think, it is not conscious, it must be plugged into the body to function. The body and the spirit of man work together, the spirit must be plugged into the body to function: Even so faith must be plugged into works, and works come by faith, so that godly faith [trust and belief] results in the works of faith.

Faith without works cannot stand on its own. If we have faith, if we believe God, we will do what God says; which is our works of faith.

We cannot do what God says if we do not believe [have faith] in Him, any more than the spirit can function without the body. If we have faith and we have no works our faith is meaningless, it is a waste of time. Believing without acting on that belief is a waste of time; it won't get anyone anywhere.

Therefore my friends, let us be full of faith in God the Father and our perfect High Priest and follow him in doing the Works of Faith; fully living by every Word of God without any hint of turning or compromise!

Hebrews 11:1 Now faith is the substance of things hoped for [Godly faith is an unshakable belief and trust that every Word of God is true, resulting in obedience to live by every Word of God.], the evidence of things not seen. **11:2** For by it the elders obtained a good report.

Nineteen hundred years ago Paul spoke of physical things being made from invisible things; which was confirmed by E=MC squared, which means that energy is mass times the speed of light squared or multiplied by itself. The opposite is also true that mass consists of energy. The Creator God who was spirit [pure energy] made matter by converting energy to matter!

Paul understood this by faith; which thing is today confirmed by discovery of the facts. Matter is energy concentrated into matter. Just like ice is a form of water and water is a form of vapor!

11:3 Through faith we understand that the worlds were framed by the word of God, so that things which are seen were not made of things which do appear.

11:4 By faith Abel offered unto God a more excellent sacrifice than Cain, **by which he obtained witness that he was righteous, God testifying of his gifts**: and by it he being dead yet speaketh.

That is, Abel died and yet he is spoken of to this day, and he will be raised up in the resurrection.

11:5 By faith Enoch was translated that he should not see death; and was not found, because God had translated him: for before his translation he had this testimony, that he pleased God.

How can we obey God if we do not believe that God exists? and how can we please God if we do not believe he exists?

11:6 But without faith it is impossible to please him: for he that cometh to God must believe that he is [exists], and that he is a rewarder of them that diligently seek him.

11:7 By faith Noah, being warned of God of things not seen as yet, moved with fear, [believed God and acted on that belief to] prepared an ark to the saving of his house; by the which he condemned the world [Noah's example set him apart from the worldly whho would not believe the warnings.], and became heir of the righteousness which is by faith.

This is a lesson that all those who do not believe the warnings and turn to God to live by every Word of God in sincerity and truth will also be destroyed.

11:8 By faith Abraham, when he was called to go out into a place which he should after receive for an inheritance, **obeyed; and he went out, not knowing whither he went. 11:9** By faith he sojourned in the land of promise, as in a strange country, dwelling in tabernacles [The Feast of Tabernacles requires that we dwell in temporary shelters to make the very point that if we are called of and faithful to God we are strangers in an ungodly world.] with Isaac and Jacob, the heirs with him of the same promise: **11:10** For he looked for a city which hath foundations, whose builder and maker is God

We are to be focused on the spiritual things of the whole Word of God just as Abraham was; and we are to be built on the whole Word of God; which is Moses, the Writings, the Prophets and the Apostles [the Holy Scriptures] with Jesus Christ being the Chief Stone of the foundation: All of which was inspired by God!

Abraham believed God and therefore he acted on what God told him to do. To believe God is one thing; to actually act on what God says and to obey him, is what pleases God.

We must believe before we can obey, but if we believe and do not obey, there is no sacrifice for our sin and there is no reconciliation with God for us.

As long as we continue to reject living by every Word of God, we can believe all we want and it won't do us any good at all. We must believe and then we must act on that belief and start doing what God wants us to do.

Our reconciliation with God and our relationship with Him depends upon us living by every Word of God, and one of those commandments is to honor thy father and thy mother.

In order to keep that commandment, we must be willing to do anything that God the Father tells us to do. Was there any law that said Abraham had to move to a different land? Was there any law that told Noah to build this ark?

We are obligated by the commandment do what God our Father tells us to do, and He told Abraham to leave that land and He told Noah to build that boat.

We are to obey God our Father in whatever He tells us to do. This concept of obedience goes far beyond just the commandments. Yes, we are to keep all of His commandments but we are also to love Him with all our hearts, to serve Him with all the strength that God gives us and to try and to please Him in every way; which means doing whatever God says; always, always, always, at all times.

11:11 Through faith also Sara herself received strength to conceive seed, and was delivered of a child when she was past age, because she judged him faithful who had promised. **11:12** Therefore sprang there even of one, and him as good as dead, so many as the stars of the sky in multitude, and as the sand which is by the sea shore innumerable.

Out of Sarah and Abram came a son by God's promise; out of Abram who was a very old man would come as "many as the stars of the sky in multitude, and as the sand which is by the sea shore enumerable. What if they in their great age had not believed that promise, and not added the works of faith to their belief and had not come together; the promise would have been of no effect! The birth of Isaac was by faith in the promise of God, coupled with the works of faith!

11:13 These all died in faith, not having received the promises, but having seen them afar off, and were persuaded of them, and embraced them, and confessed that they were strangers and pilgrims on the earth.

Notice that they ALL died: which means that Enoch and Elijah also died.

These all died in faith. Enoch was translated that he should not see death; in other words, he was moved from one place to another so that he would not be murdered or killed for his faith and then later on he died.

Those who reject worldliness for godliness are making a clear statement that they are not of this world and that they seek another and godly nation, the Kingdom of God; and if any person turns aside from their zeal to keep the whole Word of God which is the constitution of the Kingdom of God and goes back into worldliness; they become worldly again.

11:14 For they that say such things declare plainly that they seek a country. **11:15** And truly, if they had been mindful of that country from whence they came out, they might have had opportunity to have returned.

That is what dwelling in tabernacles or temporary structures at the Feast of Ingathering is all about. To teach us that this flesh is temporary and that we are to seek a better promised land; a resurrection and change from flesh into spirit and eternal life.

It is to remind us that we are temporary sojourners and foreigners in this society and that we must seek a better society and a better and eternal Promised Land, which is found in the Kingdom of God.

We are really just temporary sojourners in this flesh and we should all be looking forward to a better and more permanent place to dwell, a change to spirit and the promise of eternal life: Which is the gift of God for all those who sincerely repent, who turn from sin and commit to sin no more and who are reconciled to God the Father and given God's Holy Spirit.

Those who endure and overcome will then be given eternal life in a new spirit body at the resurrection when they are changed to spirit.

11:16 But now **they desire a better country, that is, an heavenly: wherefore God is not ashamed to be called their God: for he hath prepared for them** [prepared for the faithful who believe and have the works of faith] **a city.**

Abraham had received promises that Isaac would be the father of countless descendants and yet not understanding the command to kill Isaac after such promises had been made, Abraham still obeyed.

11:17 By faith Abraham, when he was tried, **offered up Isaac: and he that had received the promises offered up his only begotten son, 11:18** Of whom it was said, **That in Isaac shall thy seed be called: 11:19 Accounting that God was able to raise him up, even from the dead;** from whence also he received him in a figure.

Figuratively speaking, Abram received Isaac back from the dead because he was about to kill him and God delivered Isaac.

11:20 By faith [in God's promises] Isaac blessed Jacob and Esau concerning things to come. **11:21** By faith [in God's promises] Jacob, when he was a dying, blessed both the sons of Joseph; and worshipped, leaning upon the top of his staff. **11:22** By faith [in God's promise that he would bring Israel out of Egypt] Joseph, when he died, made mention of the departing of the children of Israel; and gave commandment concerning his bones.

11:23 By faith Moses, when he was born, was hid three months of his parents, because they saw he was a proper child; and they were not afraid of the king's commandment.

11:24 By faith Moses, when he was come to years, refused to be called the son of Pharaoh's daughter; **11:25** Choosing rather to suffer affliction with the people of God, than to enjoy the pleasures of sin for a season; **11:26** Esteeming the reproach of Christ greater riches than the treasures in Egypt: for he had respect unto the recompence of the reward.

Moses esteemed who? Paul shows here that he KNEW that Jesus Christ was the God who was the Husband of Israel under the Mosaic Covenant.

By faith in the promise of God, Moses chose to reject Egypt and follow the God of his father Abraham.

11:27 By faith he forsook Egypt, not fearing the wrath of the king: for he endured, as seeing him who is invisible.

Moses obeyed the call of God from the burning bush in Sinai and by faith Moses believed God and killed the Passover in Egypt. If Moses had said I believe and had not had the works of faith in commanding the killing of the lambs; what would have happened to Israel?

11:28 Through faith he kept the passover, and the sprinkling of blood, lest he that destroyed the firstborn should touch them. **11:29** By faith they passed through the Red sea as by dry land: which the Egyptians assaying to do were drowned.

What if Joshua had said "I believe you can do it LORD;" and then did not demonstrate his faith with the works of faith and did not march around Jericho?

11:30 By faith the walls of Jericho fell down, after they were compassed about seven days.

What if Rahab had not saved the spies and what if she had not tied the scarlet ribbon [a red ribbon like the red blood of the lambs in Egypt, representing being under the protection of the Lamb of God] to her window? Have you ever wondered why a scarlet ribbon? The red ribbon was a symbol of being under the protection of the blood of the Lamb of God!

11:31 By faith the harlot Rahab perished not with them that believed not, when she had received the spies with peace.

11:32 And what shall I more say? for the time would fail me to tell of Gedeon, and of Barak, and of Samson, and of Jephthae; of David also, and Samuel, and of the prophets: **11:33** Who through faith [**and the works of faith, doing mighty deeds in obedience to God**] subdued kingdoms, wrought righteousness, obtained promises, stopped the mouths of lions.

11:34 Quenched the violence of fire [Shadrach, Meshach and Abednego], escaped the edge of the sword, out of weakness were made strong, waxed valiant in fight, turned to flight the armies of the aliens.

11:35 Women received their dead raised to life again: and others were tortured, not accepting deliverance; that they might obtain a better resurrection: **11:36** And others had trial of cruel mockings and scourgings, yea, moreover of bonds and imprisonment:

11:37 They were stoned, they were sawn asunder, were tempted, were slain with the sword: they wandered about in sheepskins and goatskins; being destitute, afflicted, tormented; **11:38** (Of whom the world was not worthy:) they wandered in deserts, and in mountains, and in dens and caves of the earth.

All of these faithful called out over the past 6,000 years and they were FULL of the works of Faith, yet they still died; and now they wait in their graves for the promise of the resurrection to eternal life in the Promised Land of eternity!

Yet today, so many of the Ekklesia are afraid to take a stand to question and prove the words of men by God's Word; afraid to learn and to live by every Word of God; afraid to take a stand against deceivers and idols of men!

11:39 And these all, having obtained a good report through faith, received not the promise: **11:40** God having provided some better thing for us, that they without us should not be made perfect.

All of these ancient called out people [and very many others] mentioned by Paul, through faith performed the works of faith. They didn't say, "Oh,

I've got faith. Praise the Lord," and then do nothing. They had the FAITH to be DOERS of the Will and the whole Word of God!

NO watering down, NO compromise, NO dimming of their light of example to appease the world!

They were valiant people, courageous people, godly people; and they were made strong by the power of their belief in God and the power of God's Spirit dwelling within them: Which God gave to them because of their belief and their willingness to ACT on that belief and to be filled with the works of faith to put Almighty God first and to act and do whatever God wanted them to do.

They had faith. Abel believed God and acted on that belief having the works of faith.

These people acted on their faith and they did what God wanted them to do. They lived by every Word of God.

Faith without the works of faith is a dead faith.

They did not fear to take a stand nor did they love this world, they looked forward to another and a better world; being willing to give up their lives in this world to follow the whole Word of God and attain that better world: While most today would not even give up a meal in a restaurant on God's Holy Sabbath Day!

Like Esau, today's called out Ekklesia has sold its birthright for a bowl of pottage; for the pleasures of this world and for fear of trials.

> **Revelation 21:7 He that overcometh** [overcomes all sin and lives by every Word of God] **shall inherit all things; and I will be his God, and he shall be my son. 21:8** But the fearful, [Those fearing the deceiving idols of men in leadership positions or those afraid of persecution and fearing men more than God so that they compromise with God's Word will be corrected and ultimately destroyed if they refuse to repent.] and unbelieving, and the abominable, and murderers, and whoremongers, and sorcerers, and idolaters, and all liars, shall have their part in the lake which burneth with fire and brimstone: which is the second death.
>
> **Matthew 24:11 And many false prophets shall rise, and shall deceive many. 24:12 And because iniquity shall abound, the love of many** [Today, to our great shame the zeal of many of the Called Out for God and God's Word has been replaced by a zeal to blindly

follow idols of men; very many loving the corporate church organization or human leaders more than they love God!] **shall wax cold. 24:13 But he that shall endure unto the end, the same shall be saved**.

Those who continue in godliness and reject all temptation to turn away from living by any part of the whole Word of God, will be saved in the resurrection to eternal life.

Hebrews 12

Let us be encouraged by the steadfast works of faith of so many others and let us be diligent to reject sin and to follow their example of patient works of zeal for the whole Word of God; especially following the example of Jesus Christ and overcoming by God's indwelling Spirit.

Hebrews 12:1 Wherefore seeing we also are compassed about with so great a cloud of witnesses, let us **lay aside every weight, and the sin which doth so easily beset us, and let us run with patience the race** [the labor of overcoming] **that is set before us**, **12:2** Looking unto Jesus the author and finisher of our faith; who for the joy [of saving many and being restored to spirit and eternal life] that was set before him endured [death] the cross, despising the shame, and is set down at the right hand of the throne of God.

Consider how Jesus Christ endured all temptations, trials and persecution to be triumphant over Satan and sin; KNOW that he can do the same things dwelling in us through the agency of the Holy Spirit.

12:3 For consider him that endured such contradiction of sinners against himself, lest ye be wearied and faint in your minds.

In this generation many have not yet been put to death for godliness as Christ was; but the time is fast approaching when a great correction will be applied to save the fallen away Ekklesia, and very many will suffer greatly and many will sincerely repent and die for our calling: Joining the many martyrs that have gone before.

12:4 Ye have not yet resisted unto blood [today few have died for God the Father, as Christ did], striving against sin.

Very soon the unrepentant Ekklesia will be rejected by Christ (Rev 3:14-22) into severe correction. That correction is for our GOOD so that we may turn to the Eternal God and be saved. It is an affliction of the flesh to save the spirit: Therefore do not despise the correction of the LORD who is working to save us just like he saved Job [Iyob].

Do not lose heart and give up, because the trial is only for a very short time and comes so that Almighty God can save and perfect us.

12:5 And ye have forgotten the exhortation **which speaketh unto you as unto children, My son, despise not thou the chastening of the Lord, nor faint when thou art rebuked of him: 12:6 For whom the Lord loveth he chasteneth, and scourgeth every son whom he receiveth. 12:7 If ye endure chastening, God dealeth with you as with sons; for what son is he whom the father chasteneth not? 12:8 But if ye be without** [If we refuse to be corrected and refuse to learn and to obey God our Father, we are not the sons of God.] **chastisement, whereof all are partakers, then are ye bastards, and not sons.**

We are not legitimate sons if we will not accept the guidance, instruction and correction of God our Father. To be legitimate sons of God the Father, we must accept and keep every Word of God our Father, and act with sincere repentance upon his correction.

12:9 Furthermore **we have had fathers of our flesh which corrected us, and we gave them reverence: shall we not much rather be in subjection unto the Father of spirits, and live** [If we live by every Word of God our Father we will receive eternal life.]? **12:10** For they verily for a few days chastened us after their own pleasure; but he, [God the Father and Jesus Christ correct us for our advantage, not for their own pleasure.] **for our profit that we might be partakers of his holiness.**

Of course our correction will be grievous, and in the flesh we will suffer greatly, but it God's correction will save us bringing us to God and his holiness and his gift of eternal life

12:11 Now no chastening for the present seemeth to be joyous, but grievous: **nevertheless afterward it yieldeth the peaceable fruit of righteousness** unto them which are exercised thereby

When we go astray from the Word of God our Father, and become stubborn and self-willed wanting our own ways, God will correct us.

If we respond positively to that correction with sincere repentance by turning to love the truth and to reject error, learning to respect the authority and the wisdom of the whole Word of God; then we will be saved from death by our Father's merciful correction.

If we rebel and reject God's correction to continue to reject truth and to follow idols of men and their false traditions and false teachings; then we are not worthy to be called the sons of God and we will be rejected.

If we reject truth to insist on our own false ways, then God will reject us. If we accept and follow the whole Word of God, God will accept and bless us.

In Revelation 3, Jesus Christ stands at the door knocking, but we must let him in or he will reject us because we will not accept HIM.

Therefore accept the correction of God our Father in heaven and lift ourselves up from whence we have fallen; and turn to love and to keep the whole Word of God our Father.

12:12 Wherefore lift up the hands which hang down, and the feeble knees; **12:13** And make straight paths for your feet, lest that which is lame be turned out of the way; but let it rather be healed.

Let us be filled with the holiness of God, to become holy as God is holy; through sincere repentance and the diligent keeping of the whole Word of God our Father.

12:14 Follow peace with all men, and holiness, without which no man shall see the Lord: **2:15** Looking diligently lest any man fail of the grace of God; lest any root of bitterness springing up trouble you, and thereby many be defiled;

How can we fail of the grace of God?

Grace is a gift: It is forgiveness for repented past sins, given only to those who repent and stop sinning. If we do not repent, if we do not stop sinning, there is no forgiveness. There is no grace for us. We will fail of the grace of God.

Let us not despise the birthright of our calling and turn from it for the pleasures of the flesh by profaning the Sabbath, and let us not fall to the temptation of any other sin. Let us not turn from our zeal to follow the whole Word of God in order to follow idols of men and their false traditions. Let us not sell the birthright of our calling for the easy way that leads to damnation.

12:16 Lest there be any fornicator [pornea, a spiritual adulterer who follows others and not the Husband of our baptismal commitment], or profane person, as Esau, who for one morsel of meat sold his birthright.

12:17 For ye know how that afterward, when he would have inherited the blessing, he was rejected: for he found no place of repentance, though he sought it carefully with tears.

Be very, very careful not to reject God and not to reject any part of the whole Word of God,

Remember what James said, **"If you have broken the law in one point, you have broken the whole law** (Jas 2:10)." We must live by every Word of God, continually correcting ourselves as we learn.

12:18 For ye are not come unto the mount that might be touched [the physical Mount Sinai, which was physical and could be seen and touched] and that burned with fire, nor unto blackness, and darkness, and tempest, **12:19** And the sound of a trumpet, and the voice of words; which voice they that heard intreated that the word should not be spoken to them any more: **12:20** (For they could not endure that which was commanded, And if so much as a beast touch the mountain, it shall be stoned, or thrust through with a dart: **12:21** And so terrible was the sight, that Moses said, I exceedingly fear and quake:)

If offenders in the Mosaic Covenant died without mercy; how shall the offenders against the Word of God the King of the Universe and the New Covenant escape their destruction if they turn aside from following the God of their spiritual calling to the New Covenant and make a mockery of the sacrifice of the very Creator himself, by living in self-justified sin?

12:22 But ye are come unto mount Sion, and unto the city of the living God, the heavenly Jerusalem, and to an innumerable company of angels,

Can sin enter into the presence of God? NO!

We have access to God the Father in heaven only if we are without any sin; which comes only through sincere repentance and the application of the perfect sacrifice of Jesus Christ, our High Priest. If we then make a mockery of our High Priest by continuing in sin; how shall he then intercede for us? and what sin or spiritual uncleanness will God the Father tolerate? NONE WHATSOEVER!

> **1 Corinthians 3:17** If any man defile the temple of God [with self-justified sin], him shall God destroy; for the temple of God is holy, which temple ye are.

Hebrews 12:23 To the general assembly and church [the individual faithful brethren] of the firstborn [Jesus Christ], which are written in heaven, and to God the Judge of all, and to the spirits of just men made perfect, **12:24** And to Jesus the mediator of the new covenant, and to the blood of sprinkling, that speaketh better things that that of Abel.

Men are made just and perfected through sincere repentance, the application of the sacrifice of the Lamb of God and then going forward to live by every Word of God, which is godly righteousness.

Once our PAST sins have been sincerely repented of and forgiven, we are to use God's Spirit and his power to become perfect. We are not to make excuses for, or try to justify willful sins; we are to go and sin no more!

We must continually grow and continually overcome until we reach perfection. For it is written:

> **2 Timothy 3:16** All scripture is given by the inspiration of God, and is profitable for doctrine, for reproof, for correction, for instruction in righteousness: That the man of God may be perfect, thoroughly furnished unto all good works.

It is through the study of and the keeping of every Word of God through the power of Christ dwelling in us that we can live a Christ-like life.

It is through sincere repentance and a dedicated commitment to sin no more and the application of the sacrifice of Jesus Christ that we may receive the gift of the power of the Holy Spirit to enable us to overcome; because God the Father will empower us with his Spirit of power and self-control and of a sound mind.

God will give us the strength and the power to take control of our actions, and to resist and overcome temptation if we remain faithful to Him.

To try to justify breaking any part of the whole Word of God automatically breaks the Great Commandment, which is to honor God our Father. If our

Heavenly Father wants us to do something, we must never just ignore it to do what we want like a rebellious child.

God would not have told us to do something, if HE did not think it was important. We must put God our Father FIRST! We do not have the right to judge the Word and Will of God our Father in heaven!

It is our responsibility to keep our part of our baptismal covenant and obey God our Father and our espoused Husband: To live by every Word of God!

Hebrews 12:24 And to **Jesus the mediator** [High Priest] **of the new covenant**, and to the blood of sprinkling [the application of the sacrifice of Christ that truly removes sin], that speaketh better things that that of Abel.

Christ's sacrifice is a better sacrifice than the animal sacrifices which began with Abel and were expanded in the Mosaic Covenant: The sacrifice of the Creator of all things being a far better sacrifice than all of the physical animal sacrifices ever made.

12:25 See that ye refuse not [Do NOT reject any part of the whole Word of God.] **him that speaketh. For if they escaped not who refused him** [If those who did not obey the Mosaic Covenant could not escape punishment, how can we escape punishment for trampling on the New Covenant?] **that spake on earth, much more shall not we escape, if we turn away from him that speaketh from heaven:**

If we turn aside from keeping any part of the New Covenant, which is the whole Word of God written on our hearts (Jer 31:31) we cannot escape destruction, for making a mockery of the sacrifice of the very Creator God.

12:26 Whose voice then shook the earth: but now he hath promised, saying, Yet once more I shake not the earth only, but also heaven.

The very voice of the God who became flesh as Jesus Christ SHOOK Mount Sinai with the Mosaic Covenant utterances: and he has now shaken and destroyed that Mosaic Covenant, and replaced it with a permanent and better New Covenant which can never be shaken (Jer 31).

12:27 And this word, Yet once more, **signifieth the removing of those things that are shaken, as of things that are made, that those things which cannot be shaken may remain.**

12:28 Wherefore we receiving a kingdom [at the resurrection to spirit and the establishment of the Kingdom of God] which cannot be moved [which is eternal], let us have grace [God's gift of persevering faith], whereby we may serve God acceptably **with reverence and godly fear: 12:29 For our God is a consuming fire.**

Right now God is shaking [testing] his people to see who will be left standing; and only those who are standing on his Word will remain standing.

God is testing and trying and sifting his people to see who stands on his Word, and who would rather put their trust in the false traditions of men and interpret God's Word through the eyes of some man.

It doesn't matter whether a man calls himself an apostle or a prophet or any such thing. What matters is whether their words are consistent with God's Word; and if their words are not consistent with God's Word then that man is neither prophet, nor apostle, nor man of God; no matter what he claims or how impressive he is.

A true man of God is always consistent with the whole Word of God; and if he does make a mistake and it is pointed out and he sees it in God's Word, then he will quickly repent!

A man who defends false teachings and is willing to reject parts of God's Word, or to use lies to defend false traditions; is NOT a man of God!

Almighty God has a very high standard and he holds all people to that standard.

This is not like some kind of game like little children playing doctor or playing church or playing school.

This is reality and this is the power of the very Creator of the universe, and the power of the God the Father, the Ruler of the universe.

The Creator is not going to give responsibilities over others to anyone unless that person can prove through a lifetime of service that he is absolutely loyal to God his King and to his eternal High Priest Jesus Christ [Melchizedek].

The Great King Emperor of the entire universe, Almighty God: is not going to have lesser kings [people under him in authority] who are going to sneak around behind his back and do whatever they feel like doing, and who will judge his Word on the basis of what they think is important!

The King of the universe absolutely requires that all of his instructions be followed!

God knows what he is doing: He is wiser than us and he understands and knows what is going to work out to be the very best for all of his children.

God knows what he is doing and if we want to become kings and priests of God in the order of Jesus Christ [Melchizedek], then we are going to have to prove to him that we are faithful and loyal in all things large and small!

Hebrews 13

Hebrews 13:1 Let brotherly love continue. Be not forgetful to entertain strangers: for thereby, some have entertained angels unawares.

Be full of Godly love. God is love and if you are a godly person, full of his Spirit, you will be filled with his love which means you will be passionately living by every Word of God.

Everyone loves their own; the real test arises in how we react to our enemies. True godly love does not mean that we tolerate sin, but that we forgive those who sin and that we warn the sinner in hope that he will turn from his sinful ways and be saved.

> **Matthew 5:43** Ye have heard that it hath been said, Thou shalt love thy neighbour, and hate thine enemy.
>
> **5:44** But I say unto you, **Love your enemies, bless them that curse you, do good to them that hate you, and pray for them which despitefully use you, and persecute you; 5:45 That ye may be the children of your Father which is in heaven: for he maketh his sun to rise on the evil and on the good**, and sendeth rain on the just and on the unjust.

5:46 For if ye love them which love you, what reward have ye? do not even the publicans the same? **5:47** And if ye salute your brethren only, what do ye more than others? do not even the publicans so?

5:48 Be ye therefore perfect, even as your Father which is in heaven is perfect

Do we love only our own and think less of others?

Unless we repent; we shall stand ashamed before our Lord.

13:3 Remember them that are in bonds, as bound with them. [Think of yourself as being in the same chains as the other person or having the same trials as others.] **Remember them which suffer adversity, as being yourselves also in the flesh.**

Sex is a beautiful wonderful creation of God, but it must be used in the manner ordained and commanded by God; any unlawful use of sex diminishes and demeans the human being made in the image of God.

13:4 Marriage is honorable in all, and the bed undefiled: but whoremongers and adulterers God will judge.

God condemns fornication and adultery; which now abounds in the Ekklesia; BOTH physically and spiritually.

To esteem anyone more than your spouse is emotional adultery; and to esteem any human being as your moral authority is spiritual adultery against our espoused Husband Jesus Christ!

Sex and marriage are for one man and one woman and make of the two persons one flesh.

Sexual activity is to be reserved for the marriage state. It is to be reserved for the union between a man and his [female] wife: And what they do with each other must be based on love and mutual respect and a desire to please one another and is intended by God to cement them together as one flesh and ultimately of one mind.

Therefore, sexual activities even within marriage must be based on and full of love and concern for the other, and should not be selfish.

Our attitude in our marriages should not be "You must do this for me because I want it; or I am the boss" No, the attitude of BOTH parties should be "What can I do for you? How can I please you?" That attitude should be in BOTH our physical marriages and in our espousal to Jesus Christ!

John Kennedy put this very aptly when he said, "Ask not what your country can do for you, ask what you can do for your country:" And that is true of marriage and with our relationship with God.

God has done so much for us and our attitude in our relationship with God should be: how we can best serve, follow and please God our Father in heaven and Jesus Christ our espoused Husband!

Jesus Christ gave himself for his creation. We should remember that and consider that example and be willing to serve God the Father and Jesus Christ as they serve us.

We should be eagerly passionately seeking to wholeheartedly live by every Word of God and to do those things which are pleasing to God.

> **Ephesians 5:20** Giving thanks always for all things unto God and the Father in the name of our Lord Jesus Christ;
>
> **5:21 Submitting yourselves one to another in the fear of God.**
>
> **5:22 Wives, submit yourselves unto your own husbands, as unto the Lord.**
>
> **5:23** For the husband is the head of the wife, even as Christ is the head of the church: and he is the saviour of the body.
>
> **5:24** Therefore as the church is subject unto Christ, so let the wives be to their own husbands in every thing.
>
> **5:25 Husbands, love your wives, even as Christ also loved the church, and gave himself for it;**

On Passover night Christ washed the feet of the disciples to demonstrate to them not just humility, but a life of service to one another.

Hebrews 13:5 Let your conversation [conduct] be without covetousness, [without any selfishness and self-seeking; or seeking dominance of others] and be content with such things as you have: for he has said, I will never leave thee, nor forsake thee. **13:6** So that **we may boldly say, the Eternal is my helper, and I will not fear what man shall do unto me.**

13:7 Remember them that have the rule over you, who have **spoken unto you the word of God.** [This is talking about those ministers who speak the TRUE Word of God. It is NOT talking about those ministers who speak their own words, but those who teach the whole Word of God, calling all to a genuine "from the heart" repentance and the passionate Christ-like keeping of every Word of God.] whose faith follow, considering the end of their conversation.

Prove out and consider the fruits of their conduct, whether they present evil teachings contrary to scripture and gendering to destruction, or teach godly conduct bringing eternal salvation!

13:8 Jesus Christ is the same yesterday, and today, and forever.

God's character does not change. The character of Jesus Christ does not change. Christ said, **"I have kept my Father's commandments** (John 15:10)."

He will continue to keep God the Father's commandments for he said**, "If you have seen me, you have seen the Father (John 14:9)."**

God the Father and Jesus Christ are one in total unity with each other. They cooperate and work together. They have the same attitude, the same approach, the same beliefs, understanding, purposes and desires.

The Son keeps the Father's Word and if the Son [Jesus Christ] through God's Spirit is dwelling in you, he will be keeping God the Father's Word within you!

The Spirit of God cannot turn against God's commandments or any part of the whole Word of God. The Holy Spirit is the Spirit of TRUTH (John 15:26) and by its very nature, it keeps God's Word which is TRUTH (john 17:17) and it empowers us to do likewise if it is dwelling in us.

Those who are willing to lie to maintain past false traditions now known to be in error: Do not love the truth! They are not of God's Holy Spirit, but of another spirit which loves lies!

13:9 Be not carried about with divers and strange doctrines. For it is a good thing that the heart be established with grace; [the free application of the sacrifice of Christ to the sincerely repentant] not with meats [not with the physical sacrifices of the Mosaic Covenant and the Aaronic priesthood]**, which have not profited them that have been occupied therein**.

Remember Paul is writing to the Hebrews [the Jews and Levites in Judea], and the subject is the change in the priesthood, covenants and the sacrificial system.

13:10 We have an altar, whereof they have no right to eat which serve the tabernacle.

We cannot serve two masters; either we seek to serve the priesthood of the dead Mosaic Covenant, or we serve God the Father and Jesus Christ the High Priest of the eternal New Covenant.

Which is better; that which cannot atone for sin and which has passed away; or that which HAS atoned for all PAST sincerely repented sin?

13:11 For the bodies of those beasts, whose blood is brought into the sanctuary by the high priest for sin [sin offerings], are burned without the camp

The altar of the New Covenant is before God the Father in heaven, and our sacrifice is Jesus Christ, the very Creator; the Lamb of God.

Jesus Christ was crucified outside the temple and city, indicating that the Mosaic Covenant represented by the physical Jerusalem and Mosaic temple was ended, and that a New Covenant was being made sure.

13:12 Wherefore Jesus also, that he might sanctify the people with his own blood, suffered without the gate. **13:13** Let us go forth therefore unto him without the camp, bearing his reproach. **13:14** For **here have we no continuing city, but we seek one** [the resurrection to spirit of the New Covenant] **to come.**

Jesus Christ was killed outside the city, demonstrating that his priesthood, the priesthood of Melchisedec; was to be a different, a separate, a new priesthood and yet a very old priesthood because this priesthood of Melchisedec actually predated the Aaronic priesthood.

We seek a city to come; which is, the New Jerusalem, the heavenly city.

13:15 By him therefore let us offer the sacrifice of praise to God continually, that is, the fruit of our lips giving thanks to his name. **13:16** But to do good and to communicate forget not: for with such sacrifices God is well pleased.

Do not forget brethren, to be grateful for the things that you have, even during times of poverty. Don't focus so much on your trials or on your troubles; but rather focus on the spiritual riches of your calling and on the heritage of the birthright of your calling which God has stored up for you in his kingdom.

We have been called and given a birthright to become kings and priests forever. We have been called to eternal life. We need only submit to God the Father and to live by every Word of God, which brings eternal life as a good child of our Father.

God is not asking anything really difficult of us: He is asking us to live a way which brings peace and harmony and life.

It is Satan's hatred of God and Satan's hatred of God's ways which causes him to persecute those people who do keep the Word of life. It is not a burden to keep the Word of God. God's Word is light and easy to keep, as Jesus said, **"My yoke is easy and my burden light** (Mat 11:30)."

The true heavy burden is the burden that Satan places upon us, trying to discourage us to give up and quit. Even the poorest among the brethren, the sickest, the people who have the most problems have a tremendous amount to rejoice for.

We need to keep our eyes focused on the future, on God's promises, on our true love for our Father and our espoused Husband, and on the inestimable value of the birthright of our calling. NEVER despise the value of the birthright of our calling as Esau did.

All those who account themselves as teachers of God must give an account to our Head Jesus Christ for what we teach.

How is it that so many teach the brethren to follow idols of men, and teach to follow traditions that they KNOW are false even lying to maintain them, while decrying any zeal to keep the whole Word of God? How is it that such men do not tremble and exceedingly shake in fear of the just retribution of their idolatry? How can they escape the wrath of God?

13:17 Obey them that have the rule over you [in the Lord], and submit yourselves [to the whole Word of God]: for they [Godly teachers] watch for your souls, as they that must give account, that they may do it with joy, and not with grief: for that is unprofitable for you.

Consider that we are to submit to those who are teaching us the TRUTH and the whole Word of God. We are to take what leaders, elders and others teach, and judge it against the whole Word of God. Then, ONLY if the teaching is consistent with God's Word, and if we can prove the doctrine out of God's Word; should we submit to that teaching.

Now, consider the other side of that coin. If you are a teacher; be very, very sure that what you are teaching is absolutely consistent with the whole Word of God.

The heart and soul, the very key of any godly teacher, is that he will always teach people to question him and prove him out by scripture; and he will MEAN THAT; and will never exalt himself.

He will never claim to be an apostle or prophet to gain a following, but will let people judge for themselves what he is by his fruits, according to the command of Jesus Christ in Matthew 7. A godly man will always fearlessly teach sincere repentance from sin and a passionate Christ-like zeal to live by every Word of God without any shadow of compromise.

Paul says that we must live with a clean conscience before God, which clean conscience is that we are pleasing our LORD and faithfully following him, and living by every Word of God.

Paul then asks the brotherhood in Jerusalem to pray that he can come to them soon.

13:18 Pray for us: for we trust we have a good conscience, in all things willing to live honestly. **13:19** But I beseech you the rather to do this, that I may be restored to you the sooner.

Paul prays that God the Father will make us all perfect in godliness, to keep the whole Word of God with the good work's of faith, and strengthen us to do the Will of God; and to please God the Father in all things through the indwelling power of the Holy Spirit.

13:20 Now the God of peace, that brought again from the dead our Lord Jesus, that great shepherd of the sheep, through the blood of the everlasting [new] covenant,

13:21 Make you perfect in every good work to do his will, working in you that which is wellpleasing in his sight, through Jesus Christ; to whom be glory for ever and ever. Amen.

Who are we to please: Whose will are we to do? **God the Father's will!**

12:22 And I beseech you, brethren, suffer [accept, obey] the word of exhortation: for I have written a letter unto you in few words. **13:23** Know ye that our brother Timothy is set at liberty; with whom, if he come shortly, I will see you. **13:24** Salute all them that have the rule over you, and all the saints. They of Italy salute you.

13:25 Grace [God's Mercy] be with [upon] you all. Amen.

The New Covenant Priesthood of Zadok

God has given a prophetic pledge of a New Covenant Temple and of the renewal of physical sacrifices, Ezekiel 40-48 and included in that prophecy was a promise that physical Levites and physical Priests from the line of Zadok [a descendant of Levi] would be called into the New Covenant to serve as a part of the priesthood of Jesus Christ.

That is not a promise of a restoration of all of the priesthood of Aaron, it is a promise to the descendants of faithful Zadok ONLY!

The promise to Zadok is not a promise of the restoration of the Aaronic priesthood, because this promise was not given to all the sons of Aaron, most of whom had not been faithful in their service and fell away time after time!

This promise was given to Zadok and to the descendants of Zadok ONLY! This because of the loyalty of Zadok and his sons during the kingdom of David beginning in 2 Samuel 15 and continuing into 1 Kings.

The promise to Zadok does not mean that the Mosaic Covenant will be restored or that they will be Aaronic priests of the Mosaic Covenant! To think so, one would have to reject the entire book of Hebrews! For Paul tells us several times and in various ways in the book of Hebrews that the Mosaic Covenant with its Aaronic priesthood has ended and has been replaced by the High Priesthood of Jesus Christ!

The promise to the descendants of Zadok means that men who are the descendants of the faithful sons of Zadok, will be called into the New Covenant; and will serve in the New Covenant Temple as the priests of the New Covenant, officiating over the physical things of the Ezekiel Temple.

This promise has two distinct meanings:

1 That some of the descendants of Zadok would be among the called out and the Chosen in the resurrection to spirit and will be among the spirit priesthood of Jesus Christ in that way,

2 That some of the descendants of Zadok will live on into the Millennial Kingdom and will serve in the Ezekiel Temple in the physical necessities of the Temple!

In BOTH cases they will be priests of the New Covenant priesthood of Jesus Christ and not priests of the Aaronic priesthood!

David was loyal to God and he will rule Israel forever as a resurrected spirit; and because Zadok and his sons were loyal to God and to David and Solomon, they will serve God in the Ezekiel Temple as PHYSICAL priests of Jesus Christ in the New Covenant Temple.

Zadok has a promise from Almighty God, that because of his and his son's faithfulness [trained up in the faithfulness of Zadok] in service to God under the Mosaic Covenant; his descendants will be called into the New Covenant and will serve in the New Covenant Temple!

The physical sacrifices of the Mosaic Covenant were an allegory of the sacrifice of Jesus Christ; to teach Israel that the wages of sin is death, and to teach Israel about the need for a better and more perfect sacrifice for sin.

Sacrifices will be restored in the New Covenant Temple for the same reason, as a practical demonstration, lesson and teaching method.

The descendants of Zadok will officiate in the physical sacrifices and the physical things of the Ezekiel Temple and will teach these principles: While the resurrected spirit priests and kings freed from the physical duties of the Ezekiel Temple by the descendants of Zadok, will teach the spiritual understandings of these things to the whole world.

God gave the Mosaic Covenant as an allegory and foundation of the New Covenant.

The New Covenant is merely the Mosaic Covenant with a better sacrifice and better promises, and the addition of the Holy Spirit to write the whole Word of God in our minds and on our hearts so that we may keep them.

The New Covenant is a much better Covenant and the Mosaic Covenant by reason of its weakness has passed away and been replaced by the New as Paul teaches through the whole book of Hebrews.

Jeremiah 31:31 Behold, the days come, saith the Lord, that I will make a new covenant with the house of Israel, and with the house of Judah:

31:32 Not according to the covenant that I made with their fathers in the day that I took them by the hand to bring them out of the land of Egypt; which my covenant they brake, although I was an husband unto them, saith the Lord:

31:33 But this shall be the covenant that I will make with the house of Israel; After those days, saith the Lord, **I will put my law in their inward parts, and write it in their hearts; and will be their God, and they shall be my people.**

Jeremiah 33:16 In those days shall Judah be saved, and Jerusalem shall dwell safely: and this is the name wherewith she shall be called, The LORD our righteousness [The Righteousness of the LORD is There]. **33:17** For thus saith the LORD; David shall never want a man to sit upon the throne of the house of Israel [referring to the now resurrected spirit and eternal David himself]; **33:18 Neither shall the priests the Levites** [through the descendants of Zadok] **want a man before me to offer burnt offerings, and to kindle meat offerings, and to do sacrifice continually**

This is a promise that the descendants of Zadok will yet serve God in a physical New Covenant priesthood and offer physical sacrifices in the New Covenant: It is not a promise that the Mosaic Covenant will endure, for Jeremiah 31:31 plainly speaks of a New Covenant; and the Old is replaced by the New as Paul plainly says in Hebrews.

Jeremiah 33:20 Thus saith the LORD; if ye can break my covenant of the day, and my covenant of the night, and that there should not be day and night in their season; **33:21** Then may also my covenant be broken with David my servant, that he should not have a son to reign upon his throne; and with the Levites the priests, my ministers. **33:22** As the host of heaven cannot be numbered, neither the sand of the sea measured: so will I multiply the seed of David my servant, and the Levites that minister unto me.

This is NOT speaking of the Mosaic Covenant but is speaking of the New Covenant; the entire context of Jeremaih 33 is the restoration of Israel in the millennium New Covenant Kingdom of God. We know this is speaking of the New Covenant because the gift of the Holy Spirit which was never promised in the Mosaic Covenant and is a promise exclusive to the New Covenant, will be poured out **on all flesh** Joel 2:28 in the Millennial New Covenant Kingdom of God!

Zadok (a descendant of Aaron (1 Chron 6:50-53) and his sons served in Solomon's Temple and the physical descendants of Zadok will serve in the Ezekiel Temple, in place of the other sons of Aaron! However they will not serve as Mosaic priests, but as physical priests of Jesus Christ of the New Covenant.

1 Chronicles 29:22 And they made Solomon the son of David king the second time, and anointed him unto the LORD to be the chief governor, and Zadok to be priest.

2 Chronicles 31:10 And Azariah the chief priest of the house of Zadok answered him, and said, Since the people began to bring the offerings into the house of the LORD, we have had enough to eat, and have left plenty: for the LORD hath blessed his people; and that which is left is this great store.

God promises that the descendants of the priests who remained faithful when the other Mosaic priests went astray, shall serve in the physical things of the New Covenant Temple.

This is not a promise of a continuing Mosaic Covenant and it does not mean that they will be Aaronic priests of the Mosaic Covenant.

Most of the physical priesthood of Aaron was rejected for their continual rebellion against God; while Zadok and his sons were faithful and have a promise from God that for their faithfulness, their descendants will serve as physical priests of the New Covenant in the Ezekiel Temple.

Ezekiel 44:15 But the priests the Levites, **the sons of Zadok, that kept the charge of my sanctuary when the children of Israel went astray from me,** they shall come near to me to minister unto me, and they shall stand before me to offer unto me the fat and the blood, saith the Lord GOD:

In the consecration of the altar, blood is the means by which it is purified and atoned for: picturing that sin must be atoned for by the death of the sinner or by the effectual sacrifice of Jesus Christ the Lamb of God.

Leviticus 8:15 And he slew it; and Moses took the blood, and put it upon the horns of the altar round about with his finger, and purified the altar, and poured the blood at the bottom of the altar, and sanctified it, to make reconciliation upon it.

The New Covenant Temple will also be sanctified by the blood of sacrifices and the Ezekiel Temple will be a place of physical sacrifice. Therefore it is needful that physical priests of the New Covenant serve in the Ezekiel Temple.

Ezekiel 43:20 You are to take some of its blood and put it on the four horns of the altar and on the four corners of the upper ledge and all around the rim, and so purify the altar and make atonement for it.

The sacrifices to be offered in the Ezekiel Temple in the New Covenant, are the same as those offered in the Mosaic Covenant, as recognized in this list:

Ezekiel 45:17 And it shall be the prince's part to give burnt offerings, and meat offerings, and drink offerings, in the feasts, and in the new moons, and in the sabbaths, in all solemnities of the house of Israel: he shall prepare the sin offering, and the meat offering, and the burnt offering, and the peace offerings, to make reconciliation for the house of Israel.

The personal offerings for cleansing/atonement for impurity and sin are also instructional New Covenant offerings.

Regarding the New Covenant Temple Ezekiel writes:

Ezekiel 44:25 And they shall come at no dead person to defile themselves: but for father, or for mother, or for son, or for daughter, for brother, or for sister that hath had no husband, they may defile themselves. **44:26** And after he is cleansed, they shall reckon unto him seven days. **44:27** And in the day that he goeth into the sanctuary, unto the inner court, to minister in the sanctuary, he shall offer his sin offering, saith the Lord GOD.

Ezekiel 40:39 And in the porch of the gate were two tables on this side, and two tables on that side, to slay thereon the burnt offering and the sin offering and the trespass offering.

This is from the formula for the trespass offering from Leviticus:

Leviticus 5:16 and the priest shall make an atonement for him with the ram of the trespass offering, and it shall be forgiven him.

The physical priests that perform the New Covenant physical sacrificial services, are physical helpers of the New Covenant priesthood of Jesus Christ, serving in the physical things of the Ezekiel Temple and are not priests of the Mosaic Covenant, but are converted into the New Covenant!

These physical priests of the New Covenant will also be teaching what the offering sacrifices really mean.

Leviticus 10:8 And the LORD spake unto Aaron, saying, **10:9** Do not drink wine nor strong drink, thou, nor thy sons with thee, when ye go into the tabernacle of the congregation, lest ye die: it shall be a statute for ever throughout your generations: **10:10 And that ye may put difference between holy and unholy, and between unclean and clean; 10:11 And that ye may teach the children of Israel all the statutes which the LORD hath spoken unto them by the hand of Moses.**

Ezekiel speaks of the physical priests of the New Covenant, the descendants of Zadok; as being teachers of the people. This is because the physical sacrificial system is an instructional allegory of the sacrifice of Jesus Christ the Lamb of God.

Ezekiel 44:22 Neither shall any priest drink wine, when they enter into the inner court [courtyard]. **44:23** And they **shall teach my people the difference between the holy and profane, and cause them to discern between the unclean and the clean.**

Moses prophesies of the New Covenant in this manner.

Deuteronomy 30:1 And it shall come to pass, when all these things [specifically the great tribulation] are come upon thee, the blessing and the curse, which I have set before thee, and thou [they shall remember the whole Word of God to keep it] shalt call them to mind among all the nations, whither the LORD thy God hath driven thee, **30:2 And shalt return unto the LORD thy God, and shalt obey his voice according to all that I command thee this day,** thou and thy children, **with all thine heart, and with all thy soul; 30:3** That then the LORD thy God will turn thy captivity, and have compassion upon thee, and **will return and gather thee from all the nations, whither the LORD thy God hath scattered thee. 30:4** If any of thine be driven out unto the outmost parts of heaven, from thence will the LORD thy God gather thee, and from thence will he fetch thee:

30:5 And the LORD thy God will bring thee into the land which thy fathers possessed, and thou shalt possess it; and he will do thee good, and multiply thee above thy fathers. **30:6** And **the LORD thy God will circumcise thine heart, and the heart of thy seed, to love the LORD thy God with all thine heart, and with all thy soul, that thou mayest live. 30:7** And the LORD thy God will put all these curses upon thine enemies, and on them that hate thee, which persecuted thee.

30:8 And **thou shalt return and obey the voice of the LORD, and do all his commandments which I command thee this day.**

As a matter of interest today's Temple Faithful in Israel consists of one main extended family which is preparing to serve in the coming Ezekiel Temple. They are filled with zeal to serve in the coming new physical temple which will be built by Messiah after he comes.

Could they be the descendants of Zadok who will serve in the New Covenant Temple after they have been brought into the New Covenant when Messiah comes?

Physical Sacrifices in the New Covenant

All sacrifices must be made at the Jerusalem temple and since there is no temple in Jerusalem right now no physical sacrifices can be made. However once Christ comes and builds the Ezekiel Temple, physical sacrifices will be restored. Yet the physical sacrifices in the New Covenant Ezekiel Temple will not be made as part of the Mosaic Covenant: they will be offered as part of the New Covenant!

Physical laws are intended to teach us spiritual lessons. For example the laws of clean and unclean animals is intended to teach us to put a difference between sin and godliness, a difference between the Holy and the Profane; and to get us into a life time habit of avoiding all uncleanness physically and the uncleanness of association with sin spiritually.

There are two purposes; one is to teach the actual lesson and the second part is to instil a habit of obedience of God that will last forever.

The physical sacrificial system was not specific to the Mosaic Covenant and began as soon as the first woman and man sinned in the garden. When sin entered the need for an atonement for sin became essential to save mankind.

Later God expanded the sacrificial system to Moses; each and every animal and type of sacrifice was an allegory of the sacrificial work of our LORD, the Lamb of God.

The very first aspect of offering a physical sacrifice is repentance; presenting a physical offering was a way of saying "I'm sorry, I will not do that again".

Not meaning to trivialize in any way but an example is when we present a gift and apology to someone whom we have offended. When we have sinned against God and have offended Him, we must repent [stop dong the offensive thing] and make an offering [sacrifice] to God.

Repentance is saying that we are sorry for what we did, and saying "I am sorry" means that we will never do it again.

Consider that when we give a gift and say we are sorry; that our friend might well say: "If you had not done that, you would not need to say you are sorry, I would much rather that you had not done the deed than to hear you say sorry and receive your gift."

God would much rather that we did not sin in the first place then that we should offer sacrifice for having offended with sin. God wants a humble person poor in the spirit of self-will who will live by God's Word and not need to say "I am sorry" for sinning, because he is not offending God and sinning.

That is what God means when he says: **Psalm 51:16-17** For thou desirest not sacrifice; else would I give it: thou delightest not in burnt offering. The sacrifices of God are a broken spirit [a spirit poor in stubborn self-will, humble teachable and obedient to live by every Word of God]: a broken and a contrite heart, O God, thou wilt not despise.

God wants to forgive, but sacrifice must be made for our good; so that we will learn that sin brings death; and only when we learn how very serious sin is, can we be fully motivated to STOP SINNING!

Hosea 6:6 For I desired mercy, and not sacrifice; and the knowledge of God more than burnt offerings. In burnt offerings and sacrifices for sin thou hast had no pleasure.

In order to understand Hosea 6:6 properly, one must understand the sense of the Hebrew text. In it a rhetorical negation is used to point up antithesis more emphatically (cf. Deut 5:3).

"Moreover, the negation in Hebrew often supplies the lack of a comparative - i.e., without excluding the thing denied, the statement implies only the importance of the thing set in contrast to it (Hos 6:6). In short, the Hebrew idiom permits denial of one thing in order to emphasize another (cf. for a NT parallel Luke 14:26). The idiom does not intend to deny the statement but only to set it in a secondary place (so Frost)."

God desires obedience and mercy, nevertheless all have sinned and come short of the glory of God (Rom 3:23) and sacrifices are needed to teach us that the consequences of sin is death.

Physical sacrifices are a reminder of sin and the need for the sacrifice of the Lamb of God, but they cannot atone for sin on a spiritual level. They are a practical lesson on the need for sincere repentance and a graphic example of the wages [end result] of sin [which is death] that was paid in our place by the very Creator made flesh.

Hebrews 10:4-12 For it is not possible that the blood of bulls and of goats should take away sins. Wherefore when he cometh into the world, he saith, Sacrifice and offering thou wouldest not, but a body [the sacrifice of Christ] hast thou prepared me: Then said I, Lo, I come (in the volume of the book it is written of me,) to do thy will, O God.

Above when he said [Paul is quoting Hosea 6:6], Sacrifice and offering and burnt offerings and offering for sin thou wouldest not, neither hadst pleasure therein; which are offered by the law; Then said he, Lo, I come to do thy will, O God. He taketh away the first, that he may establish the second.

By the which will we are sanctified through the offering of the body of Jesus Christ once for all. And every priest standeth daily ministering and offering oftentimes the same sacrifices, which can never take away sins: But this man, after he had offered one sacrifice for sins for ever, sat down on the right hand of God;

The physical sacrificial system was given to teach us that sin requires a sacrifice to atone for sin, it was also given to teach us about the various aspects of the sacrifice of the Lamb of God.

When Christ was sacrificed and that sacrifice was accepted by God the Father on Wave Offering Sunday; the sacrifice of the Lamb of God was perfect and complete and need never be repeated, however as men repent that sacrifice needs to be applied often. Let it be made clear that Christ's sacrifice was perfect - which was covered in the Hebrews study - and

Christ need never die again; but his sacrifice must be applied as often as men sin and repent.

The physical sacrifices were an instructional allegory to teach us about the sacrifice of Jesus Christ the Lamb of God.

The sacrifice of Christ did away with sin and reconciles the sincerely repentant to God the Father, something which the physical sacrifices could not do; but Christ's sacrifice did not do away with the need for the physical sacrifices as a graphic instructional reminder that the wages of sin is death and as a means of instruction about the sacrifice of Christ.

The physical sacrifices were instituted from the foundation of the world and came into effect as soon as sin entered the world, as an example that the Lamb of God would need to be sacrificed to atone for the sins of the sincerely repentant.

From the very beginning it was understood that man would sin and would need the atoning sacrifice of their Creator made flesh.

Revelation 13:8 And all that dwell upon the earth shall worship him, whose names are not written in the book of life of **the Lamb slain from the foundation of the world**.

These physical sacrifices were a graphic example that the wages of sin is death, and were a type or instructional allegory of the sacrifice of the Lamb of God.

These physical sacrifices continued and were accepted as appropriate by the first century Ekklesia right up to the destruction of the temple in c 70 A.D. The apostles at Jerusalem even encouraging Paul to sponsor the required sacrifices for certain Nazarites.

Acts 21:23 Do therefore this that we say to thee: We have four men which have a vow on them; **21:24** Them take, and purify thyself with them, and be at charges (the sacrifice of a lamb, Numbers 6) with them, that they may shave their heads: and all may know that those things, whereof they were informed concerning thee, are nothing; but that thou thyself also walkest orderly, and keepest the law.

Bear in mind that after the tabernacle was built it became unlawful to offer sacrifices anywhere else, and later that law was transferred to the temple when the Ark was moved to the temple: Therefore when the temple was destroyed it became unlawful to offer physical sacrifices until the Ark was remade and a new temple was built.

Jesus knowing that the temple would be destroyed taught the spiritual Passover service to his disciples.

Because physical sacrifices are unlawful until the new temple is built, Nazarite vows are unlawful for the present time as well.

Leviticus 17:8 And thou shalt say unto them, Whatsoever man there be of the house of Israel, or of the strangers which sojourn among you, that **offereth a burnt offering or sacrifice, 17:9 And bringeth it not unto the door of the tabernacle** [the altar in the inner court at the entrance to the Most Holy Place] **of the congregation, to offer it unto the Lord; even that man shall be cut off from among his people.**

God told Daniel that once the prince who would come would destroy the city, the sacrifice would be stopped [by the destruction of the temple; which was destroyed by Prince Titus of Rome in c 70 A.D.], and that the physical Daily Sacrifice would not begin anew until after the consummation [the coming of Christ to cleanse the temple mount and build the Ezekiel Temple].

Once Christ comes the Ezekiel Temple will be built and physical sacrifices will be restarted

WHY? For exactly the same reasons that physical sacrifices had been offered from Abel to the destruction of the temple; as a graphic lesson on the NEED for Christ's sacrifice to atone for sin and as an instruction in the various aspects of the sacrificial work of the Lamb of God.

The sacrificial system began when Eve and Adam sinned and it will continue as long as flesh exists. The sacrificial system was never ended - even Paul sponsored sacrifices for certain Nazarites long after the resurrection of Christ - it was merely suspended for the period in which the temple remained destroyed and will begin anew when a new temple is built.

There will be a big difference from the past however; because, instead of making physical offerings in ignorance about what they were doing and what it meant; in the millennium the physical sacrifices will be made as a graphic instructional lesson and the people will be taught the spiritual MEANING of what they are doing!

The point of a New Covenant Temple is to focus the whole world on God the Father and Jesus Christ the King of kings; the point of the Temple and sacrifices is to graphically teach all people the need to stop sinning and to teach them the various aspects of the sacrifice of Jesus Christ, the Lamb of God.

As for the Holy Spirit being poured out on all flesh (Joel 3:28), the Holy Spirit does not make one instantly perfect but leads one into godliness if we are willing to follow and live by every Word of God.

Receiving the Spirit is only the beginning point of our spiritual education, not the end

Micah 4:2 And many nations shall come, and say, Come, and let us go up to the mountain of the Lord, and to the house of the God of Jacob; and he will teach us of his ways, and we will walk in his paths: for the law shall go forth of Zion, and the word of the Lord from Jerusalem.

James

James 1

James is the English form of the Greek form of the Hebrew name Jacob. In his own language he would have been called Yakov [Jacob].

James 1:1 James, a servant of God and of the Lord Jesus Christ, to the twelve tribes which are scattered abroad, greeting.

This message is to all of the twelve tribes and not just the Jews. It is also a message to all of Spiritual Israel.

1:2 My brethren, count it joy when you fall into various temptations [or trials], **1:3** knowing this, that the trying of your faith [belief and trust] worketh patience. **1:4** But let patience have her perfect work, that ye may be perfect [endure and patiently grow and overcome so that we might attain to godly holiness] and entire [we are to be complete in internalizing the whole nature of God], wanting nothing. [lacking nothing in the keeping of the whole Word of God]

James encourages us to become perfect through the diligent keeping of the whole Word of God, and in patiently enduring the trial and temptation associated with zeal for keeping God's Word, enduring every trials and temptations which Satan throws in our direction.

In overcoming sin and trials we develop patient perseverance in striving toward perfection in godliness; and eventually with the power of God's

Spirit we can overcome and achieve that perfection; not achieving through the strength of our flesh or our own efforts alone, but becoming godly through the power of God.

1:5 If any of you lack wisdom, **let him ask of God**, that giveth to all men liberally, and upbraideth not; and it shall be given him.

James tells us that we need to ask for and then we must actively seek, godly wisdom; through diligent study and the application of God's Word to every circumstance.

When we sincerely repent and turn away from sinning, turning towards living by every Word of God; the sacrifice of Christ is applied to us and we may then enter the presence of God the Father and ask that God's Spirit of understanding and power be given to us.

1:6 But let him ask in faith, nothing wavering or diverging. For he that wavers or doubts is like a wave of the sea tossed with the wind and driven. **1:7** For let not that man think that he shall receive any thing of the Lord."

If we do not believe God's Word enough to diligently obey and seek to please him, do not think that we are going to receive anything from God.

We must KNOW that God exists and that God keeps his promises; and we must add to that knowledge the works of faith, loving and diligently keeping the whole Word of God and seeking God's will and seeking to please him will all of our beings. Only then can we expect a positive answer to our petitions.

> **1 John 3:22** And whatsoever we ask, we receive of him, **because we keep his commandments, and do those things that are pleasing in his sight.**

James 1:8 For a double-minded [doubting] man is unstable in all his ways."

It is only by knowing that God exists and that God's Word will not be broken, that we can believe and trust God enough to obey and please him.

If we ask for something according to God's will, Word and Promises, and doubt him and his promises so that we are not zealous and passionate to learn and to keep the whole Word of God, if we do not seek to do God's will and to please God in every way; we will not receive our requests.

We must learn to TRUST [which is Faith] God enough to do his will, before we can expect God to bless us.

1:9 Let the brother of low degree rejoice in that he is exalted.

A person who has a low place in this life can rejoice knowing that he is called to become a king or a priest, or both king and priest in the kingdom of God. He has a high reward if he has faith in God, if he trusts and believes God and if he acts on that trust and belief and diligently lives by every Word of God, doing God's will.

1:10 But the rich, in that he is made low: because as the flower of the grass he Shall pass away. **1:11** For the sun is no sooner risen with a burning heat, but it withereth [like] the grass, and the flower thereof falleth, and the grace of the fashion of it perisheth: so also shall the rich man fade away in his ways.

The rich man who gives up his physical riches for God's sake and for the kingdom's sake should rejoice in that he is humbled now so that he will be made fit for the riches of eternal life; and he should know that physical things mean nothing because like the flowers they will wither and pass away.

This applies not just to giving away wealth it also applies to those who lose their good jobs and must take inferior ones due to persecution. Often God tests us to see how much we love him and how much we willing to give for that pearl of great price.

1:12 Blessed is the man that endures temptation: for when he is tested, [if he passes the test] he shall receive a crown of life, which the Eternal has promised to them that love him [love him enough to follow him and to keep his Word].

If we love someone we will seek to please them and if we truly love God, we would never walk around saying, "Oh, I love the Lord" while not obeying him: What we would do is to enthusiastically try to please Him by doing what He says.

1:13 Let no man say when he is tempted, I am tempted of God: for God cannot be tempted with evil, neither tempteth he any man: **1:14** But every man is tempted, when he is drawn away of his own lust, and enticed. **1:15** Then when lust hath conceived, it bringeth forth sin: and sin, when it is finished, bringeth forth death."

When we see some unlawful thing and we dwell on it and begin to desire it in our hearts and we let that desire grow and develop in us, eventually we are going to do it. When God sees something evil he does not dwell on it as if it were some desirable thing; he immediately rejects it as the loathsome filth it really is.

The key to overcoming temptation is that when we are tempted we must immediately reject it and not let the temptation take root within us.

We need to recognize the consequences of sin by thinking beyond the immediate pleasure; not dwelling on the temptation and wrongfully thinking that it is desirable!

1:16 Do not err, my beloved brethren. 1:17 Every good gift and every perfect gift is from above, and cometh down from the Father of lights, with whom is no variableness, no changing, nor even a shadow of turning."

God knows the way that is right and he sticks to it and there is not even a shadow not even the remotest possibility that He is going to turn away from the righteousness of his Word; which should be the case with all of us.

1:18 Of his own will begat he us with the word of truth [which is the whole Word of God], **that we should be a kind of firstfruits of his creatures. 1:19 Wherefore, my beloved brethren, let every man be swift to hear** [always be seeking to learn] **slow to speak and slow to anger.**

Anyone who is quick tempered is not in control of himself and he needs to learn to get control of himself, he needs to learn to listen, to think and to make sound judgments before proceeding.

1:20 For **the wrath of man worketh not the righteousness of God**.

A man who cannot control his anger cannot do what is right in God's sight and is easily led astray. Righteous anger is anger that is under control and governed by the law of righteousness which is the whole Word of God.

1:21 Therefore lay apart all filthiness and superfluity of naughtiness [sinful shallowness], and **receive with meekness the engrafted word, which is able to save your lives.**

Godly righteousness is to turn away from the filthiness of sin and all uncleanness and worldliness; and to be zealous to learn and to keep the whole Word of God with meekness before God because it is the only thing of lasting value and is able to save our lives.

1:22 be ye doers of the word, and not just hearers only, deceiving your own selves.

If a man hears God's Word and says, "Oh, that's great" and does not actually act on it and keep it, he is really deceiving himself. He is not so special after all, he just thinks he is.

It is he who lives by every Word of God and has the Works of Faith who is special in God's eyes.

1:23 For if any be a hearer of the word, and not a doer, he is like unto a man beholding his natural face in a glass: **1:24** For he beholds himself, and goes his way, and straightway forgets what manner of man or person he was. But whoso looketh into the perfect law of liberty…"

God's law is a law which brings us liberty from bondage to Satan and sin. It delivers us from the chains of sin, from the burdens of slavery to to Satan and sin.

1:25 But who so looketh unto the **perfect law of liberty and continues therein**, he being not a forgetful hearer, but **a doer of the work, this man shall be blessed in his deeds. 1:26** If any man among you seems to be religious, and does not control his tongue, but deceives his own heart, this man's religion is vain.

Those people who are always talking the good talk and then not walking the good walk, have a vain and empty religion.

Those who erupt in uncontrolled anger have a serious spiritual problem.

1:27 Pure religion and undefiled before God and the Father is this, to visit the fatherless and widows in their affliction, and **to keep himself unspotted from the world**.

"To visit the fatherless and widows in their affliction," also means to have empathy, to have concern, to love others, to care about them and to care about the condition they are in; and to act on that caring and do something about it and to try our best to help eliminate or alleviate the suffering of others: To be kindhearted and generous to those suffering or in need.

"To keep unspotted from the world," means to turn away from the sins of Satan's world; and the only way to do that is to sincerely repent of those sins, to reject any compromise with the Word of God; and to passionately embrace God's ways to live by every Word of God and to wholeheartedly seek to please God!

Then the sacrifice of Jesus Christ will be applied to us, and we can enter into a relationship with God the Father who will give us His Spirit and empower us to keep His Word and Will, and empower us to keep ourselves unspotted by the sins of the world.

James 2

James 2:1 My brethren, have not the faith of our Lord Jesus Christ, the Lord of glory, with respect of persons.

This is a major, major, major problem in today's spiritual Ekklesia: People respecting persons above their respect for the Word of God. That is, they do not hold everyone up to the standard of God's Word.

They do not hold certain people up to the standard of God's Word, making idols of them. Yet they will turn around and attempt to hold other people to their own ways even when their own ways are contrary to God's Word. This makes them respecters of persons, rather than respecters of God; which is the sin of idolatry; it is the sin of allowing people to come between us and God.

There is also the great sin of respecting those who give more or who flatter us. Many have been ordained and promoted because they excelled at flattery, and many others because they gave more than other brethren.

2:2 For if there come into your assembly a man with a gold ring, in goodly apparel, and there comes in also a poor man in vile raiment; **2:3** And ye have respect to him that weareth the gay clothing, and say unto him, "Sit thou here in a good place" and say to the poor, "Stand thou there, or sit here under my stool." **2:4** Are ye not then partial in yourselves, and are become judges of evil thoughts? **2:5** Hearken, my beloved brethren, Hath not God chosen the poor of this world rich in faith, and heirs of the kingdom which he hath promised to them that love him?

2:6 But ye have despised the poor. Do not rich men oppress you, and draw you before the judgment seats? **2:7** Do not they blaspheme that worthy name by which ye are called?

2:8 If ye fulfill the royal law according to the scripture, Thou shall love thy neighbour as thyself, ye do well: **2:9** But if ye have respect to persons, ye commit sin, and are convicted of the law as transgressors.

2:10 For **whosoever shall keep the whole law, and yet offend in one point, he is guilty of all.**

If we break any part of God's Word we are guilty of breaking the whole law.

Being respecters of persons is wrong and respecting the rich over the poor is wrong. Respecting the poor over the rich is also wrong and respecting some man because he claims some grand title or claims to be somebody while departing from the Word of God, is wrong.

We are not to study the Scriptures as interpreted or explained by this man or that man: We are to judge the words of all men, by the Holy Scriptures of Almighty God!

We are to study the Scriptures and when someone explains something, we are to test what he has said against the standard of the Scriptures.

We are not to test the Scriptures against some man's view of them; we are to test that man's view against what the scriptures actually say.

2:11 For he that said, Do not commit adultery, also said, Do not kill. Now if thou commit no adultery, yet if you kill, thou art become a transgressor of the law. **2:12 So speak ye, and so do** [according to the whole Word of God, for we shall all be judged by every Word of God], as they that **shall be judged by the law of liberty**. **2:13** For he shall have judgment without mercy, that hath showed no mercy; and mercy rejoices against judgment.

If we show no mercy to others, no mercy will be shown to us by God in our own judgment. If we break the smallest law we are guilty of breaking the whole law itself.

If we cook a meal on God's Sabbath, or have a barbecue etc; we will face the same judgment as the homosexual or murderer if we do not repent; for the wages of sin is death.

Faith and the Works of Faith

2:14 What doth it profit, my brethren, though a man say he hath faith, and have not works? Can faith save him? **2:5** If a brother or sister be naked, and destitute of daily food, **2:16** and one of you say unto them, Depart in peace, be ye warmed and filled; notwithstanding ye give them not those things which are needful to the body, what doth it profit?

2:17 Even so **faith, if it hath not works, is dead, being alone. 2:18** Yea, a man may say, You hast faith, and I have works. **Show me thy faith without thy works, and I will show thee my faith by my works. 2:19** Thou believest that there is one God; thou doest well: the devils also believe, and tremble.

The demons believe God yet they will not obey God's Word, therefore their belief brings them nothing but the sure knowledge of their coming judgment.

2:20 But wilt thou know, O vain man, that **faith without works is dead**?

2:21 Was not Abraham our father justified [by his deeds] by works when he [obeyed God] had offered Isaac his son upon the altar? **2:22** Seest thou how faith wrought [worked with] with his works and **by works was faith made perfect**? **2:23** And the scripture was fulfilled which saith, Abraham believed God, and it was imputed unto him for righteousness: and he was called the Friend of God.

2:24 Ye see then how that by works a man is justified, and not by faith only. **2:25** Likewise also was not Rehab the harlot justified by works, when she had received the messengers, and had sent them out another way? **2:26** For **as the body without the spirit is dead, so faith without works is dead.**

Yes, there is a spirit in our body, it is a spirit of man, a spirit in man; and without the body it doesn't function, it doesn't think, it is not conscious.

Our spirit must be plugged into the body because the spirit of man and the body work together. Just so, faith must be plugged into works, and works into the faith; so that trust and belief result in the works of faith.

Faith without works cannot stand: If we have faith, if we believe God, we will do what God says; which is our works of faith.

We cannot do what God says if we do not believe [have faith that his Word is true] Him; any more than the body can function without the human spirit.

If we have faith and no works, our faith is meaningless: it is a waste of time. Believing without acting on that belief is a waste of time; it won't get us anywhere.

James 3

We are to grow and learn and perfect ourselves by continually and diligently seeking more knowledge and understanding; and then APPLYING what we learn in our lives .

James 3:1 My brethren, be not many masters [teachers, leaders], knowing that we [leaders and teachers] shall receive the greater condemnation [a more intense scrutiny].

This refers to wanting to be masters or teachers of this way. Don't just jump up and decide you want to be a preacher or a teacher and that you want to teach the Word of God to others, without carefully considering the fact that God will hold you responsible for what you teach.

Someday we will stand before God and he will hold us accountable and judge us on the basis of what we have told others and on the basis of whether we have pointed them toward God or whether we have deceived and misled people away from a zeal for the Word of God.

There are many who want to be elders and to teach, but what they really want is a personal following; they want to think of themselves as being a somebody. This is pride, when a true godly teacher must be humble and without carnal pride.

Anyone who studies the false traditions of men and then stands on them, or leads people away from a zeal for God into a zeal to follow some man, is going to be judged by God as a false prophet or teacher.

While someone who points all people toward God will be judged as a godly teacher and will have his reward. There is a very serious responsibility involved in being teachers because of their influence on others.

Do not decide you can stand up and teach until you weigh the matter and consider the responsibilities that you are shouldering. This is very important and very vital.

It is good to teach the Word of God, but it is wrong to teach people error and lead them astray. Someone who wants to teach must be very, very, very careful to consider all of these things and the heavy burden of responsibility that we are taking on ourselves. We should not treat these things lightly and just go out and say anything we feel like saying.

Many men teaching falsely have led many astray from the ways of God. The following is a warning to all, and a special warning to the teachers, for a godly teacher will offend many; because the Word of God is a sharp two edged sword of TRUTH that cuts deeply against all sin; and we have all sinned.

The TRUTH will cut and offend ALL of us, unless we have the sincerely humble repentant attitude that is a gift of God. If we are filled with God's Spirit of loving obedience to all of God's Word, then we will be delighted when we are shown our shortcomings and sins, so that we may correct ourselves and become right with our Beloved.

If we are offended by Biblical correction; sin and an unrepentant unconverted attitude is in us. We are in trouble and we need to seek our God immediately and with all our hearts.

3:2 For in many things we [godly teachers] offend everyone. If any man offend not in word, the same is a perfect man, and able also to bridle the whole body.

It is impossible to be godly teachers and avoid offending the ungodly; therefore we must choose to speak the truth and avoid offending God; there is NO "business model" outreach for a true servant of God!

3:3 Behold, we put bits in the horses' mouths that they may obey us; and we turn about their whole bodies. **3:4** Behold also the ships, which though they be so great [so large], and are driven of fierce winds, yet when they are turned about with a very small helm, whithersoever the governor listeth [in whatever the direction the pilot wants the ship to go].

Speaking ungodly things leads people into sin and brings damnation on both the false teacher and those who follow him.

3:5 Even so the tongue is a little thing, and boasteth great things. Behold how great a matter a little fire kindles. **3:6** And the tongue is a fire, a world of iniquity: so is the tongue among our members, that it [when uncontrolled, can bring much destruction] defiles our whole bodies, and sets on fire the course of nature; and it is set on fire of hell.

Our speech is tamed and brought under control by sincere repentance and the power of the Holy Spirit which is the power of a sound mind of self-control.

3:7 For every kind of beasts, and of birds, and of serpents, and of things in the sea, can be tamed, and has been tamed of mankind: **3:8** But the tongue can **no man** tame; . . .

The wicked man lacks the ability to understand or speak the things of God and speaks all manner of carnal things in rebellion against the whole Word of God, but God can tame the tongues of men by converting the mind and heart:

> **Matthew 12:34** O generation of vipers, **how can ye, being evil, speak good things? for out of the abundance of the heart the mouth speaketh.**

James 3:8 . . . . it is an unruly evil, full of deadly poison. **3:9** Therewith bless we God, even the Father; and therewith curse we men, which are made after the similitude of God. **3:10** Out of the same mouth proceeds blessing and cursing. My brethren, these things ought not so to be. **3:11** Doth a fountain send forth at the same place sweet water and bitter? **3:12** Can the fig tree, my brethren, bear olive berries? Can a vine bear figs? So can no fountain also yield salt water and fresh.

3:13 Who is a wise man and endued with knowledge among you? Let him show out of a good [let us demonstrate wisdom by godly conduct and words] **conversation** [words and conduct] **his works,** with meekness and wisdom. **3:14** But if ye have bitter envying and strife in your hearts, **glory not, and lie not against the truth**. **3:15** This [worldly] wisdom descends not from above, but is earthly, sensual, and devilish."

A quick uncontrolled temper and bitter envying and strife are of Satan the devil.

3:16 for where envying and strife is, there is confusion and **every evil thing.**

3:17 But the wisdom that is from above is first pure, then peaceable, gentle, and easy to be intreated, full of mercy and good fruits, without partiality, and without hypocrisy" [or deceit] **3:18** And the fruit of righteousness is sown in peace of them who make peace."

James 4

We might ask, from whence comes strife and divisions in today's Ekklesia? Is it not from our pride and desire to get our own way and to have the pre-eminence, as much as it has to do with doctrinal disagreement?

James 4:1 From whence come wars and fightings among you? Come they not hence, even of your lusts that war in your members [our fighting has its roots in the worldly lusts of our flesh]? **4:2** Ye lust, and have not: ye kill, and desire to have, and cannot obtain: ye fight and war, yet ye have not, because ye ask not.

Very many of our brethren and elders seek selfishly for their own pre-eminence or to have their own ways. Leaders seek a following for themselves, their idols of men, or corporate idols, or cherished false traditions; instead of teaching a true zeal to live by every Word of God. Too many becoming filled with pride, want the adulation of the brethren when we should be humbly serving our Maker and God our Father in heaven.

4:3 Ye ask, and receive not, because ye ask amiss, that ye may consume it upon your lusts.

We commit spiritual adultery against the Husband of our baptismal espousal by seeking the friendship of the world with our worldly business model outreach and our desire for material things as we envy the "successful" wicked of this world.

4:4 Ye [spiritual] **adulterers and adulteresses** [disloyal to God], **know ye not that the friendship of the world is enmity with God? whosoever therefore will be a friend of the world is the enemy of God.**

4:5 Do ye think that the scripture saith in vain, The spirit that dwelleth in us lusteth to envy? **4:6** But he giveth more grace [God is merciful to the sincerely repentant who obey him and keep his Word.]. Wherefore he saith, **God resisteth the proud** [All those who think so much of themselves and their own ways that they turn their noses up at any zeal to live by every Word of God.], **but giveth grace unto the humble.**

God forgives the sincerely repentant who tremble at his Word and commit to go forward and sin no more.

Today the Ekklesia is full of spiritual adulterers who love worldliness and their idols of men, and have no zeal for the things of God.

To our great shame we brag about how we are friends with the worldly wicked. To say that we are friends with this king, and that prime minister, and this ruler, and those people; reveals that we value the friendship of the worldly more than we value the Word of God; for if we taught the truth of the whole Word of God we would not be seen as friends by the chiefs of the worldly.

It is wrong to compromise with the Word of God and to try and be close friends with the worldly and this wicked society. It is also wrong to conduct ourselves in a worldly manner, or to covet the pleasures of the worldly wicked, or to desire the friendship of the world's wickedness.

We are to set an example of keeping God's laws, of living God's way and of overcoming this world and enduring; so that we can become righteous leaders and rulers in the future and so that we can teach these wicked men the ways of God by being a LIGHT of godly example.

We are not to seek the friendship of wickedness by going to these people and mumbling some double-talk nonsense about; a strong hand from someplace is coming to save us from our troubles.

We are to stand up, to stand solidly on God's Word and to lay it out, and tell it like it is, and tell them that they are doing wrong, loudly proclaiming that they should stop doing what is wrong and start doing what is right, which is the only real solution to their problems.

That is what should have been told to these people, not some smooth thing while seeking their friendship and then going to the brethren and lying, saying, "I'm such a great man because I'm a friend of all these great people."

If you think the leaders of this world are so great, just stop for a moment and consider the mess this world is in. These so-called great leaders are responsible for that mess, they created the present conditions and situation by their sins, and by leading the rest of humanity into sin.

Oh yes, the rest of humanity would have sinned anyway, no doubt. But these leaders have a certain responsibility and they failed to fulfill it and they are far from being great men.

The great men in this world are nothing in the eyes of God. It is the weak in worldliness that God has called; and He has called them because they are humble and they are meek, and they are willing to listen; and they are willing to sincerely repent and they are willing to live by every Word of God. God will glorify and exalt them if they are faithful and overcome, by resurrecting them and making them kings and priests and causing them to inherit eternal life in His kingdom.

We should also go back here in verse one, "From whence come wars and fighting's among you? Come they not hence, even of your lusts that war in your members?" Isn't this why there are so many different groups in today's Ekklesia? Because they are all led by different people who lust to become the leader, who lust to become the next apostle or somebody great; and who want a following after themselves and are not willing to cooperate with each other.

If they all put God's Word first and they all worshiped God with a whole heart; they would be forgiving and they would be cooperative and there would be a lot less division than there is today.

Our human spirit envies, it lusts; and we are to overcome that evil spirit by the Spirit of God dwelling in us! We are NOT to give place to our natural lusts and envies, No not for a second.

4:7 Submit yourselves therefore to God. Resist the devil, and he will flee from you.

Satan cannot stand before the power of God. Keep your baptismal commitment to follow the Lamb of God in all things; be zealous for the whole Word of God to learn and to keep and to teach it. Cleanse ourselves from all sin by our zeal to reject all error and embrace the truth and the Word of God with a wholehearted zeal.

4:8 Draw nigh to God, and he will draw nigh to you. Cleanse your hands, ye sinners; and purify your hearts, ye double minded.

4:9 Be afflicted [fast], and mourn, and weep [in sincere wholehearted repentance]: let your laughter be turned to mourning [over our wicked sins, seeking the forgiveness of our God for our many spiritual adulteries and idolatry], and your joy [Turn back from joying in the pleasures of sin, for they will bring our destruction; and mourn over them seeking the mercy of our Mighty Savior.] to heaviness.

4:10 Humble yourselves in the sight of the Lord, and he shall lift you up.

The following is not about forbidding to condemn sin, it is about spreading false rumors, knowingly making false accusations and judging others by our own ideas; instead of judging all things by the standard of the whole Word of God.

4:11 Speak not evil one of another, brethren. He that speaketh evil of his brother [with false statements], and judgeth his brother [judging by our own ways], speaketh evil [sets himself up over God's Word by exalting his own ways above God's Word] of the law, and judgeth the law [exalts his own words over God's Word]: but if thou judge the law, thou art not a doer of the law, but a judge.

We are not to judge by our own ways, traditions or standards, exalting ourselves and our own traditions above the Word of God, instead we are to exalt the whole Word of God and to prove [judge] all things by the just standards of the whole Word of God. as the scripture commands (1 Thes 5:21).

James does not mean that we should tolerate sin and not speak out against evil doers. He does mean that we should not falsely condemn those who are zealous to keep the Word of God and who are faithful to God. There are many calling themselves God's people who condemn the zealously faithful to God, because they themselves are NOT faithful to keep the Word of God and they want to follow idols of men and false traditions.

Many fear those who are zealous to keep the Word of God, because they fear losing the personal followings they crave! They see zeal to obey God in the brethren as a threat to their own control and supposed personal authority.

This, because they are not zealous for God themselves and they want to lead people away from any zeal for God and lead people to follow themselves and their own false ways. Those who desire to exalt themselves [using God's name to do so] are evil men just as Jesus, Jude and others have warned would come into the Ekklesia in the last days.

We MUST reveal the evil and call the perpetrators to repentance, in love. That is not speaking evil of them, it is speaking the truth in the hope that the warning will lead to true repentance and the saving of the person.

If any condemn others for any zeal for the Word of God; they are attacking the Law and Word of God!

4:12 There is one lawgiver, who is able to save and to destroy: who art thou that judgest another? **4:13** Go to now, ye that say, To day or to morrow we will go into such a city, and continue there a year, and buy and sell, and get gain: **4:14** Whereas ye know not what shall be on the morrow. For what is your life? It is even a vapour, that appeareth for a little time, and then vanisheth away.

Our lives are not guaranteed to last until tomorrow, therefore always be close to God.

Go today, ye that say, tomorrow or today we will go into such a city, and continue there a year, and buy and sell, and get gain: Whereas ye know not what shall be on the morrow. For what is your life? It is even as a vapour, that appears for a little time, and then vanishes away. For that ye ought to say, If the Lord will, we shall live, and do this, or that. But now ye rejoice in your boastings: all such rejoicing is evil.

To keep a proper focus on the transitory nature of our physical lives; it is better to say; "I hope to," or "I plan to" or "if God wills" rather than "I will do this or that". By the same token we should live our lives in godliness as if we will die and be judged by our Creator before the next day.

The tribulation and the resurrection have been spoken of since at least the days of Christ, and how many have died since then? They have all gone to their judgment and perhaps so will some of us before the final 3 1/2 years.

4:15 For that ye ought to say, If the Lord will, we shall live, and do this, or that.

Do not boast in physical wealth and possession, numbers of followers or friendships with worldliness, buildings, etc; but work hard so that the Shining Light of godliness may burn brightly in us for all the world to see!

4:16 But now ye rejoice in your boastings: all such rejoicing is evil.

4:17 Therefore to him that knoweth to do good, and doeth it not, to him it is sin.

If we have the opportunity to do good or we know that something is the right thing to do and we don't do it, that is a sin, as says the law.

> **Leviticus 19:17** Thou shalt not hate thy brother in thine heart: thou shalt in any wise rebuke thy neighbour, and not suffer sin upon him.

We should not condemn persons but we should definitely stand on God's Word and we should warn the sinner, which is an act of godly love.

We are to teach the righteousness of God [which is the keeping of the whole Word of God] to all peoples beginning with the Ekklesia; and we are to rebuke all sin:

> **Isaiah 58:1 Cry aloud, spare not, lift up thy voice like a trumpet, and shew my people their transgression, and the house of Jacob their sins.**

James 5

Those who seek and focus on physical wealth and pleasures instead of the spiritual riches of the Word of God, will be perverted away from the Word of God and will compromise with God's Word to gain worldly riches.

Physical riches have no lasting value since they will perish; therefore set your heart on the spiritual things that are permanent and that will matter for eternity.

James 5:1 Go to now, ye rich men, weep and howl for your miseries that shall come upon you. **5:2** Your riches are corrupted, and your garments are moth eaten. **5:3** Your gold and silver is cankered; and the rust of them shall be a witness against you, and shall eat your flesh as it were fire for ye have heaped treasure together for the last days.

To gain wealth by fraud or turning aside from a zealous keeping of the whole Word of God is a great sin. Very many leaders and elders in today's Ekklesia are frauds who use the name of God to deceive and gain followers after themselves.

Can our worldly riches save us from the great correction of Almighty God? NO, therefore set your hearts on godly things!

> **Ezekiel 7:19** They shall cast their silver in the streets, and their gold shall be removed: their silver and their gold shall not be able to

deliver them in the day of the wrath of the Lord: they shall not satisfy their souls, neither fill their bowels: because it is the stumblingblock of their iniquity.

Speaking of this society and also of the elders who extort from the brethren and rob widows and orphans

James 5:4 Behold the hire [wages] of the labourers who have reaped down your fields, which is of you kept back by fraud, cries: and the cries of them which have reaped are entered into the ears of the Lord of sabaoth.

The Lord of HOSTS [armies] hears the cries of the oppressed and he will avenge them.

5:5 Ye [the wicked] have lived in pleasure on the earth, and been wanton; ye have nourished your hearts, as in a day of slaughter [the fleecing of the flock]. **5:6** Ye have condemned and killed the just; and he [the just person] doth not resist you."

The saints have been persecuted continually, counted as sheep for the slaughter and they have not resisted or fought with weapons of war, because they know that God's kingdom is not of this world and not of this age. For Jesus Christ said, "My kingdom is not of this world. If it were then my servants would fight."

The day is coming when Jesus Christ will return to gather up God's saints to the Marriage of the Lamb before God the Father in Heaven (Rev 15, 19): And shortly after that, he will come down to the earth with those saints and they will fight all wickedness (Jude).

They will fight sin, evil and wickedness, and those who insist upon doing wickedness. And they will bring the earth into submission and subjection to the whole Word of God and establish the Kingdom of God.

That time will come; but for now we submit without resisting, even as Jesus Christ submitted without resisting; for it is not yet our time.

5:7 Be patient therefore, brethren, unto the coming of the Lord.

Patiently wait for the end time events and the redemption of the faithful in God's good time.

Behold, the husbandman waiteth for the precious fruit of the earth, and hath long patience for it, until he receive the early and the latter rain. **5:8 Be ye also patient; establish your hearts: for the coming of the Lord draws near.**

Do not bear grudges against those who abuse us, because animosity and hatred grows into a bitterness which will destroy us spiritually.

We are forgiven only as we forgive others. Our true enemy who is inspiring these things is not the people doing them but Satan. Remember the words of Christ:

> **Luke 23:34** Then said Jesus, **Father, forgive them; for they know not what they do.**

> **Zechariah 13:6** And one shall say unto him, **What are these wounds in thine hands? Then he shall answer, Those with which I was wounded in the house of my friends.**

James 5:9 Grudge not one against another, brethren, lest ye be condemned: behold, the judge stands before the door. **5:10** Take, my brethren, the prophets, who have spoken in the name of the Lord, for an example of suffering affliction, and of patience.

Suffer all things patiently just as the prophets and apostles did, and as Jesus Christ did. In this world seek to foresee trouble and to wisely avoid it whenever possible; without compromising with the Word of God.

> **Proverbs 27:12** A prudent man foreseeth the evil, and hideth himself;

> **Matthew 10:16** Behold, I send you forth [into the world] **as** sheep in the midst of wolves: be ye therefore wise **as** serpents, and **harmless as doves**.

Those who are faithful and endure all things to the end of their lives will have the reward of eternal life.

James 5:11 Behold, we count them happy which endure. Ye have heard of the patience of Job, and have seen the end of the Lord; that the Lord is very pitiful [full of mercy], and of tender mercy [forgiving the repentant].

Avoid the making of oaths and vows for they are a trap, because none of us can keep our own word by our own strength.

5:12 But above all things, my brethren, swear not, neither by heaven, neither by the earth, neither by any other oath. But let your yea be yea; and your nay, nay; lest ye fall into condemnation.

In our daily activities; if we are downcast we should pray about our troubles, and if we are happy we should rejoice in our God: meaning that we should be focused on our God the Giver of all good things.

5:13 Is any among you afflicted? Let him pray. Is any merry? Let him sing psalms.

5:14 Is any sick among you? Let him call for the [true godly elders only, because God does not hear the prayers of the wicked] elders of the church; and let them pray over him, anointing him with oil in the name of the Lord.

5:15 And the prayer of faith [Godly faith is believing in God and keeping what God says in his Word.] shall save the sick [spiritually sick], and **the Eternal shall raise him up** [In the resurrection to spirit]; **and if he have committed sins, they shall be forgiven him.**

What does it mean "The Eternal shall raise him up?"

This is about forgiveness of sincerely repented sins and the resurrection of the dead. The sins of the sincerely repentant will be forgiven and they shall be resurrected or raised up in the resurrection to spirit.

The prayer of faith shall save the spiritually sick. Does that mean the physically sick will be instantly healed?

No, it does not always mean instantaneous physical healing, although that certainly can and often does happen.

A person may be sick for a reason. God may be trying to teach some kind of lesson [see Job], and if we obey him and are anointed with oil in the name of the Lord, the prayer of faith, that is believing prayer coupled with the works of faith shall save the sick. That is, if we have committed sins and are sincerely repentant and resolve to sin no more, they shall be forgiven us and God will raise us up in the resurrection.

There is also the issue of FAITH; it is faith in God, demonstrated by obedience to the whole Word of God, which brings forgiveness of sins and spiritual healing.

It is our faith in God and sincere repentance accompanied by the works of faith which is to obey God, that brings spiritual healing; and NOT any faith in the anointer. Why then call for prayers at all? Because Christ said that whenever two or three agree on anything lawful it would be granted (Mat 18). Yet the healing is not always physical, for physical things are transitory.

5:16 Confess your faults one to another, and pray one for another, that ye may be healed. The effectual fervent prayer of a righteous man avails much.

Does that mean standing up in front of a congregation and confessing all your sins to everyone?

No, it does not. It means to confess your sins to God in sincere repentance! Healing comes from learning what our sins are and sincerely repenting of them!

Confessing also applies if you sinned against a particular person, you need to go to that person and say, "I am really sorry, I have done such and such, I was wrong, I sinned. Please forgive me."

Only if your sin is a public sin, would it need a public apology.

This is about sincere repentance before God and when necessary reconciling with your brother. It is not about standing up and confessing in front of the whole world. It is about reconciling with your brother; about making what you have done wrong, right again; making it good, making it right; as per Christ's instructions in Matthew 18.

Yes, Elijah was a man like ourselves and not a god, God heard his prayer because of his faithfulness and zeal for the whole Word of God. That was an example for us, that we will also be heard according to our faithfulness and zeal to keep the whole Word of God

5:17 Elias was a man subject to like passions as we are, and he prayed earnestly that it might not rain: and it rained not on the earth by the space of three years and six months. **5:18** And he prayed again, and the heaven gave rain, and the earth brought forth her fruit.

When we see our brother caught up in sin; it is our moral duty to warn him (Ezekiel 33)

5:19 Brethren, if any of you do err from the truth, and one convert him; **5:20** Let him know, that he which converteth the sinner from the error of his way shall save a soul from death, and shall hide a multitude of [if we warn others and they repent, we have caused their sins to be covered] sins.

How can one convert another from his sin if there is no rebuke of sin, or instruction in righteousness provided?

If we see our brother stepping out in front of a truck; is it godly love to say nothing? or would God want us to shout a warning? Remember the commission of the watchman in Ezekiel 33. We have a COMMAND and a COMMISSION from God to warn our brothers; our own life depends on loving God and our neighbors enough to SHOUT A WARNING! Remember the Law of God:

> **Leviticus 19:17** Thou shalt not hate thy brother in thine heart: thou shalt in any wise rebuke thy neighbour, and not suffer sin upon him.

We should not condemn persons but we should definitely stand on God's Word and we should warn the sinner, which is an act of godly love.

We are to teach the righteousness of God [which is the keeping of the whole Word of God] to all peoples beginning with the Ekklesia; and we are to rebuke all sin:

> **Isaiah 58:1 Cry aloud, spare not, lift up thy voice like a trumpet, and shew my people their transgression, and the house of Jacob their sins.**

Covering a multitude of whose sins? If we go to someone that is sinning, and they repent and they are converted and they STOP sinning, we have saved their life, and the sins that have been covered are the sins that the person has repented of.

If we want our own sins to be covered, we must sincerely repent of them, and STOP sinning.

The only way that sin can be covered, is if we sincerely repent and go forward, committed to sin no more! Then the sacrifice of Christ will be applied to us, blotting out our past sins and only then we shall be justified by Christ. The only way that the gift of grace or pardon will be given to us is if we sincerely repent and STOP sinning, if we stop doing the offending behavior.

If we stop breaking God's Word, we can be forgiven. If we don't stop, how can we be forgiven?

How can we possibly be forgiven if we are continually repeating the same sin, continually repeating the same criminal act of breaking the law of the Kingdom? Earning the same wages of death over and over again?

If we are continually repeating criminal acts, we will be judged a criminal and we must pay the penalty for our crimes.

It is only if we stop being a criminal, stop committing the criminal act, stop breaking the law of the Kingdom; only then can we be forgiven our sincerely repented past sins NOT future sins, only then will our sins be covered by the sacrifice of the Lamb of God!

Grace or forgiveness for PAST sins is NOT a license to continue in future sin!

First Peter

1 Peter 1

1 Peter 1:1 Peter, an apostle [apostle means servant] of Jesus Christ, to the strangers scattered throughout Pontus, Galatia, Cappadocia, Asia, and Bithynia,

From before the foundations of the world God the Father had determined to call out a few people to be raised up in an early harvest of humanity. This early harvest is represented by the early Biblical Spring Festivals while the main harvest of humanity is represented by the Biblical Fall Festivals.

It was already decided and therefore foreknown by God before the world began; that God would call out a people and test them to choose a fit collective bride for the Son over the first six thousand years of humanity. It was foreknown that many would be called out to sincere repentance and the application of the sacrifice of Christ by God the Father; and Set Apart to becoming godly through the Holy Spirit.

1:2 Elect according to the foreknowledge of God the Father, through sanctification of the Spirit, unto obedience and sprinkling of the blood of Jesus Christ: Grace unto you, and peace, be multiplied.

Peter writes to the elect saints who were called by God the Father and were sanctified by the Holy Spirit to keep the whole Word of God; Called Out of sin to obey God and covered by the sprinkling of the blood of Jesus Christ, the blood of the New Covenant sacrifice of Christ.

The Mosaic Covenant was ratified by the sprinkling of animal sacrificial blood on the people; and the New Covenant is ratified by the sprinkling of the blood of Jesus Christ upon the people; Jesus Christ the Lamb of God being our sacrifice.

Grace is the forgiveness of God, meaning that we would be forgiven all our iniquities and that the sincerely repentant could be reconciled into a peaceful relationship with God the Father. and with other faithful likeminded brethren through their individual unity with God the Father and Jesus Christ.

1:3 Blessed be the God and Father of our Lord Jesus Christ, which according to his abundant mercy hath begotten us again unto a lively hope by the resurrection of Jesus Christ from the dead,

If we are faithful and filled with Christ-like zeal to love and to live by every Word of God like Christ did and does, we shall likewise inherit eternal life and an incorruptible spirit body, and many other spiritual blessings.

1:4 To an inheritance incorruptible, and undefiled, and that fadeth not away, reserved in heaven for you,

The faithful to zealously live by every Word of God are reserved to eternal salvation by the Awesome Power of our Mighty God.

1:5 Who are kept by the power of God through faith [including the works of faith] unto salvation ready to be revealed in the last time.

We have the hope of a resurrection to spirit and eternal life and the proof of that hope is the reality that Jesus Christ was resurrected and given eternal life.

If we keep the whole Word of God and love God enough to seek to please him with a whole heart, enduring all things to the end of our lives; we will receive an inheritance of an incorruptible and undefiled eternal spirit body.

We can remain faithful by GOD'S power and not by our own strength.

We MUST remain in complete unity with God!

Unity with God comes through faith in God and the works of faith, not only believing but being DOERS of the WORD, internalizing the mind and nature of God in us, through the uncompromising keeping of the whole Word of God!

The faithful overcomers are chosen and resurrected will come as the seventh trump begins to sound; BEFORE the seven last plagues are poured out. Their salvation comes when the chosen are resurrected to life as spirit and given the gift of eternal life and presented to God the Father.

Our trials are to be accounted precious for they are forming us into the kind of people that God wants us to be, perfecting us in godliness.

1:6 Wherein ye greatly rejoice, though now for a season, if need be, ye are in heaviness through manifold temptations: **1:7** That the trial of your faith, being much more precious than of gold that perisheth, though it be tried with fire, might be found unto praise and honour and glory at the appearing of Jesus Christ:

Our faith is much more precious than gold that perishes, because God is creating in us the very nature of God; through testing, trials and the development of our faith.

God is developing a godly nature in the faithful, which is going to last for eternity.

Faith means to believe, to trust, and to act on that belief, to do what God says and wants; which then results in the salvation of our souls, our lives.

We are saved by our sincere repentance and the application of Christ's sacrifice [bringing the forgiveness of God], and by our willingness to turn from sin towards our God and diligently living by every Word of God.

1:8 Whom having not seen, ye love; in whom, though now ye see him not, yet believing, ye rejoice with joy unspeakable and full of glory:

Being called out of sin to God, believing and acting on that calling and belief to sincerely repent and commit to sin no more, and adding to our belief the works of faith which is obedience and living by every Word of God (Mat 4:4), brings eternal salvation through the application of the sacrifice of Christ!

1:9 Receiving the end of your faith, even the salvation of your souls.

The prophets prophesied of Christ and human salvation through Christ's perfect life and sacrifice and the resurrection of the faithful to life eternal; all being gifts of God.

1:10 Of which salvation the prophets have enquired and searched diligently, who prophesied of the grace [mercy] that should come unto you:

The Spirit of Christ and God the Father was in all the prophets.

The Holy Spirit of God is the very mind and nature of God; which if we follow it to zealously internalize the nature of God [which is defined by the whole Word of God], we shall be resurrected to spirit like Christ was resurrected.

The Holy Spirit was in all the prophets, signifying that God had called and put his spirit in many, many people since Abel; since the very beginning, and showing that God has called certain people throughout all of history to be his people, and to be a part of a New Covenant which was made official in 31 A.D. with the acceptance of Christ for us as our High Priest by God the Father.

This gift of God's Spirit to the ancients - Abel, Noah, Abraham, Moses, Elijah, David, John Baptist and so many more - reveals that the seven days of the Feast of Unleavened Bread picture the calling out of a kind of first fruits of the New Covenant for six thousand years followed by a thousand year Sabbath of rest in the presence of the Creator.

Those people [called out before Christ was sacrificed] were called in faith, looking forward to the sacrifice of Christ. And now we, who are called in this latter day, can look backward in faith that Christ was resurrected and sits at the right hand of God the Father as the High Priest of the New Covenant.

1:11 Searching [the ancient prophets tried to search out and understand these things] what, or what manner of time **the Spirit of Christ which was in them** did signify, when it testified beforehand the sufferings of Christ, and the glory that should follow.

The Holy Spirit was in all the prophets and men of God from righteous Abel; and the whole Word of God was inspired through the agency of that Spirit by the Creator Jesus Christ!

The Word of God was inspired by Jesus Christ to the prophets who wrote God's Word for OUR instruction. The prophets did not understand much of what they wrote, which things are now being explained by the inspiration of the Holy Spirit in these last times.

God has promised that very much understanding would be sealed until the very last days; and only be revealed at the very end, and also that what has been forgotten would be restored in the last days by his servants.

This "Sealing" and "Revealing" is further explained in Revelation 5 and Daniel 12.

Those who reject the increase of understanding promised by the scriptures, preferring to cling to past error and false traditions; are rejecting truth and are rejecting the Word of God.

> **Daniel 12:9** And he said, Go thy way, Daniel: for the **words are closed up and sealed till the time of the end. 12:10** Many shall be purified, and made white, and tried; but the wicked shall do wickedly: and **none of the wicked shall understand; but the wise shall understand.**
>
> **Daniel 12:4** But thou, O Daniel, shut up the words, and seal the book, even to the time of the end: many shall run to and fro, and knowledge shall be increased.

1 Peter 1:12 Unto whom [God revealed his Word unto the prophets] it was revealed, that not unto themselves [these things were not revealed to the understanding of the ancient prophets who did not understand what they were writing], but **unto us they did minister** [they served God in writing these things for us in our time] **the things, which are now reported unto you by them that have preached the gospel unto you with the Holy Ghost sent down from heaven;** which things the [even the angels did not know these things until Jesus overcame and rose to heaven to unseal these things (Rev 5) and then reveal them to us on his own schedule] angels desire to look into.

The prophets wrote the Word of God throughout history without a full understanding. A more complete understanding of these prophecies and the gospel were reserved for the very end time.

We in this very last time, just before the tribulation and the resurrection to spirit, are not to be slack about the precious jewels of wisdom that God is revealing to us in these latter days.

In the very last days of this society we are being given a knowledge and an understanding of the Word of God that was the earnest desire of the prophets themselves to know.

Those who love the Eternal embrace these truths with great joy and gratitude to God for HIS revelations, but the wicked reject the truth and the increase of godly knowledge which was promised by our God so long ago.

We are to dedicate ourselves to a godly diligence to become holy as God is holy, to become like God, by internalizing the whole Word of God within ourselves through an enthusiastic zeal to learn and live by every Word of God.

1:13 Wherefore gird up the loins of your mind, be sober [be serious about our calling], and hope to the end for the grace [forgiveness for sincerely repented sin] that is to be brought unto you at the revelation [coming of Christ and the resurrection to spirit] of Jesus Christ;

Let us be obedient to God our Father [the law commands us to honor our fathers] in heaven, not following our own ways, but being diligent to live by the whole Word of God, (Mat 4:4); so that we might internalize the very nature of God, which is defined by the whole Word of God; to become just like our Father in heaven!

1:14 As obedient children, not fashioning yourselves according to the former lusts in your ignorance: **1:15 But as he which hath called you is holy, so be ye holy in all manner of conversation; 1:16 Because it is written, Be ye holy; for I am holy.**

Peter informs us that we should be holy as God the Father is holy and as Jesus Christ is holy. The Father of course keeps his own Word and the son, Jesus Christ said, "I have kept my Father's commandments:" And we are also to keep their Word through the power of their Spirit in us.

1:17 And if ye call on the Father, who without respect of persons judgeth according to every man's work [according to God's Word], pass the time of your sojourning here [in the flesh] in fear: **1:18** Forasmuch as ye know that ye were not redeemed with corruptible things, as silver and gold, **from your vain conversation received by tradition from your fathers**;

In the past we have learned and lived by the vain traditions of our physical fathers; out of which we have been called by God the Father and redeemed by the blood sacrifice of our Creator. Therefore let us put aside all past error and false traditions and let us love and embrace the truth and the whole Word of God with joyful enthusiastic passionate zeal!

1:19 But with the precious blood of Christ, as of a lamb without blemish and without spot:

Let us live our lives in the knowledge that we will be judged by God the Father, judged by every Word of God according to all our deeds: We will not be judged by what some man says about God's Word.

Every individual has a personal responsibility to put God first; and we are to test everything that any man teaches by the standard of God's Word, because it is God's Word by which we will be judged.

We should fear God and not men. There is a great deal of fear in the assemblies regarding the ministry and organizational authorities. People are afraid to question, afraid to speak out, afraid to prove things by God's Word; and that is wrong.

We are to fear God and not men, for it is God who can destroy both body and spirit in the lake of fire. No man can do that. Do not be intimidated by men, no matter who they claim to be or how high and mighty they might think themselves. They are nothing compared to God and we will each be judged by God and God's Word, not by what any man says.

We are not redeemed from the vain traditions of our elders by corruptible things. Our redemption is not with gold or silver or by the blood of lambs or goats or bullocks.

We are redeemed with the precious blood of Christ, the very Lamb of God, perfect and without blemish and without any spot of sin.

Yes. Jesus Christ was/is the Lamb of God, who has slain from the very foundations of the world, as it is written in Revelation. This was, as Peter says in Verse 20: "It was foreordained before the foundations of the world" that Jesus Christ would atone for the sins of humanity his creation. It was all part of the plan from the very beginning.

1:20 Who verily **was foreordained before the foundation of the world**, but was manifest [revealed, made known] in these last times for you, **1:21** [We] Who by him do believe in God, that raised him up from the dead, and gave him glory; that your faith and hope might be in God.

We are not to have faith and hope [trust] in any man or group of men. Our faith and hope is to be in unity with Almighty God the Father who raised up Jesus Christ to eternal life, and who will judge us by his every Word.

1:22 Seeing ye have **purified your souls** [purified ourselves by repentance and the keeping the whole Word of God] **in obeying the truth** through the Spirit [learning to love God and the brethren] unto unfeigned love of the brethren, see that ye love one another with a pure heart fervently: **1:23**

Being born again, not of corruptible seed, but of incorruptible [living by God's Word and not living by the vanity of worldliness], by the word of God, which liveth and abideth for ever.

Explaining the "Born Again" confusion

We are to abandon the old person and become a new person in Christ and in God the Father. We are to discard our sinful living contrary to the Word of God and embrace God to live by every Word of God; the old sinful man figuratively dying in the watery grave of baptism and a new person rising up out of baptism as a new person in godliness.

Nevertheless we are still physical persons and we will not be fully "born again' in the sense of being changed to spirit, until the resurrection to spirit.

At our baptism we are conceived [joined with God's Spirit], as a new being in Christ and in godliness; but we are still like an embryonic spiritual child learning and growing until we complete the race and are chosen to be reborn in a new body made of spirit.

When we receive God's Spirit at conversion a new being is conceived; from there it must grow and develop into a new person until it is finally fully changed from a body of flesh and reborn as a being made of spirit at the resurrection to spirit.

1:24 For all flesh is as grass, and all the glory of man as the flower of grass. The grass withereth, and the flower thereof falleth away:

Only the Word of the Lord endures forever. The true Gospel is the whole Word of God endures forever. The Gospel of the Kingdom is only a part of the whole Gospel.

Teaching the Gospel of Christ and the Gospel of Salvation, which is sincere repentance and a passionate enthusiastic zeal to live by every Word of God, has been abandoned in order to cause people to follow idols of men and the false traditions of men.

1:25 But the word of the Lord endureth for ever. And this is the word which by the gospel is preached unto you.

The ministry and various leaders can be a tremendous influence for good. They can also make mistakes, and they can be a tremendous influence for evil if they are false.

We must test every word that every person, every man and indeed every spirit and angel speaks, against the standard of the Word of God: because the words of men and spirits are nothing unless they are absolutely consistent with the whole Word of God.

Only the Word of the LORD endures forever and the whole Word of God is the true Gospel.

1 Peter 2

1 Peter 2:1 Wherefore laying aside all malice, and all guile, and hypocrisies, and envies, all evil speakings,

Let us put away everything that divides us from God and his Word, and separates us from the teachings of Christ; let us eagerly hunger and thirst for the spiritual nourishment of the whole Word of God just as a babe cries out for milk.

2:2 As newborn babes, desire the sincere milk of the word, that ye may grow thereby: **2:3** If so be ye have tasted that the Lord is gracious.

Let us come to God the Father through Jesus Christ the living stone and rock of our salvation. Let us diligently follow Christ to also become living stones, and to become a part of the living spiritual house [the temple, the dwelling place] of God the Father.

2:4 To whom coming, as unto a living stone, disallowed indeed of men, but chosen of God, and precious, **2:5 Ye also, as lively stones, are built up a spiritual house, an holy priesthood, to offer up spiritual sacrifices**, acceptable to God by Jesus Christ.

Jesus Christ is the chief foundation stone of the true spiritual Ekklesia; the foundation on which the Ekklesia is to be built.

Ephesians 2:19 Now therefore ye are no more strangers and foreigners, but fellowcitizens with the saints, and of the household of God;

2:20 And are built upon the foundation of the apostles and prophets [those who wrote the scriptures represent the whole Word of God], **Jesus Christ himself being the chief corner stone;**

2:21 In whom all the building fitly framed together groweth unto an holy temple in the Lord: **2:22** In whom ye also are builded together for an habitation of God through the Spirit.

1 Peter 2:6 Wherefore also it is contained in the scripture, Behold, I lay in Sion a chief corner stone, elect, precious: and he that believeth on him shall not be confounded.

Often we think this applies to the worldly being offended in Christ, not realizing that Christ is a rock of offence to almost all brethren in the church of God today.

What? Are we not Christians? Do we not follow Christ? The answer to that is NO!

How? Because we do not DO what Christ taught and DID!

We follow the false traditions of men which make the Word of God of no effect; making idols of men, in place of being zealous to learn and to live by every Word of God.

> **Matthew 15:6** . . . Thus have ye made the commandment of God of none effect by your tradition. **15:7** Ye hypocrites, well did Esaias prophesy of you, saying, **15:8** This people draweth nigh unto me with their mouth, and honoureth me with their lips; but their heart is far from me. **15:9 But in vain they do worship me, teaching for doctrines the commandments of men.**

By being disobedient to any part of the Word of God we reject the author of that Word: Jesus Christ and God the Father!

Today, those who call themselves God's people reject God by following idols of men, corporate entities and false traditions; in place of living by every Word of God!

1 Peter 2:7 Unto you therefore which believe he is precious: but unto them which be disobedient, the stone which the builders disallowed, the same is made the head of the corner, **2:8** And **a stone of stumbling, and a rock of offence, even to them which stumble at the word, being disobedient**

[disobedient to the Word of God and leading the brethren astray from godliness into following men]: whereunto also they were appointed

It was predetermined from the beginning to allow many false teachers to come into the Ekklesia to TEST the brethren's faithfulness to God (Mat 24, Jude).

> **Jude 1:4** For there are certain men crept in unawares, who were before of old ordained to this condemnation, ungodly men, turning the grace of our God into lasciviousness [a license to continue in sin], and denying the only Lord God [the Father], and our Lord Jesus Christ [by following idols of men and refusing to live by every Word of God].

1 Peter 2:9 But **ye are a chosen generation,** [chosen to become a] **a royal priesthood** [of the High Priesthood of Jesus Christ], **an holy nation** [a godly spiritual Israel], **a peculiar** [special] **people**; that ye should shew forth the praises of him [should be an example of the Light of God the Father] who hath called you out of darkness into his marvellous light [the Light of the whole Word of God];

We who were sinners of all nations, have been called by God the Father to himself through Jesus Christ, to join together to become one people in zeal for God; so that through sincere repentance and living by every Word of God through the power of God's Spirit (Mat 4:4); we might be granted God's mercy and become an example and a Shining Light of godliness to all people.

> **Matthew 5:14** Ye are the light of the world. A city that is set on an hill cannot be hid. **5:15** Neither do men light a candle, and put it under a bushel, but on a candlestick; and it giveth light unto all that are in the house. **5:16** Let your light so shine before men, that they may see your good works, and glorify your Father which is in heaven.

1 Peter 2:10 Which in time past were not a people, but are now the people of God: which had not obtained mercy, but now have obtained mercy.

If we set a proper example in keeping God's Word, the wicked will see our example and while they reject it now, they will remember that example in the day that their eyes are opened and they will glorify God in that day.

2:11 Dearly beloved, I beseech you as strangers and pilgrims [in this world], **abstain from fleshly lusts**, which war against the soul [spirit];

2:12 Having your conversation [words and conduct] honest among the Gentiles [among the unconverted]: that, whereas they speak against you as evildoers, they may by your good [godly example and works of faith] works, which they shall behold, **glorify God in the day of visitation** [of Christ's coming].

Submit to every law of governments, as long as they do not conflict with the Word of God; and if they make laws forbidding us to keep God's laws, or requiring us to sin, we are to flee that jurisdiction [this includes fleeing out of the jurisdiction of membership in apostatizing church organizations].

2:13 Submit yourselves to every ordinance of man for the Lord's sake: whether it be to the king, as supreme; **2:14** Or unto governors, as unto them that are sent by him for the punishment of evildoers, and for the praise of them that do well.

2:15 For so is the will of God, that with well doing [keeping God's law and the law of the land and doing good works] **ye may put to silence the ignorance of foolish men**: **2:16** As free [freed from bondage to sin and false traditions, but not misusing that freedom to disrespect the present authorities], and not using your liberty for a cloke of maliciousness, but as the servants of God.

Put God first and then honor those in authority over us.

2:17 Honour all men. Love the brotherhood. Fear God. Honour the king. **2:18** Servants, be subject to your masters with all fear; not only to the good and gentle, but also to the froward.

If we are punished by men for doing wrong in society we have nothing to glory over; but if we obey God and are punished by men for obeying God, we have a reward reserved for us in heaven.

2:19 For this is thankworthy, if a man for conscience toward God endure grief, suffering wrongfully. **2:20** For what glory is it, if, when ye be buffeted for your faults, ye shall take it patiently? but **if, when ye do well, and suffer for it, ye take it patiently, this is acceptable with God.**

We are to follow the example of Jesus Christ and endure all things to persevere in the calling of God, because God is allowing the trials in our lives to perfect us and to make us into the people that God wants us to become.

2:21 For even hereunto were ye called: because Christ also suffered for us, leaving us an example, that ye should follow his steps: **2:22** Who did no sin, neither was guile found in his mouth: **2:23** Who, when he was reviled, reviled not again; when he suffered, he threatened not; but committed himself to him that judgeth righteously: **2:24** Who his own self bare our sins in his own body on the tree, that we, being [we are to be dead to sin] dead to sins, should live unto righteousness [we are to live by every Word of God which is righteousness]: by whose stripes ye were [spiritually healed from sin] healed.

2:25 For ye were as sheep going astray [falling into sin and straying away from our Shepherd]; but are now returned [At this time some have been called to return to God the Father through Jesus Christ and others will be called in God's time.] unto the Shepherd and Bishop [We have been called to return to God the Father through His High Priest, Jesus Christ [Melchizedek], the Good Shepherd] of your souls [lives].

1 Peter 3

Instructions for Wives

1 Peter 3:1 Likewise, ye wives, be in subjection to your own husbands; that, if any obey not the word, they also may without the word be won by the conversation [by the conduct and example] of the wives; **3:2** While they behold your chaste conversation [godly example in godliness with loyalty and reverence to their husbands] coupled with fear [respect].

Let wives be adorned with true godliness and the righteousness of keeping the whole Word of God as a Shining Light of example for others. Let wives be subject to all godliness and after that to be a true help to their husbands and not aggressive or disrespectful.

3:3 Whose adorning let it not be that outward adorning of plaiting the hair, and of wearing of gold, or of putting on of apparel; **3:4** But let it be the hidden man of the heart, in that which is not corruptible, even the ornament **of a meek and quiet spirit, which is in the sight of God of great price. 3:5 For after this manner in the old time the holy women also, who trusted in God, adorned themselves** [with righteousness], **being in subjection unto their own husbands: 3:6 Even as Sara obeyed Abraham, calling him lord: whose daughters ye are, as long as ye do**

well, and are not afraid [to be godly, keeping God's Word] **with any** [having no fear to do what is godly] **amazement** [terror].

Godly women are the daughters of Sara as long as they are not afraid to be godly and to do well, living by every Word of God.

Instructions for husbands

Husbands behave with wisdom and do not act and react selfishly or emotionally in anger or frustration. Have respect for your wives and live peaceably with them; for how can we come before God with an attitude of anger against the one we have pledged before God to love?

3:7 Likewise, ye husbands, dwell with them according to knowledge, giving honour unto the wife, as unto the weaker vessel, and as being heirs together of the grace of life; that your prayers be not hindered.

Instructions for All

This instruction is for the whole body of believers in their relations towards one another. If we are to behave thusly toward our neighbours, how much more are we to behave thusly to our spouses?

3:8 Finally, be ye all of one mind [with God], having compassion [be forgiving] one of another, love as brethren, be pitiful, be courteous: **3:9** Not rendering evil for evil, or railing for railing: but contrariwise blessing; knowing that ye are thereunto called, that ye should inherit a blessing.

Refrain from spreading false rumors or teaching the brethren to turn away from their zeal to keep God's Word and avoid all evil, which is the breaking of any part of the Word and Will of God; and always do good, which is living by every Word of God.

3:10 For he that will love life, and see good days, let him refrain his tongue from evil, and his lips that they speak no guile: **3:11** Let him eschew [loathe and avoid] evil, and do good; let him seek peace [seek peace with God first and then with people], and ensue it.

God hears the prayers of those who do his will and keep his Word; but he will not hear the prayers of those who lack any zeal to keep his Word.

3:12 For **the eyes of the Lord are over the righteous** [the zealous keepers of the whole Word of God], **and his ears are open unto their prayers: but the face of the Lord is against them that do evil.**

If we do what is good and peaceable only the wicked will seek our harm, because they are pricked in their conscious and despise the example that makes them feel uncomfortable.

3:13 And who is he that will harm you, if ye be followers of that which is good?

Be not afraid of trials, rather persevere to always have a good conscious before God through living by God's Word; and study diligently so that we may be always able to answer others; and always set an example of godliness.

3:14 But and if ye suffer for righteousness' sake, happy are ye: and be not afraid of their terror, neither be troubled; **3:15** But sanctify the Lord God in your hearts [set ourselves apart from sin, and dedicate ourselves to the godliness of the LORD]: and **be ready always to give an answer to every man that asketh you a reason of the hope that is in you with meekness and fear** [humility before God]: **3:16** Having a good conscience; that, whereas they speak evil of you, as of evildoers, they may be ashamed that falsely accuse your good conversation [words and conduct] in Christ.

If we must suffer from men, let it be for pleasing God; rather than for any evil deed on our part.

3:17 For **it is better, if the will of God be so, that ye suffer for well doing, than for evil doing.**

3:18 For Christ also hath once suffered for sins, the just for the unjust, that he might bring us to God, being put to death in the flesh, but quickened [resurrected] by the Spirit:

3:19 By which also he went and preached unto the spirits [Strong's G43151 2) the spirit, i.e. the vital principal by which the body is animated 2a) the rational spirit, the power by which the human being feels, thinks, decides 2b) the soul] in prison [souls of men in bondage to sin];

Jesus Christ also inspired Noah by the Holy Spirit to warn the people in bondage to sin, warning them for 120 years before the flood.

3:20 Which sometime [had been disobedient to God] were disobedient, when once the longsuffering of God waited in the days of Noah, while the ark was a preparing [for 120 years], wherein few, that is, eight souls were saved by water.

Baptism [immersing, washing] is not merely washing clean the fleshly body, but is to show the washing away of all sin by figuratively destroying the old sinful person in a watery grave; to then rise up a new person clean from sin and dedicated to sinning no more.

The flood of Noah was an allegory of baptism, for the world was destroyed by water and those folks will yet rise up to turn from their disobedience and become new beings in Christ!

Sincere repentance and a baptismal commitment to sin no more then brings the application of the atoning sacrifice of Jesus Christ, reconciling us to God the Father and bringing a good conscious for us towards God. The effectiveness of the sacrifice of Christ was made sure by his resurrection to glory and his acceptance by God the Father for us.

Eight persons went through the flood of Noah as a type of salvation for the godly.

Millions of persons died in the flood as a type of the death of the old sinful person [an allegory of baptism] and they will rise to become new godly persons in Christ in their due time.

Therefore the flood of Noah was an allegory of baptism, which is the death of the sinner in baptism and the rising up of a new being in Christ-like godliness, to become a new person putting away all sin to wholeheartedly live by every Word of God.

3:21 The like figure [Noah's flood is a like figure of baptism] whereunto even baptism doth also now save us (not the putting away of the filth of the flesh, but the answer of a good conscience [The water of baptism is not meant to wash away physical dirt, but represents the washing away of all repented sin. The rising up out of the water of baptism a new sincerely repentant godly spiritual person in Christ and the application of the sacrifice of Christ, is what saves us from all sincerely repented PAST sin: It does NOT justify remaining in sin in future.] toward God,) by the resurrection of Jesus Christ: **3:22** Who is gone into heaven, and is on the right hand of God; angels and authorities and powers being made subject unto him.

1 Peter 4

Let us cease from all sin and live by every Word of God just like Jesus Christ did and does.

1 Peter 4:1 Forasmuch then as Christ hath suffered for us in the flesh, arm yourselves likewise with the same mind [we are to be filled with the same Christ-like determination to live by every Word of God]: for he [those that] that hath suffered in the flesh hath ceased from sin [suffering for godliness is proof that we have turned from worldliness and rejected sin]; **4:2** That he no longer should live the rest of his time [the remainder of our lives] in the flesh to the lusts of men [we who sinned in times past, must STOP sinning and live in godliness], but to the will of God.

In the past we lived to satisfy the lusts of our flesh, but now we who are called to God through Christ are to live in Christ-like zeal according to every Word of God.

4:3 For the time past of our life may suffice us to have wrought the will of the Gentiles, when we walked in lasciviousness, lusts, excess of wine, revellings, banquetings, and abominable idolatries: **4:4** Wherein they think it strange that ye run not with them to the same excess of riot, speaking evil of you:

The wicked speak evil of those who will not join them in their sins.

All humanity will ultimately have to face the Judge and give an account for their works.

4:5 Who [every person will be made to account for their actions] **shall give account to him that is ready to judge** the quick [the living] and the dead [those who have died will be raised up to their judgment].

The Gospel is preached to sinners so that when they are raised back up to the flesh, they will remember and repent and be saved. They died in the flesh being wicked, and they will be raised up to flesh for an opportunity to repent and to live by the whole Word of God in their period of judgment.

4:6 For for this cause was the gospel preached also to them that are dead [The Gospel was preached to many who sincerely repented to live by every Word of God. They will be resurrected to eternal life in godliness.], **that they might be judged** [we die while in the flesh] **according to men in the flesh, but live according to God in the spirit** [God's faithful will receive eternal life in the resurrection to spirit.].

4:7 But the end of all things is at hand: be ye therefore sober [serious], and watch unto [be diligent in] prayer.

This was written for us in that all flesh is subject to death, and for our day with the end of this society and the coming of our LORD now very close at hand.

4:8 And above all things have fervent charity [true godly love] among yourselves: for charity [loving God by keeping His Word; and loving our brothers and sisters enough to warn them to turn away from sin and to live by every Word of God, which love will cover their sincerely repented sins] shall cover the multitude of sins.

Let us be friendly and sharing with the brethren; and brethren, do not take undue advantage of others. Let each person work and not be a burden to others.

4:9 Use hospitality one to another without grudging.

4:10 As every man hath received the gift [a gift of the Spirit], even so minister the same [help and edify one another according to God's gifts as they are given to each one] one to another, as good stewards of the manifold grace of God.

Do all things for the glory of God and be a shining personal example of the righteousness of God; which is to passionately love and live by every Word of God in all our thoughts, words and deeds.

4:11 If any man speak, let him speak [we are to speak as befitting godly people] as the oracles of God; if any man minister, let him do it as of the ability which God giveth: that God in all things may be glorified through Jesus Christ, to whom be praise and dominion for ever and ever. Amen.

We are to expect trials of our faith and zeal; be not dismayed by trials for our God is working with us to make us fit to be a part of the eternal collective bride of Christ.

> **John 15:20** Remember the word that I said unto you, The servant is not greater than his lord. If they have persecuted me, they will also persecute you; if they have kept my saying, they will keep yours also.

Speaking of the imminent great tribulation in our time, as well as the trials when Jerusalem was surrounded by the Roman's in the first century when the faithful brethren fled to Pella; Peter warns us not to be moved away from God and reminds us of the things that Jesus suffered.

1 Peter 4:12 Beloved, think it not strange concerning the fiery trial which is to try you, as though some strange thing happened unto you: **4:13** But rejoice, inasmuch as ye are partakers of Christ's sufferings; that, when his glory shall be revealed, ye may be glad also with exceeding joy.

Because, having suffered for righteousness sake just as Christ did we will have a part in the resurrection to eternal life, just as Jesus Christ was resurrected to eternal life.

If you are reproached for being zealous to keep God's Word and Will; rejoice for you are in the company of Jesus Christ, who was also reproached for faithfulness to God the Father.

4:14 If ye be reproached for the name of Christ, happy are ye; for the spirit of glory and of God resteth upon you: on their part he is evil spoken of, but on your part he is glorified.

Keep yourself pure from all sin so that we need not suffer for our own sins and be zealous to learn and to keep the whole Word with a deep and abiding love for all truth and all things godly.

4:15 But let none of you suffer as a murderer, or as a thief, or as an evildoer, or as a busybody in other men's matters.

4:16 Yet if any man suffer as a [faithful doer of the Word of God] Christian, let him not be ashamed; but let him glorify God on this [because he is faithful to God and suffers for his faithful loyalty, which enduring will bring the good blessing of eternal life] behalf.

Brethren, the called out are being tested and judged right now as to whether we will be fit to be resurrected to eternal life as Jesus Christ was. Only those who are of the same mind as Christ, who are full of Christ-like zeal for God the Father and the whole Word of God will be among the Chosen for the resurrection to eternal spirit.

4:17 For the time is come that **judgment must begin at the house of God: and if it first begin at us**, what shall the end be of them that obey not the gospel of God? **4:18** And if the righteous scarcely be saved, where shall the ungodly and the sinner appear?

When we face trials for our diligence to live by every Word of God the Father, let us not back down or compromise to try to reduce the burden by our own efforts; rather let us redouble our love, commitment and zeal to live by every Word of God, and let us commit our lives into the hands of our Mighty Deliverer and Savior, who will raise us up on that day!

4:19 Wherefore let them that suffer according to the will of God commit the keeping of their souls to him in well doing, as unto a faithful Creator

1 Peter 5

Instructions for Elders

1 Peter 5:1 The elders which are among you I exhort, who am also an elder, and a witness of the sufferings of Christ, and also a partaker of the glory that shall be revealed:

5:2 Feed the flock of God which is among you [with the pure and undefiled milk and the solid meat of the whole Word of God], taking the oversight thereof, not by constraint, but willingly; not for filthy lucre [not as a mere job for a pay cheque, or for the adulation of men], but of a ready mind; [a mind willing to serve God]

The elders are to serve first by setting a godly example.

5:3 Neither as being lords over God's heritage, but **being ensamples to the flock.**

Those who exhort the people to passionate godliness, teaching the whole Word of God and powerfully rebuking all sin; will have a good reward.

> **2 Timothy 4:1** I charge thee therefore before God, and the Lord Jesus Christ, who shall judge the quick and the dead at his appearing and his kingdom;

4:2 Preach the word; be instant in season, out of season; reprove, rebuke, exhort with all long suffering and doctrine.

Those who do not rebuke all sin, those who do not set a godly example and those who are not diligent to teach passionate zeal to live by every Word of God; will be required to give an account and will be judged by our Master.

Matthew 7:15 Beware of false prophets, which come to you in sheep's clothing, but inwardly they are ravening wolves.

A wolf feeds himself first, and ravages the flock.

Ezekiel 34 the entire chapter is about those shepherds in BOTH physical and spiritual Israel who are wolves and feed themselves with all the good things of the flock, while neglecting to feed the flock with ever Word of the Truth of God in due season.

Those who are political and seek the chief seats, who seek self-aggrandizement and personal advantage; are the wolves hiding among the sheep.

Today there are very many such wolves who do not feed the sheep the true Gospel of warning, repentance, and diligent faithful obedience to God unto salvation and eternal life.

Ezekiel 34:1 And the word of the LORD came unto me, saying, 34:2 Son of man, prophesy against the shepherds of Israel, prophesy, and say unto them, Thus saith the Lord GOD unto the shepherds; Woe be to the shepherds of Israel that do feed themselves! should not the shepherds feed the flocks?

Matthew 7:16 Ye shall know them by their fruits. Do men gather grapes of thorns, or figs of thistles? 7:17 Even so every good tree bringeth forth good fruit; but a corrupt tree bringeth forth evil fruit.

If any man teaches tolerance for sin out of a phony false love; if any elder tolerates sin [the breaking of any part of God's Word, not the breaking of some organizational edict] without rebuke; if any organization does not preach a message of warning and repentance to the world; They are corrupt branches that will be pruned off at the judgment!

The True Good Shepherd and his faithful servants feed the flock with the words of truth and with the teachings that lead to salvation; strongly rebuking all sin.

We are to follow that True Good Shepherd on High, diligently living by every Word of God so that we internalize God the Father and the Son and grow into complete spiritual unity with God!

> **John 15:1** I am the true vine, and my Father is the husbandman.
>
> **15:2** Every branch in me that beareth not fruit he taketh away: and every branch that beareth fruit, he purgeth it, that it may bring forth more fruit.
>
> **15:3** Now ye are clean through the word which I have spoken unto you.
>
> **15:4** Abide in me, and I in you. As the branch cannot bear fruit of itself, except it abide in the vine; no more can ye, except ye abide in me.
>
> **15:5** I am the vine, ye are the branches: He that abideth in me, and I in him, the same bringeth forth much fruit: for without me ye can do nothing.
>
> **15:6** If a man abide not in me, he is cast forth as a branch, and is withered; and men gather them, and cast them into the fire, and they are burned.
>
> **Matthew 7:18** A good tree cannot bring forth evil fruit, neither can a corrupt tree bring forth good fruit. **7:19** Every tree that bringeth not forth good fruit is hewn down, and cast into the fire.

The good tree is that Ultimate Good Shepherd who is working to bring the whole flock into a fullness of complete unity with God the Father! We are to follow that Good Shepherd who gave his all, who gave his very life for the Father's flock and did not seek his own.

We are to follow the example that was set for us and faithfully serve God the Father by feeding his flock with the very Word of God, the very nature of God; without fear or compromise; regardless of what men think or do.

There are some good shepherds among us even now who teach the true way of salvation and are alert watchmen discerning the signs of the times. They may be kept down, ridiculed and even persecuted by others, yet the Father will reward them.

> **Luke 12:42** And the Lord said, Who then is that faithful and wise steward, whom his lord shall make ruler over his household, to give them their portion of meat in due season?

12:43 Blessed is that servant, whom his lord when he cometh shall find so doing.

12:44 Of a truth I say unto you, that he will make him ruler over all that he hath.

Matthew 7:19 Every tree that bringeth not forth good fruit is hewn down, and cast into the fire.

The evil servant.

Luke 12:45 But and if that servant say in his heart, My lord delayeth his coming; and shall begin to beat the menservants and maidens, and to eat and drink, and to be drunken;

Those who exalt themselves, abuse others and seek their own pleasures will be abased

12:46 The lord of that servant will come in a day when he looketh not for him, and at an hour when he is not aware, and will cut him in sunder, and will appoint him his portion with the unbelievers.

12:47 And that servant, which knew his lord's will, and prepared not himself, neither did according to his will, shall be beaten with many stripes.

12:48 But he that knew not, and did commit things worthy of stripes, shall be beaten with few stripes. For unto whomsoever much is given, of him shall be much required: and to whom men have committed much, of him they will ask the more.

Matthew 7:20 Wherefore by their fruits ye shall know them.

We can know the good shepherds by their love of God and by their diligent keeping and teaching of every Word of God and by their diligence to do the will of HIM who called them.

Matthew 23:11 But he that is greatest among you shall be your servant.

23:12 And whosoever shall exalt himself shall be abased; and he that shall humble himself shall be exalted.

Matthew 7:21 Not every one that saith unto me, Lord, Lord, shall enter into the kingdom of heaven; **but he that doeth the will of my Father which is in heaven.**

7:22 Many will say to me in that day, Lord, Lord, have we not prophesied in thy name? and in thy name have cast out devils? and in thy name done many wonderful works? **7:23** And then will I profess unto them, I never knew you: depart from me, ye that work iniquity.

7:24 Therefore whosoever heareth these sayings of mine, *and doeth them,* I will liken him unto a wise man, which built his house upon a rock: **7:25** And the rain descended, and the floods came, and the winds blew, and beat upon that house; and it fell not: for it was founded upon a rock.

Those who internalize the nature of God the Father and Jesus Christ, those who become one with them in total spiritual unity through a deep love for God and all the things of God, those who love the passionate keeping of every Word of God and who set a good example of godliness and FEED THE FLOCK with the good pasture of the Word of God, watering them with godliness; are building on the foundation of the Word of God: Which shall NEVER be moved.

The good and faithful teacher will receive a good reward of eternal life and the knowledge that he has helped to save many, as well as a good office in the eternal priesthood and kingship of Jesus Christ.

1 Peter 5:4 And when the chief Shepherd shall appear, ye shall receive a crown of glory that fadeth not away.

Let everyone humble themselves before God and work in cooperation with one another so that we may all exercise the gifts that God has given to each of us for the edifying of the whole body, in an orderly manner.

5:5 Likewise, ye younger, submit yourselves unto the elder [let the young in the faith submit to the older or wiser]. Yea, **all of you be subject one to another, and be clothed with humility: for God resisteth the proud, and giveth grace [mercy] to the humble. 5:6 Humble yourselves therefore under the mighty hand of God, that he may exalt you in due time: 5:7 Casting all your care upon him; for he careth for you.**

The tempted and persecuted are not alone because all of the faithful brethren have been or will be tempted and afflicted while in this world in the flesh.

5:8 Be sober [serious and controlled], be vigilant [always watchful]; because **your adversary the devil, as a roaring lion, walketh about, seeking whom he may devour** [Satan seeks to tempt or deceive away from God.]: **5:9** Whom resist stedfast in the faith, knowing that the same afflictions are accomplished in your brethren that are in the world.

The faithful brethren who are in the flesh in this world, all face trials like we do.

God the Father will establish those who persevere in his Word and will give them eternal life in a body of spirit; just as he raised up Christ.

5:10 But the God of all grace, who hath called us unto his [God the Father's] eternal glory [God the Father has called us to salvation and eternal life through Jesus Christ.] by Christ Jesus, after that ye have suffered a while, [God will] make you perfect, stablish, strengthen, settle you.

5:11 To him [to God the Father] be glory and dominion for ever and ever. Amen.

5:12 By Silvanus, a faithful brother unto you, as I suppose, I have written briefly, exhorting, and testifying that this is the true grace [godly love] of God wherein ye stand.

Peter wrote from Jerusalem and he was using the name "Babylon" as a euphemism for Jerusalem which is also called spiritual Egypt and Sodom (Rev 11:8). At that time wicked Jerusalem was soon to be surrounded by the Romans and facing complete destruction, which came in 70 A.D.

5:13 The church that is at Babylon [Jerusalem], elected [also called to God] together with you, saluteth you; and so doth Marcus my son [Mark, Peter's son in the faith who assisted Peter at Jerusalem].

5:14 Greet ye one another with a kiss of charity. Peace be with you all that are in Christ Jesus. Amen.

It was the custom for the brethren to greet one another with a big loving hug and a kiss of affection on the cheek or neck as many of us still do today.

Second Peter

2 Peter 1

Peter addresses this Epistle to all these who are zealous to learn and to live by every Word of God.

2 Peter 1:1 Simon Peter, a servant and an apostle of Jesus Christ, **to them that have obtained like precious faith** [Faith in God to perform the works of faith, which are to believe and obey God and to live by every Word of God the Father.] **with us through the righteousness of God** [which is the keeping of every Word of God] and [the atoning sacrifice of] our Saviour Jesus Christ:

1:2 Grace [Mercy from God] and peace [with God] be multiplied unto you through the knowledge of God [faith and knowledge married to the works of faith; which works of faith are obedience to live by every Word of God], and of Jesus our Lord, **1:3** According as his divine power hath given unto us all things that pertain unto life and godliness, through the knowledge of him that hath called us to glory and virtue:

Jesus Christ in his ministry explained the intent of the law and the Word of God and revealed the way of salvation through sincere repentance, a baptismal commitment to sin no more and the application of the sacrifice of the Lamb of God.

By sincerely repenting of all past sin to go forward living by every Word of God through the power of Christ dwelling in us; we can internalize the very nature of God the Father to become holy as God is holy.

1:4 Whereby are given unto us exceeding great and precious promises: that **by these ye might be partakers of the divine nature,** having escaped the corruption [Through the Gospel of Salvation we can escape the decay and death that comes through bondage to sin.] that is in the world through lust.

1:5 And beside this, giving all diligence, add to your faith virtue [well doing, the good works of faith, which are to live by every Word of God]; and to virtue knowledge;

We are to grow in truth, faith and knowledge and to gain a fuller knowledge of God, through daily diligent study, eagerly accepting the truth and rejecting all error for the truth.

Faith means to believe, trust and obey.

We must add to faith virtue; and virtue is the action of obedience; and we must add to virtue; knowledge.

Knowledge is knowing what we should be doing, which knowledge comes through a diligent study of every Word of God and seeking knowledge from God in prayer and continual thought on the Word and Law of our God, Psalm 119.

1:6 And to knowledge temperance [self-control]; and to temperance patience; and to patience godliness [becoming like God through a zealous keeping of the whole Word of God]; **1:7** And to godliness brotherly kindness [We must put Love for God and the zealous keeping of the whole Word of God first, and immediately after that the second great commandment is to love thy neighbor as thy self.]; and to brotherly kindness charity [Strong's G26. Charity here means true godly love, which is to love God and man more than one loves oneself].

If we do these things we shall be filled with God's Spirit of understanding, bearing much spiritual fruit.

God is not divided against himself and his Spirit will not inspire anyone to break or compromise with any part of God's Word.

God is united with himself, and his Spirit in us is God's very mind and nature; it will inspire us to keep the whole Word of God, and it will empower us to keep God's Word: Thus building in us the very nature of God, the divine nature.

Every Word of God in the letter, spirit and intent, constitute godly LOVE; and only by keeping the whole Word of God in BOTH the letter and the intent, can we be filled with the nature of God; which is godly LOVE.

1:8 For if these things be in you, and abound, they make you that ye shall neither be barren nor unfruitful in the knowledge of our Lord Jesus Christ.

If we do not zealously learn and keep the whole Word of God and love God first above all else, while secondly loving our brothers and humanity enough to speak the truth to them; we have fallen back into sin and have been turned aside from God.

1:9 But **he that lacketh these things** [They which lack a good knowledge of God and sound doctrine, and lack temperance (self-control) and patience and virtue (a passionate keeping of the whole Word of God) are spiritually blind (Laodicean, Rev 3).] **is blind, and cannot see afar off, and hath forgotten that he was purged from his old sins.**

Let all the called out to God the Father through Jesus Christ be diligent to root out all error and sin, and passionate to learn and to live by every Word of God.

1:10 Wherefore the rather, brethren, **give diligence to make your calling and election sure**: for if ye do these things, ye shall never fall:

The duty of the spiritually called out is to diligently study and apply every Word of God in faithful obedience to God; and through that process to internalize the very nature of God to eternal salvation!

1:11 For so [By doing the things mentioned above, in sincere repentance from all sin and in internalizing the whole Word and nature of God the Father; we shall receive eternal life.] an entrance shall be ministered unto you abundantly into the everlasting kingdom of our Lord and Saviour Jesus Christ.

The elders and teachers are to continually rebuke all sin and are to diligently teach a passionate zeal to keep the whole Word of God. As Paul also instructs:

> **2 Timothy 4:1** I charge thee therefore before God, and the Lord Jesus Christ, who shall judge the quick and the dead at his appearing and his kingdom; **4:2** Preach the word; be instant in season, out of season; reprove, rebuke, exhort with all long suffering and doctrine.

2 Peter 1:12 Wherefore **I will not be negligent to put you always in remembrance of these things, though ye know them, and be established in the present truth.**

Even those well established in the whole truth of God need to be continually reminded of all godly things; lest we forget.

1:13 Yea, I think it meet [proper, necessary], as long as I am in this tabernacle [alive in the flesh], **to stir you up by putting you in remembrance; 1:14** Knowing that shortly I must put off this my tabernacle [after writing this Epistle from Jerusalem, Peter would soon die in the flesh], even as our Lord Jesus Christ hath shewed me.

Peter wrote his Epistles as a kind of farewell message before his death in approximately 64 A.D.

1:15 Moreover I will endeavour that **ye may be able after my decease to have these things always in remembrance.**

Peter gives his eyewitness testimony to the Messiah-ship of Jesus Christ and the teachings of the whole Word of God. Peter is an eye witness to the ministry of Christ, and to the transfiguration on the mount, having seen the righteousness of Christ and heard the voice from heaven attesting to the righteousness of Christ as the Deliverer of humanity.

1:16 For we have not followed cunningly devised fables, when we made known unto you the power and coming of our Lord Jesus Christ, but were eyewitnesses of his majesty. **1:17** For he received from God the Father honour and glory, when there came such a voice to him from the excellent glory, This is my beloved Son, in whom I am well pleased. **1:18** And this voice which came from heaven we heard, when we were with him in the holy mount.

Peter then exhorts us to seek understanding and to study prophecy.

We know about Christ through the prophets, and we are warned that no prophecy stands alone. All the prophets MUST fit together precisely to provide the big overall picture. One of the ways to test our understanding of the prophets is to compare and make sure that a pet belief does not contradict some other scripture.

The Word of God is one consistent whole, made up of many parts: And every single part fits together with every other part to make a greater whole. It is like a great mosaic, and we cannot take one little piece out of its context and think we have the true whole overall understanding.

No. We must look at the whole big picture and every part has to fit together with everything else.

1:19 We have also a more sure word of prophecy; whereunto ye do well that ye take heed, as unto a light that shineth in a dark place, until the day dawn, and the day star arise in your hearts:

No prophecy and no scripture stands alone, but all scripture must be consistent with all other scripture. We are to study by putting all scriptures on any subject together. God's Word on a subject is here a little and there a little; and ungodly men take scripture out of its subject context and twist it to justify their sins.

> **Isaiah 28:9** Whom shall he teach knowledge? and whom shall he make to understand doctrine? them that are weaned from the milk, and drawn from the breasts.

The knowledge of God comes to those that are mature to learn and internalize the Word of God through diligent study, putting all scriptures together on any given subject and not forgetting to study synonyms.

> **28:10** For precept must be upon precept, precept upon precept; line upon line, line upon line; here a little, and there a little:

> **28:11** For with stammering lips and another tongue [a little here and a little there] will he [God] speak to this people [so that God might prove and test our zeal to study, learn and understand His Word].

> **28:12** To whom he said, This is the rest wherewith ye may cause the weary to rest; and this is the refreshing: yet they would not hear.

> **28:13** But the word of the Lord was unto them precept upon precept, precept upon precept; line upon line, line upon line; here a little, and there a little; that they might go, and fall backward, and be broken, and snared, and taken.

2 Peter 1:20 Knowing this first, that no prophecy of the scripture is of any private interpretation.

1:21 For the prophecy came not in old time by the will of man: but holy men of God spake as they were moved by the Holy Ghost.

The prophets worked under the inspiration of Jesus Christ through the Holy Spirit of God. Scriptural doctrine and prophecy are God inspired and therefore true. In order to properly understand God's Word, all the different parts have to be put together in the correct way to complete the puzzle.

2 Peter 2

Peter warns us as Paul, Jesus and Jude also warn us; that in this end time the called out spiritual Ekklesia would be full of false teachers who teach the brethren to follow themselves as idols of men and deny the authority of Christ and the Word of God by paying lip service while rejecting any zeal to live by every Word of God.

They falsely present themselves as God's ministers saying "follow me;" instead of saying "zealously follow the whole Word of God!"

2 Peter 2:1 But there were false prophets also among the people, even **as there shall be false teachers among you, who privily shall bring in damnable heresies, even denying the Lord that bought them** [Brethren, this is happening in TODAY'S brotherhood with many elders and leaders denying God's authority by refusing any zeal to live by every Word of God without compromise, while they pay lip service to God to deceive the brethren!], and bring upon themselves swift destruction.

Yes, Paul spoke the truth when he prophesied that there would be a "great falling away" from true godliness (2 Thess 2:3), in the end time.

Today, because sound doctrine has NOT been taught, MANY false teachers have crept into the Ekklesia and very MANY brethren have fallen away from the sound doctrine of the whole Word of God.

Some false teachers even teach the nonsense that the worldly are fallen away from what they were never a part of, in order to propagate the lie [which is contrary to God's many warnings] that the Ekklesia cannot fall away.

Why? So they can lead the Ekklesia even further away from God; speaking lies in the name of truth and teaching wickedness in the name of spiritual growth.

> **2 Timothy 4:1** I charge thee therefore before God, and the Lord Jesus Christ, who shall judge the quick and the dead at his appearing and his kingdom;
>
> **4:2** Preach the word; be instant in season, out of season; reprove, rebuke, exhort with all long suffering and doctrine.
>
> **4:3** For the time will come when they will not endure sound doctrine; but after their own lusts shall they heap to themselves teachers, having itching ears;
>
> **4:4** And they shall turn away their ears from the truth, and shall be turned unto fables.

2 Peter 2:2 And **many shall follow their pernicious** [malignant, noxious, poisonous, corrupting, ruinous, deadly, lethal, fatal] **ways;** by reason of whom the way of truth shall be evil spoken of.

Isn't that the truth? Isn't that exactly what has happened in this latter day?

Today the truth of God is evil spoken of by VERY MANY, because of the many false teachers who have taken over in today's Ekklesia, leading many astray.

In today's spiritual Ekklesia there is an idolatrous zeal for human leaders and corporations as they substitute their false traditions for the Word of God and do what THEY think is right instead of doing what God SAYS is right.

This is exactly what the Abomination of Daniel 12 does; substituting his own false traditions for the Word of God!

2:3 And through covetousness shall they with feigned [false and deceitful teachings] words make merchandise of you [deceive the brethren]: whose judgment [the judgment and destruction of such wicked church leaders is now almost at hand] now of a long time lingereth not, and their damnation slumbereth not.

Any leader or elder who justifies sin and even a hint of any tolerating or compromising with sin; or who rejects scripture, or who tries to twist it to justify their own traditions: IS A FALSE TEACHER and is a FALSE PROPHET!

2:4 For if God spared not the angels that sinned, but cast them down to hell, and delivered them into chains of darkness, to be reserved unto judgment; **2:5** And spared not the old world, but saved Noah the eighth person, a preacher of righteousness, bringing in the flood upon the world of the ungodly; **2:6** And turning the cities of Sodom and Gomorrha into ashes condemned them with an overthrow, making them an ensample unto those that after should live ungodly;

God calls the faithful out from among the wicked so that he can correct the wicked without harming the faithful.

2:7 And delivered just Lot, vexed with the filthy conversation [evil conduct] of the wicked: **2:8** (For that righteous man dwelling among them, in seeing and hearing, vexed his righteous soul from day to day with their unlawful deeds;)

God knows how to deliver those who love him enough to keep his Word with passion; and he knows how to correct the wicked; and if they remain unrepentant God will utterly destroy them in the fire of damnation.

2:9 The Lord knoweth how to deliver the godly out of temptations, and to reserve the unjust unto the day of judgment to be punished:

Those who rail the most about government really mean that they want the brethren to follow themselves. They want to be the government, the one in control, while they themselves will not submit to the authority over them; the authority of Almighty God.

They are the same people who despise the authority of the whole Word of God. They teach men to follow themselves as they rebuke any zeal to live by every Word of God. They are presumptuous deceivers, teaching for doctrine their own false traditions and human imaginations.

2:10 But chiefly them that walk after the flesh in the lust of uncleanness, and despise government. Presumptuous are they, selfwilled, they are not afraid to speak evil of dignities.

What is a "dignity" in God's eyes? Someone who is zealous for God and lives by every Word of God!

We are commanded to shine the light of God's Word on the sins of men and to reprove all sin, warning them to sincerely repent (Is 58:1, Ezek 33).

Speaking evil about dignities is about condemning those who ARE doing the will of God and zealously keeping the whole Word of God.

The faithful godly angels set an example for us when they refused to vent their personal anger at the evil ones and left such judgment to God's Word. Even so, we must not lose our temper with those who persecute the godly, but we must warn them to keep the whole Word of God; for it is God's Word that will judge them and not any outbursts of our temper.

2:11 Whereas [the faithful godly angels], which are greater in power and might, bring not railing [personal anger] accusation against them before the Lord.

The wicked men who have infiltrated today's Ekklesia and taken over nearly all their corporate churches, are leading many away from any zeal to keep the whole Word of God, to test the brethren.

They are probably sincere in their beliefs but they are not converted, being carnally worldly minded and not spiritually minded to live by every Word of God. It was ordained from the most ancient times that God would allow evil seducers to test his people.

> **Jude 1:3** Beloved, when I gave all diligence to write unto you of the common salvation, it was needful for me to write unto you, and exhort you that ye should earnestly contend for the faith which was once delivered unto the saints. **1:4 For there are certain men crept in unawares, who were before of old ordained to this condemnation, ungodly men,** turning the grace of our God into lasciviousness, and denying [by rejecting the authority of the whole Word of God] the only Lord God, and our Lord Jesus Christ.

The wicked deceivers who now lead the vast majority of today's Ekklesia; rejecting the truth and cleaving to past errors and false traditions, while demanding organizational loyalty and loyalty to idols of men in place of any zeal and loyalty for God and the whole Word of God; will perish in their own sins if they will not repent.

Those who follow them as idols of men and turn away from faithfulness to live by every Word of God will fall into great tribulation with them.

2 Peter 2:12 But these, as natural brute beasts, made to be taken and destroyed, speak evil of the things that they understand not; and shall utterly perish in their own corruption; 2:13 And shall receive the reward of unrighteousness, as they that count it pleasure to riot in the day time. Spots they are and blemishes, sporting themselves with their own deceivings while they feast with you;

These evil leaders and elders make a pretense of godliness by paying lip service to the Sabbath and the Feasts of God; while they lead people astray into polluting God's Sabbaths and Feasts.

Today the Ekklesia has been deceived into thinking of the words of men as greater than the Word of God and we are full of spiritual adultery following idols of men, corporate idols and idols of false teachings, while neither hungering nor thirsting after the truth and having a zeal to exalt men above following our LORD and departing from the diligent keeping of every Word of God.

These wicked men have deceived the spiritually weak who have not been grounded on the sound doctrine of the Word of God. They have led very many brethren to fall away from any zeal for godliness, doing so for reward like Balaam did; teaching falsely for a pay cheque and a personal following.

They like Balaam shall be rebuked by Christ for their love of money and for bringing a curse on the brethren by leading them into sin for wages.

2:14 Having eyes full of adultery, and that cannot cease from sin; beguiling unstable souls: an heart they have exercised with covetous practices; cursed children: **2:15** Which have forsaken the right way, and are gone astray, following the way of Balaam the son of Bosor, who loved the wages of unrighteousness; **2:16** But was rebuked for his iniquity: the dumb ass speaking with man's voice forbad the madness of the prophet.

Balaam was willing to sell his blessings and curses for money, just as very many leaders, elders and teachers do today.

These deceivers prophesied from old, being allowed by God to test the brethren of the called out.

Such deceivers are sons of wickedness, lacking the Light of God's Spirit, and are consigned to total everlasting destruction unless they sincerely repent.

2:17 These are wells without water, clouds that are carried with a tempest; to whom the mist of darkness is reserved for ever.

These deceivers allure the weak through temptation to compromise with worldliness, seeking to lead the brethren away from any zeal to keep the whole Word of God. They call the Sabbath and High Days holy and then refuse to keep them holy, as they exalt themselves as moral authorities above the Word of God

2:18 For when they speak great swelling words of vanity [false empty words that lead to destruction], they allure through the lusts of the flesh [We buy in restaurants on Sabbaths breaking God's commandments and polluting God's Sabbaths; FOR OUR OWN PLEASURE.], through much wantonness, those that were clean escaped from them who live in error.

The deceivers, who are now leading most of today's assemblies promise protection from tribulation and they promise spiritual salvation, as they lead the brethren to their destruction.

God is allowing this to TEST our faithfulness to Him alone.

Will we follow God: ALL THE WAY? Or will we follow men away from any zeal to keep the whole Word of God?

2:19 While they promise them liberty, they themselves are the servants of corruption: **for of whom a man is overcome, of the same is he brought in bondage.**

If the called out who have sincerely repented from all sin are deceived into being again entrapped into the sin of idolatry and spiritual adultery; if we fall for their deception then we have fallen into a worse state then we were in before we were ever called to God.

When we have been called to God and have accepted that call and then we later turn away from God; we are much worse off than if we had never been called at all, for we have had our chance and failed, while the sinner still has his opportunity before him.

2:20 For if after they have escaped the pollutions of the world through the knowledge of the Lord and Saviour Jesus Christ, they are again entangled therein, and overcome, the latter end is worse with them than the beginning.

2:21 For it had been better for them not to have known the way of righteousness, than, after they have known it, to turn from the holy commandment delivered unto them.

If we return to the filth that God has delivered us out of and we turn away from keeping the whole Word of God and we go back into the filth of sin and idolizing men and their false traditions; we are like a dog returning to its vomit.

2:22 **But it is happened unto them according to the true proverb, The dog is turned to his own vomit again; and the sow that was washed to her wallowing in the mire.**

Today there has been a great falling away of the people of God in fulfillment of prophecy, for God knew what would come in the last days.

God's called out have been enticed by deceitful men to exalt such men and our own false traditions above the Word of God, and we are now coming to the climax of this falling away in fulfillment of the words of Jude, the warnings of Paul to the Thessalonians and the warnings of Jesus Christ in Matthew 24.

2 Peter 3

Peter states that the very purpose of his epistles is to stir up the brethren to remember the scriptures. Through history and in this latter day we too need to be stirred up to remember the scriptures written by the prophets and the apostles, and not only just remember the scriptures but to be enthusiastic "Doers of the Word"

2 Peter 3:1 This second epistle, beloved, I now write unto you; in both which I stir up your pure minds by way of remembrance: **3:2 That ye may be mindful of the words which were spoken before by the holy prophets, and of the commandment of us the apostles of the Lord and Saviour:**

Today in the world and also in the Ekklesia, many have begun to think that "My Lord delays his coming." Jesus himself warned us that those who think such things and slack away from zealous godliness will be rejected by him (Mat 24: 48).

Today many in the Ekklesia scoff at those who are zealous for God, just like the worldly scoff at the warnings of correction and Christ's coming.

3:3 Knowing this first, that there shall come in the last days scoffers, walking after their own lusts, **3:4** And saying, Where is the promise of his coming? for since the fathers fell asleep, all things continue as they were from the beginning of the creation.

Because of the many false teachers and false prophets in today's assemblies, there is a spirit of unbelief in the Ekklesia, people cannot be bothered with any serious study and are happy to play "follow the Elder" for a social good time; yet God says:

> **Amos 3:7** Surely the Lord God will do nothing, but he revealeth his secret unto his servants the prophets.

We should certainly carefully TEST every word of men by the Word of God; by checking to see if the person is zealous and faithful to God and every Word of God and checking to see if what is taught is consistent with the whole Word of God.

The proof of a prophet or of any teacher or man of God, is that his words MUST be consistent with God's Word, including all of the Biblical prophets and biblical apostles.

The worldly close their eyes to the obvious and are willingly ignorant of God; just like today's spiritual Ekklesia closes its eyes to the truth and Word of God, being willingly ignorant and desiring to follow corporate idols and the false traditions of men.

2 Peter 3:5 For this they willingly are ignorant of, that by the word of God the heavens were of old, and the earth standing out of the water and in the water: **3:6** Whereby the world that then was, being overflowed with water, perished: **3:7** But the heavens and the earth, which are now, by the same word are kept in store, reserved unto fire against the day of judgment and perdition of ungodly men.

People who scoff at the prophets are scoffing at over one third of the Christ breathed Word of God and will be judged.

3:8 But, beloved, **be not ignorant of this one thing, that one day is with the Lord as a thousand years, and a thousand years as one day.**

Here we have a profound key to unlock much prophecy including the Feast Days. A key that is rejected by most today, who try to teach that seven days is as one thousand years when they give their false take on the Feast of Tabernacles.

One day is as ONE thousand years; and seven days are NOT equal to one thousand years; therefore seven days MUST refer to either just seven days, or to SEVEN thousand years. There is NO WAY that the Feast of Tabernacles could refer to a one thousand year millennium!

This FALSE teaching has been driven into the minds of people for generations and has prevented an understanding of the true meaning of the Festivals and much prophecy.

Many don't realize that what is a very long period of time to man, is a very short period of time with God. God will fulfill his Word; He will keep his promises. These things are coming and are now at the door!

All Scripture must fit together. There are many who say the Seven Day Feast of Tabernacles represents a thousand year millennium. And yet what does Peter say here? One day is with the Lord as a thousand years, and a thousand years is as one day.

How could the seven day Feast of Unleavened Bread or the Seven Day Feast of Tabernacles picture one thousand years? According to Scripture, they must picture 7,000 years or they must have nothing whatsoever to do with years.

According to God's Word, the Seven Day Feast of Tabernacles pictures 7,000 years. It does not picture any one thousand year millennium. The same thing is true of the Feast of Unleavened Bread and the seven day week! We know because God inspired Peter to say so.

3:9 The Lord is not slack concerning his promise, as some men count slackness; but is longsuffering to us-ward, not willing that any should perish, but that all should come to repentance.

The Tribulation

1 Thessalonians 5:1

Paul begins to instruct the pillars about the onset of the tribulation, first teaching that the vast majority will be taken completely by surprise.

1 Thessalonians 5:1 But of the times and the seasons, brethren, ye have no need that I write unto you. **5:2** For yourselves know perfectly that the day of the Lord so cometh as a thief in the night.

The great tribulation at end of this age of sin will come as a great surprise to the vast majority of humanity, including the vast majority of today's spiritual Ekklesia who are lax and lukewarm, rejecting the warnings and the biblical signs in favor of their false traditions.

The scriptures say that it is during a time of peace that the tribulation will come suddenly [unexpectedly]:

Daniel 8:25 And through his policy also he shall cause craft to prosper in his hand [the king of the North will make the New Europe prosperous]; and he shall magnify himself in his heart, **and by peace shall destroy many**: he shall also stand up against the Prince of princes; but he shall be broken without hand.

1 Thessalonians 5:3 For when they shall say, Peace and safety; then sudden [completely unexpected, by surprise: Strong's G1601) unexpected, sudden, unforeseen] destruction cometh upon them [Jerusalem, Judea and ultimately greater Israel], as travail upon a woman with child; and they shall not escape.

After the coming bloody Mideast war when peace is seen to be achieved; and when that peace is declared as the man of sin goes to the Holy Place; sudden and immediate destruction will come upon Jerusalem and Judah.

God Almighty will bring all the Islamic countries except Egypt [the nations of Psalm 83], against Judah and Jerusalem. Then the New Federal Europe will intervene in the name of stopping the bloodshed and bringing peace, she will also bring down the Anglo Saxon nations through non-violent economic means. See the "Coming World Events" category for details.

The children of light are pillars like the Thessalonians, who are zealous and faithful to God and his Word: Being the children of LIGHT through their zeal to live by every Word of God they will see and understand the signs and will NOT be taken by surprise.

The sinners of the world's nations and the spiritually lukewarm and spiritually blind children of darkness, including many in today's Ekklesia; will reject the scriptures and insist that Jesus was wrong in Matthew 24:15 and that there must still be 3 1/2 years before the tribulation, or that some physical temple must first be built and sacrifice begin, and so they will be deceived by their own false traditions and beliefs.

First the abomination, the man of sin, will be set up doing miracles in the Vatican and endorse a New Order in Europe, then about 75 days later he will go to the holy place.

The world's peoples and worldly brethren will not believe the warnings and they will be caught completely by surprise.

Only the pillars of today who are like the zealous of Thessaloniki will be alert and aware, and will understand and will NOT be taken by surprise; they have been forewarned and when peace is about to be declared and the man of sin schedules his visit to the holy place; the children of light will know that the tribulation is about to begin.

Jesus Christ himself said that when the abomination visits the holy place the tribulation will immediately begin (Mat 24:15).

The true Gospel being preached is NOT the sign of the beginning of any great tribulation; it is the sign of the actual coming of Christ to rule this earth..

Matthew 24:14 And this gospel of the kingdom shall be preached in all the world for a witness unto all nations; and **then shall the end come**.

The Gospel being preached is NOT the sign of the beginning of any great tribulation. After the tribulation begins the preaching of the true Gospel will be continued by God's two prophets and by God's mighty angels until the very coming of Christ with his saints!

This will take place DURING the tribulation and this preaching is NOT a sign of the beginning of the tribulation.

The sign of the beginning of the tribulation is the setting up of the final miracle working man of sin in the Vatican and his visit to the holy place around 75 days later.

24:15 When ye therefore shall see the abomination of desolation, spoken of by Daniel the prophet, **stand in the holy place,** (whoso readeth, let him understand:)

This abomination is set up doing miracles in Rome and then goes to the Holy Place [the whole Mount is Holy] about 75 days later, triggering the tribulation.

When the abomination [the final false prophet] is set up in Rome, he has only a total of 1,335 days before he is destroyed (Dan 12; Rev 19:20).

1,335 minus 1,260 for the tribulation, begins the tribulation about 75 days after the final abomination is set up in the papacy in Rome.

When you see the abomination set up in Rome and recognize him by his miracles and his endorsement of a New Europe; then know that the tribulation is imminent and will begin when he goes to the Mount.

When the scriptures tell us that some will leave the land to run to safety and some do not, it should be self-evident that a split between the zealous for godliness, and the lukewarm [for living by God's Word] of Revelation 3:14-22; is inevitable.

It should also be self-evident from the obvious apostasy in today's Ekklesia; that the prophesied falling away of many from any zeal for God, is well underway.

The spiritually wise will know that the tribulation will begin in about 75 days, when they see this abomination set up in Rome. Then God will send his Two Servants who will use their power to enable the zealous to go to God's refuge as one of their first acts.

The scripture rejecting wicked in today's Ekklesia will not understand until the tribulation is well underway. Then many of them will see their error and sincerely repent, only to be forced to prove the sincerity of their repentance by persevering in great tribulation. The great tribulation will begin when the miracle working false prophet visits the holy place around 75 days after being set up as pope in the Vatican.

24:16 Then let them which be in Judaea flee into the mountains: **24:17** Let him which is on the housetop not come down to take any thing out of his house: **24:18** Neither let him which is in the field return back to take his clothes. **24:19** And woe unto them that are with child, and to them that give suck in those days! **24:20** But pray ye that your flight be not in the winter, neither on the sabbath day: **24:21** For then shall be great tribulation, such as was not since the beginning of the world to this time, no, nor ever shall be.

It is when this final false prophet is set up doing miracles and then goes to the Holy Place about 75 days later that the great tribulation will begin: Immediately, at that time, so quickly that someone in

Judea should not even go home to fetch his coat! This we have on the direct authority of Jesus Christ (Mat 24:15).

Speaking now to the faithful and the zealous for God and his Word in this latter day:

1 Thessalonians 5:4 But ye, brethren, **are not in darkness, that that day should overtake you as a thief**.

The beginning of the great tribulation and the time of the coming of Christ will not be concealed from God's faithful zealous pillars. They SHALL KNOW, because they are the wise in Christ; for they are faithful and zealous to live by every Word of our God!

Daniel 12:10 Many shall be purified, and made white, and tried; but the wicked shall do wickedly: and none of the wicked shall understand; **but the wise** [zealous to learn and to keep the whole Word of God] **shall understand**.

1 Thessalonians 5:5 Ye [the pillars who stand on the firm foundation of the whole Word of God] **are all the children of light, and the children of the day: we are not of the night, nor of darkness.**

Those who love God enough to be zealous to learn and to keep his Word are instructed to be soberly watchful for the signs, and to be prepared so that we are NOT be taken by surprise by these things.

5:6 Therefore **let us not sleep, as do others; but let us watch and be sober.**

Let us awaken and turn to a passionate zeal to live by every Word of God and let us watch soberly and intently for the signs which God has given to us so that we may know when these things will be fulfilled.

5:7 For they [the Laodicean's of today are drunk with pride and are spiritually asleep] that sleep sleep in the night; and they that be drunken are drunken in the night.

Those who are drunk with pride and conceit and who say that there must be 3 1/2 years after a declaration of peace, in direct contradiction to Jesus Christ in Matthew 24:15 and the apostle Paul in 1 Thessalonians 5:3; will be taken by surprise for they think they know everything and really know nothing, being spiritually blind and wretched and naked, not being zealous for the Word of God and relying on their own imaginations.

Laodicea [meaning: the people will be judged]

To Laodicea Jesus identifies himself as the faithful and true witness, telling the truth about what they are truly like. They think themselves spiritually rich and have no idea what Jesus Christ really thinks of them. Jesus here tells them their problems straight out, but they are proud and willfully blind to reality.

Emphasizing that his message to Laodicea is true and coming from Christ's faithful love for them, given to them so that they might repent and be saved.

Jesus also calls himself the "beginning of the creation of God;" clearly meaning that Christ is the Creator who began the creation of all things.

Revelation 3:14 And unto the angel of the church of the Laodiceans write; These things saith the Amen, the faithful and true witness, the beginning of the creation of God;

Laodicea is spiritually lukewarm, professing godliness while living according to their own imaginations instead of living the way that God commands.

They pay lip service to godliness without any zeal to learn and live by every Word of God. Their zeal is for their own ways and what they think, it is for their own false traditions and their idols of men and not for what God says. They stand on false traditions and proudly think they know it all; refusing any spiritual growth, they are stagnant or even falling backward in their spiritual condition.

They are hot for their own traditions, and for the teachings of their idols of men about the Word of God, and cold for zealously keeping the whole Word as God, as God has commanded them. This mixture of hot for their idols of men and corporate entities, and a cold, lack of zeal to keep the Words of God makes them lukewarm and revolting to God the Father and Jesus Christ.

They are idolaters of men and the false traditions of men; proud, thinking that they know it all spiritually and therefore they refuse correction from God or man; they reject the Word of God for their own ways and they reject any growth in truth and refuse to turn from error, going deeper and deeper into error and sin.

Because these folks have rejected God the Father and Jesus Christ to follow them above our idols of men, they will be rejected by Christ into the correction of great tribulation, in the hope that through the correction of the flesh the spirit may be saved.

3:15 I know thy works, that thou art neither cold nor hot: I would thou wert cold or hot. **3:16** So then because thou art lukewarm, and neither cold nor hot, **I will spue thee out of my mouth.**

They will be rejected by Christ into severe correction

Proud and self-willed, they think they are spiritually rich and know it all, having need of no spiritual growth and rejecting the promised increase in spiritual knowledge and understanding promised for the last days (Dan 12).

They reject any part of scripture that they do not want to follow, saying it is for others; or that it is not reliable and are so proud that they have no idea how spiritually wretched, miserable and poor they really are.

They are willfully blind to their own condition and to the things of God that disprove their own false ways; They lack the garments of righteousness and are naked before God, their many sins exposed to Him; beginning with the sins of pride, stubborn self-will, self-justification and self-approval.

3:17 Because thou sayest, I am rich [spiritually], and increased with goods [spiritual knowledge], and have need of nothing [no one, not even Christ (the Word of God) can tell them anything]; and knowest not that thou art [spiritually] wretched, and miserable, and [spiritually] poor [knowing almost nothing of God as they ought to know it], and blind [willfully blind to their wretched spiritual state], and naked [naked of any true godly righteousness, not being zealous to keep the Word of God]:

Jesus Christ counsels those with the Laodicean attitude to buy spiritual gold [knowledge] in the fire of tribulation; so that they may become spiritually rich.

They are bidden to sincerely repent of their prideful sins so that the nakedness of their wickedness may be covered by the application of the sacrifice of Christ, and so that they may receive God's Holy Spirit and the white raiment of the righteousness of the zealous keeping of the whole Word of God.

They are commanded to anoint their eyes with God's Spirit and open them wide to see themselves as God sees them, and to sincerely repent from their pride and false ways and to turn away from their idols of men and false traditions to follow the Spirit of God into all truth; rejecting all error and sin to embrace godly truth that they might be saved.

3:18 I counsel thee to buy of me [spiritual] gold tried in the fire [during the period of our correction in the fire of tribulation], that thou mayest be [become spiritually rich] rich; and white raiment [the righteousness of zealously keeping the whole Word of God], that thou mayest be clothed, and that the shame of thy nakedness [that our sins might be covered by the righteousness of God] do not appear; and anoint thine eyes with eyesalve, that thou mayest see [open our eyes to see ourselves as God sees us, to see ourselves as we really are so that we can repent and be saved].

Jesus reminds these folks that he rebukes them only because he truly loves them and is not willing that they should perish. They are rejected only because they first rejected Christ, refusing to live by every Word of God, refusing to follow Christ and refusing to live by every Word of God in Christ-like zeal.

Jesus Christ tells those of the Laodicean attitude; which is the overwhelming attitude in the Ekklesia today; to REPENT of their pride and self-righteousness. and to REPENT of trusting in their idols of men and false traditions.

Jesus Christ tells us to turn to him; and to turn to a zeal for the whole Word of God, to learn it and to keep it; to turn from our false idols and false traditions and to become zealous to remove error and embrace the truth of God!

3:19 As many as I love, I rebuke and chasten: be zealous therefore, and repent.

Jesus is warning and calling each one of God's straying sheep; He wants them to open up to him, to reject idols and to follow him; to be zealous to remove sin and embrace God's righteous truth and to internalize the solid meat of the Word of God in fellowship with God the Father and Jesus Christ.

They have an open invitation from Jesus Christ who is gladly willing to accept them, if they would only open up their eyes and turn to zealous godliness!

3:20 Behold, I stand at the door, and knock: if any man hear my voice, and open the door, I will come in to him, and will sup [eat; internalize the Word of God] with him, and he with me.

The pillars of God stand on the whole Word of God, they believe and trust in the Word of God and not in idols of men and the false traditions of men.

1 Thessalonians 5:8 But let us, who are of the day, be sober, putting on the breastplate of faith and love; and for an helmet, the hope of salvation. 5:9 For God hath not appointed us [the faithful pillars are not appointed to such correction] **to wrath,** but to obtain salvation by our Lord Jesus Christ, **5:10** Who died for us, that, whether we wake or sleep, we should live together with him.

Those diligent for God and the whole Word of God should comfort one another with these things.

5:11 Wherefore comfort yourselves together, and edify one another, even as also ye do.

Peter now speaks of the coming of Christ as being a surprise to the wicked; but the coming of Christ will not be a surprise for the godly who are watching for him and who are the children of Light of God!

2 Peter 3:10 But the day of the Lord will come as a thief in the night; . . .

Peter now begins to write about the end of God's plan for physical humanity and the cleansing of the earth by fire, before God the Father and the New Jerusalem come down to the earth; and the beginning of the Feast of the Eighth Day, which is a new beginning for all humanity going forward into all eternity changed to spirit and dwelling with God.

Using the concept of duality with the coming of Christ as a precursor to the coming of God the Father, Peter uses the term "Day of the Lord" to refer to information about the final cleansing and resurfacing of the earth; before eternity with God the Father for all humanity changed to eternal spirit.

....in the which the heavens shall pass away with a great noise, and the elements shall melt with fervent heat, the earth also and the works that are therein shall be burned up.**

3:11 Seeing then that all these things shall be dissolved, what manner of persons ought ye to be in all holy conversation [words and deeds] and godliness, **3:12** Looking for and hasting unto the coming of the day of God, wherein the heavens being on fire shall be dissolved, and the elements shall melt with fervent heat? **3:13 Nevertheless we, according to his promise, look for new heavens and a new earth, wherein dwelleth righteousness**.

This refers to that time when the plan for PHYSICAL humanity has been completed and the whole earth will be cleansed by fire to purify it from all uncleanness and sin so that the New Jerusalem and God the Father may come to dwell with his changed to spirit children on this earth!

Here Peter reveals the great power of Almighty God and encourages all people to remain true to God the Father and to enthusiastically keep the whole Word of God; and by internalizing the very nature of God through pleasing him, we can look forward to spending eternity in perfect peace and harmony with God and our spiritual brethren!

That is the true meaning of the "Feast of The Eighth Day:" a New Beginning going forth into eternity in peace with God through total unity with God the Father and Jesus Christ!

3:14 Wherefore, beloved, seeing that ye look for such things, be diligent that ye may be found of him [God] in peace [with God], without spot, and blameless [without even a hint of sin].

3:15 And account that the longsuffering [God's patience with us] of our Lord is salvation; even as our beloved brother Paul also according to the wisdom given unto him hath written unto you;

Peter here warns the brethren to be on the lookout for those who would twist the words of Paul to lead men away from their zeal to live by every Word of God.

3:16 As also in all his epistles, speaking in them of these things; in which are some things hard to be understood, **which they that are unlearned and unstable wrest, as they do also the other scriptures, unto their own destruction.**

Brethren, we too have been warned. We have studied together through the Gospels and Epistles and seen the true and godly meaning and the true passionate zeal of Paul to keep the whole Word of God. Therefore beware of the twisting of the words of Paul by wicked men trying to dampen our zeal to live by every Word of God.

3:17 Ye therefore, beloved, seeing ye know these things before [we have be warned ahead of time], beware lest ye also, being led away with the error of the wicked, fall from your own stedfastness.

3:18 But grow in grace [God's mercy comes through sincere repentance and a rejection of all error to embrace the truth of every Word of God.], and in the knowledge [continually rooting out all error to seek and accept the truth of God in diligent study] of our Lord and Saviour Jesus Christ. To him be glory both now and for ever. Amen.

We are to be diligent in internalizing the mind and nature of God, growing into peace with God; unspotted by sin and blameless as to those things that separate us from God.

This is achieved through wholehearted sincere repentance and a continual growing into a full unity with God the Father; through diligent study and the uncompromising practical application of ever Word of God in our lives.

The experience of Daniel's three friends is an instructional example for us, that we are to be faithful to the whole Word of God throughout our called out lives, regardless of any fiery trials that come our way; and of we do so we will be WITH Christ and he will be WITH us!

Then when we come out of the fiery trials of the flesh we will be resurrected to spirit and not so much as the smell of sin will be upon us!

> **Daniel 3:26** Then Nebuchadnezzar came near to the mouth of the burning fiery furnace, and spake, and said, Shadrach, Meshach, and Abednego, ye servants of the most high God, come forth, and come hither. Then Shadrach, Meshach, and Abednego, came forth of the midst of the fire.
>
> **3:27** And the princes, governors, and captains, and the king's counsellors, being gathered together, saw these men, upon whose bodies the fire had no power, nor was an hair of their head singed, neither were their coats changed, nor the smell of fire had passed on them.

First John

Love and the Law of God

Almost all religions define love as positive actions towards other people and neglect putting love for God first. In short they exalt loving man above loving God and so make an idol out of humanity as more important than God.

Yes, God commands us to love our neighbor, but that is the second command; the first command is to live by every Word of God (Mat 4:4, Mat 22:36-40).

In truth the greatest love that we can give humanity is to love and obey God first, so as to set an example of the way to eternal salvation for mankind.

True godly "love" is defined as zealously living by every Word of God.

First God, then man!

If we keep God's Word first, we will automatically love and do good to others because God is love! But if we love man and do not faithfully love and obey God more; we have fallen off our foundation and we cannot know how to properly love humanity!

The Word of God is the definition of real godly love, and to be filled with God's love we MUST live by every Word of God, which defines godly love; for Faith without Works [words without actions] is DEAD.

Only those who follow Christ's example and live by every Word of GOD: who actually sincerely repent and turn from living contrary to the Word of God will be justified by the atoning sacrifice of Christ.

> **Romans 2:13** (For not the hearers of the law are just before God, but the doers of the law shall be justified [by the application of the sacrifice of Christ].

At this time Satan KNOWS that his time is now very short!

He has launched a "Full Court Press" to destroy God's people from within; as he inspired Balaam to teach the people to sin and thereby offend God to bring God's wrath down upon them.

This was foretold of the last days.

> **Revelation 2:14** But I have a few things against thee, because thou hast there them that hold the doctrine of Balaam, who taught Balac to cast a stumblingblock before the children of Israel, to eat things sacrificed unto idols, and to commit fornication.

Satan seeks to ensnare us in the sins of spiritual idolatry and spiritual fornication [pornea] by enticing us to follow others in place of our LORD.

These are BOTH physical AND spiritual sins. This is about the **sin of exalting men and organizations** [spiritual idolatry and adultery] **ABOVE the Word of God.**

This is about doing whatever the church leader or elder says instead of comparing what they say against the scripture and then; Doing What God Says.

> **Revelation 2:14** But I have a few things against thee, because thou hast there them that hold the doctrine of Balaam, who taught Balac to cast a stumblingblock before the children of Israel, to eat things sacrificed unto idols, and to commit fornication.

This is about the spiritual adultery of doing what anyone other than God our Father and our espoused HUSBAND Jesus Christ commands and not zealously living by EVERY WORD of GOD our Father!

Following men to do what they say is right instead of living by every Word of God, is now rampant in this world and in today's spiritual Ekklesia as well!

Religions today undermine the basic core doctrines of God's Word by interpreting the MEANING of God's Word according to their own imaginations, just as others have done through the ages.

They have long ago managed to divide the Word of God from the works of faith [the practical doing] and establish the sinful attitude that: Love for neighbor is the first priority and is above love for God and zeal for God's Word!

Jesus Christ made it abundantly clear that love for God is demonstrated by obedience to God; and is the foundation of true godly love of mankind!

> **Matthew 22:36** Master, which is the great commandment in the law?
>
> **22:37** Jesus said unto him, **Thou shalt love the Lord thy God with all thy heart, and with all thy soul, and with all thy mind.**
>
> **22:38 This is the first and great commandment.**
>
> **22:39** And **the second** is like unto it, Thou shalt love thy neighbour as thyself.

We are to live by every Word of God as God gave it, and NOT according to any personal or Church organizational interpretation.

> **Revelation 2:15** So hast thou also them that hold the doctrine of the Nicolaitanes, which thing I hate.

Most of today's church groups are full of the doctrine of the Nicolaitanes which Jesus Christ and God the Father HATE! This doctrine exalts men as supposed authorities BETWEEN the brethren and God.

This is a SPIRITUAL battle!

Satan is behind this perversion in a concerted attempt to turn the people away from God and into rebellion against God's Word in the disguise of a fake supposed "love," so that God himself will reject and destroy his people for not loving him or mankind as defined in the Word of God!

Brethren, if they do not quickly and sincerely repent, the MAJORITY today WILL end up being rejected by God the Father and Jesus Christ for their idolatry and spiritual adultery and Nicolaitane abuse of their brethren. (Rev 3:15).

> **Matthew 24:48** But and if that evil servant shall say in his heart, My lord delayeth his coming; **24:49** And shall begin to smite his fellowservants, and to eat and drink with the drunken; **24:50** The lord of that servant shall come in a day when he looketh not for him, and in an hour that he is not aware of, **24:51** And shall cut him asunder, and appoint him his portion with the hypocrites: there shall be weeping and gnashing of teeth.

Unless we REPENT and start keeping ALL of God's commandments with passionate enthusiasm; we will be rejected by God the Father and Jesus Christ.

We have Christ's OWN PROMISE:

> **Matthew 22:12** And he saith unto him, Friend, how camest thou in hither not having a wedding garment? And he was speechless. **22:13** Then said the king to the servants, Bind him hand and foot, and take him away, and cast him into outer darkness, there shall be weeping and gnashing of teeth. **22:14** For many are called, but few are chosen.

It is absolutely NECESSARY to seek God our Father with ALL our hearts and to be solidly grounded on the issues of Law and Grace, Faith and Works; and to KNOW and understand these things so as to fight the spiritual battle now raging in the assemblies.

1 John 1

John begins by saying that they had seen and touched the Living Word in the flesh [the LOGOS spoken of by the prophets]; Jesus Christ. John is openly declaring that Christ existed eternally and was with God the Father before he gave up his Godhood to be made flesh and manifested unto men.

1 John 1, That **which was from the beginning** [He who existed before creation], which we have heard, which we have seen with our eyes, which we have looked upon, and our hands have handled, of the Word of life; **1:2** For the life was manifested, and we have seen it, and bear witness, and show unto you that eternal life, **which was with the Father**, and was manifested unto us, [who gave up his Godhood to be made flesh and shown to us]; **1:3** That which we have seen and heard declare we unto you. that ye also may have fellowship with us: and truly our fellowship is with the Father, and with his Son Jesus Christ.

The disciples including John, had witnessed these things and they have written about what they have witnessed with their own eyes and heard with their own ears; so that other called out disciples might believe and be encouraged.

1:4 And these things write we unto you, that your joy may be full.

God is Light which is knowledge and truth, and there is no darkness of ignorance, falsehood or sin in God at all.

1:5 This then is the message which we have heard of him, and declare unto you, that **God is light, and in him,** [in God] **is no darkness at all. 1:6** If we say that we have fellowship with him [are united with God], and walk in darkness [do not live by every Word of God in Christ-like zeal], we lie, and do not the truth, [for if we are in darkness while he is light we have no fellowship with him].

> **John 8:12** Then spake Jesus again unto them, saying, I am the light of the world: he that followeth me shall not walk in darkness, but shall have the light of life.

I John 1:7 But if we walk in the light, as he is in the light, . . .

If we keep the Word of God the Father, as the Father and Christ live by it; we are living in the light of Godliness!

Those who live in the light of God the Father's Word, will be in unity with the Father and with other like-minded persons; they will be cleansed from all past darkness of sin by sincere repentance and the application of the blood sacrifice of Jesus Christ; and by internalizing and living by the whole Word of God they shall also overcome sin and become Light as God is Light!

> **Romans 2:13** For not the hearers of the law are just before God, but **the doers of the law shall be justified.**

1 John 1:7 . . . . we have fellowship [unity] one with another [through each person's unity with God], and the blood of Jesus Christ his Son cleanses us from all sin.

If we are of God and the Light of God; we will be in unity with God and in unity with all others who are also in unity with God.

When God the Father calls us into the light of his ways and his Word, a response of sincere repentance and a baptismal commitment to STOP sinning, results in the application of the sacrifice of Jesus Christ which redeems us from the repented sin and reconciles us to God the Father.

This brings us into a relationship with God the Father, who will then empower us to live by every Word of God through the gift of God's Spirit dwelling in us.

We MUST then REMAIN "IN THE LIGHT" through zealously living by every Word God as Jesus Christ did. Then our light will shine as a godly example to all men through zealously living by EVERY WORD of GOD the Father.

> **Matthew 5:16** Let your light so shine before men, that they may see your good works, and glorify your Father which is in heaven.
>
> **5:17** Think not that I am come to destroy the law, or the prophets: I am not come to destroy, but to fulfill.

Jesus Christ came to keep every Word of God the Father as an example that we should do likewise.

> **5:18** For verily I say unto you, Till heaven and earth pass, one jot or one tittle shall in no wise pass from the law, till all be fulfilled.

1 John 1:8 If we say that we have no sin, we deceive ourselves, and the truth is not in us. 1:9 if we confess [sincerely repent of our sins and commit to go and sin no more] **our sins, he is faithful and just to forgive us our sins, and to cleanse us from all unrighteousness, . . .**

If we confess our sins before God the Father and sincerely repent of them, resolving to STOP breaking God's Law and Word and to begin seeking the Father's help in overcoming all sin, then we will be cleansed from the darkness and ignorance of sin; which is living contrary to any part of the Word of God.

If we say that we have not sinned, we make God a liar, and his word is not in us.

> **Romans 3:23** For **all have sinned**, and come short of the glory of God;

1 John 2

1 John 2:1 My little children, these things write I unto you, that you sin not [Since sin is the breaking of the Word of God, John is telling us to keep the whole Word of God.]. And if any man does sin [inadvertently, or without knowing], we have an advocate with the Father, Jesus Christ the righteous.

Jesus Christ intercedes for us with God the Father when we are sincerely and wholeheartedly repentant. He is our High Priest and the ONLY Mediator between humanity and God the Father.

> **1 Timothy 2:5 For there is one God, and one mediator between God and men, the man Christ Jesus 2:6** Who gave himself a ransom for all,

1 John 2:2 And he is the propitiation [the atoning sacrifice that ransoms us from our sincerely repented sins] for our sins: and not for ours only, but also for the sins of the whole world [when they repent in the time of their calling].

Those men who say that we can compromise a little, or that Christ understands and will wink at willful sin are LIARS! They are false teachers and Antichrists!

2:3 And hereby, we do know that we know Jesus Christ, if we keep his commandments. **2:4** He that sayeth, I know him, and keeps not his commandments, is a liar, and the truth is not in him.

2:5 But whoso keepeth his word [Yes, we are to zealously live by every Word of God.], **in him truly is the love of God perfected** [Don't let yourselves be deceived, godly love is to keep the whole Word of God; true godly love is not some false human imagined emotional feel good about ourselves.]**: hereby know we that we are in him**. **2:6** He that sayeth he abides in Christ ought himself also so to walk [live or behave,] even as Christ walked [lived and lives].

If we are in Christ and he is in us, we will be doing the things that he did; and what did he do? He lived by every Word of God the Father (Mat 4:4).

> **John 15:10**: **If ye keep my commandments, ye shall abide in my love; even as I have kept my Father's commandments, and abide in his love.**

If Jesus Christ is dwelling in us, he will be keeping God the Father's Word in us!

If we are residing in Christ then our branch is plugged into the trunk of the tree (see John 15) and we are plugged into Jesus Christ; then we will be doing what Christ did and does: Which is living by every Word of God to the very end!

1 John 2:7 Brethren, I write no new commandment unto you, but an old commandment which you had from the beginning. The old commandment is the word [to keep the whole Word of God] which you have heard from the very beginning. **2:8** Again, a new commandment I write unto you, which thing is true in him and in you: because **the darkness is past, and the true light** [We are to live in the godliness of the letter and spirit of every Word of God.] **now shines.**

We are to live by every Word of God in its fullest spirit and intent as well as in the letter; with a deep enthusiastic passionate zeal to live by every Word of God with all our beings, going beyond just the letter and keeping the spirit and intent of every Word of God.

2:9 He that sayeth **he is in the light, and hateth his brother, is in darkness** even until now.

If we say that we are full of the light of God's Word, and we see our brother stumbling and we tolerate his sin instead of warning and helping him; there is no godly love in us. Godly love is to keep the whole Word of God and to warn our brethren from every wrong way that is taking him to his destruction!

> **Leviticus 19:17** Thou shalt not hate thy brother in thine heart: thou shalt in any wise rebuke thy neighbour, and not suffer sin upon him.

1 John 2:10 He that loves his brother, abides in the light [The light of Godly love is the letter and spirit of the whole Word of God; Love God first and do his will, and proper godly love for our neighbor will automatically follow; for godly love IS the keeping of the whole Word of God.], and there is none occasion of stumbling in him.

If we will not help our brother by warning him when he has stumbled and gone astray: Where is our godly love? There are sins of commission and there is the sin of failing to warn our brethren to turn from their sin.

Despite the deceiver's siren song of lies, there is NO godly love in tolerating any sin, or in failing to rebuke sin; in this sin of omission resides hatred [not love] for our brethren, because we see him going to destruction and we make no effort to warn him.

True godly love rebukes sin and warns the sinner to turn from the sin which is bringing him to destruction, in the hope that he might be saved!

2:11 But **he that hateth his brother is in darkness, and walks in darkness, and knows not where he is going, because that darkness has blinded his eyes.**

Bear no hate for others in your heart, rather warn them to wholeheartedly repent and pray that the wicked might find sincere repentance. Love the people and hate the wickedness that brings destruction.

These words are for the called out and converted disciples of Christ

2:12 I write unto you, little children, because your sins are forgiven you [Our sins are forgiven if we are sincerely wholeheartedly repentant and commit to sin no more.] for his name's [because of the application of his sacrifice] sake,

John addresses the old, the young, children and parents; reminding all of us in the faith not to love worldliness! Let us love spiritual things and not worldliness and sin!

2:13 I write unto you, fathers, because you have known him that is from the beginning. I write unto you, young men, because you have overcome the wicked one. I write unto you, little children, because you have known the Father. **2:14** I have written unto you, parents, because you have known him that is from the beginning. I have written unto you, young men, because you are strong, and the word of God abides in you, and you have overcome the wicked one.

2:15 Love not the world.

Love not the evil things of this society, nor covet physical things, neither desire the evil things that are in the world. **If any person loves this evil world, the love of God the Father is not in him.**

If we love the things of this world, if we set our heart and our desires on the things of this world, then we do not love God because the things of this world are carnal mindedness which is enmity against God.

> **Romans 8:7** Because the carnal mind is enmity against God: for it is not subject to the law of God, neither indeed can be. **8:8** So then they that are in the flesh cannot please God. They that love the pleasures of the flesh and are not subject to God cannot please Him.

The lusts of the flesh have nothing to do with the light of God. They are darkness and ignorance of the way that brings peace and life.

Will you throw the crown of your calling in the gutter to keep your business open for a few hours on the Sabbath? or will you sin by buying in restaurants or anywhere else, or by cooking on God's Sabbaths? Do you love the things of this world so very much, that a bowl of pottage is worth your crown?

1 John 2:16 For all that is in the world, the lust of the flesh, and the lust of the eyes, and the pride of life, is not of the Father, but is of the world. **2:17** And **the world passes away with the lust thereof: but he that does the will of God will abide for ever.**

Today the earth is filled with preachers and elders who are Antichrists who love personal followings and seek the pleasures of worldliness; and they have led the brethren astray to follow idols of men and corporate entities away from any zeal to live by every Word of God in the letter and the spirit and in truth and faithfulness!

It has always been the last days for every person, since no one can tell if he will die today or tomorrow. Now it is the last days of this evil society as well.

2:18 Little children, it is the last time: and as ye have heard, the [final abomination] antichrist shall come, even now are there many antichrists [Very many Antichrist's have infiltrated today's Ekklesia and deceived many brethren away from their zeal to learn and keep the whole Word of God.]; whereby we know that it is the last time.

Not every person in the assemblies is converted, for many tares, outright weeds and false wolves in sheep's clothing have entered the flock, just as foretold by Christ, Jude, Paul, Peter and others for the last days.

2:19 They went out from us, [they turned away from the doctrine and teachings of God the Father and Jesus Christ] but they were not of us [these deceivers were never converted in the first place]; for if they had been of us, they would no doubt have continued with us [If these false teachers who lead the brethren to follow idols of man had really been converted, they would have taught and lived by the whole Word of God.]: but they went out [they turned against the godliness of zeal to live by every Word of God], that they might be made known that they were not all of us.

2:20 But ye have an unction [an anointing, (the gift) of the Holy Spirit, which is given to those who obey God Acts 5:32)] from the Holy One, and you know all things.

Those who zealously obey God and live by every Word of God will have understanding from God's Spirit and will be able to discern between the godly and the ungodly.

John plainly writes that he is addressing the truly converted who are zealous for godliness.

2:21 I have not written unto you because you know not the truth, but **because you do know the truth, and there is no lie of the truth.**

John writes that anyone who denies Christ [by not allowing him to live by every Word of God within us] is an Antichrist.

In today's Ekklesia most leaders and most elders also deny Christ by refusing to allow him to live by every Word of God within us by God's Holy Spirit. Jesus himself in Matthew 24 warned us that many false teachers would infiltrate the brotherhood and would misuse the name of Christ to deceive people to follow themselves as idols of men.

Some of these men are willfully misleading the brethren while many others are very sincere in their erroneous beliefs. The ONLY way to discern false teachers from true men of God is to judge their words by the Word of God and cleave tightly to every Word of God (1 Thess 5:21).

Speaking directly and specifically to his disciples Jesus warned us that MANY deceivers would infiltrate the Ekklesia and deceive MANY, especially in these latter days!

> **Matthew 24:4** And Jesus answered and said unto them, Take heed that no man deceive you [speaking directly to his disciples about deceivers who would infiltrate the assemblies] **24:5** For many shall come in my name, saying, I am Christ; and shall deceive many.

Using the name of Jesus Christ to deceive people into following themselves and to quench any zeal to live by every Word of God, makes the leaders and elders of today's called out spiritual Ekklesia who do such things Antichrists as well.

1 John 2:22 Who is a liar but he that denies that Jesus is the Christ? He is an antichrist, that denies the Father and the Son.

If anyone denies that Jesus is the Son of God and is in full complete unity with God the Father, they are an Antichrist, if anyone says that Christ came so that we would no longer have to keep God the Father's Word then they are an Antichrists.

Brethren, to deny the doctrine, the teachings, the Word of God the Father and the Son; is to DENY THEM!

2:23 Whosoever denies the Son, the same hath not the Father,

Those who deny Christ by refusing to live by every Word of God; have no knowledge or relationship with God the Father or with Jesus Christ the Son.

They stand on their own false traditions and false opinions, and NOT on the whole WORD OF GOD.

How can those who deny Jesus Christ by refusing any zeal to obey him and to keep his teaching to live by every Word of God, denying the authority of God the Father and his Word: Claim that they are God's people?

> . . . but he that acknowledges [accepts the authority of, and obeys] the Son hath the Father also [because the Son obeys God the Father].

2:24 Let that, therefore, abide in you, which you have heard from the beginning. If that which you have heard from the beginning shall remain in you,

The words of Jesus Christ and the words of God the Father, their doctrine, their teachings, laws, statutes, commandments, precepts and judgments, the WHOLE Word of God: ARE the words of eternal life; and If they remain in us and if we keep them diligently, we shall receive eternal life in the Son, and in the Father.

If we are diligent to learn and to zealously keep the whole Word of God, then God through his Spirit will abide in us; and if we depart from any zeal for the Word of God to follow others, then God will not abide in us and his Spirit will leave us.

Brethren, many false leaders, elders and teachers have seduced very many brethren into a zeal for idols of men, and a laxity for keeping the whole Word of God!

2:25 And **this is the promise that he has promised us, even eternal life**. **2:26** These things have I written unto you **concerning them that seduce you. 2:27** But the anointing [the Holy Spirit] which you have received of him abides in you [if we remain faithful to live by every Word of God], and you need not let any man teach you: but as the same anointing [Holy Spirit] teaches you of all things.

That is, the anointing of God's Spirit leads us and empowers us to keep every Word of God; and if we follow it, it will lead us into eternal life.

If we prove all things by the Word of God, and remain steadfast in the whole Word of God to zealously follow God and not men; then we will be filled with God's Spirit and we will grow and overcome and ascend towards the Righteousness and Light of the Eternal!

If we blindly follow men without questioning or proving them, and stray from the Word of God, then the Spirit of God will be quenched and leave us; and Satan will replace God's Spirit with a kind of meaningless, without substance, emotional, feel good; false "love" that will result in our destruction! Like cotton candy it will look good, seem good and taste good, and then make us very, very sick.

The Holy Spirit will lead us into all truth if we are willing to keep the whole Word of God and continually grow in the knowledge of godly things.

2:28 And now, little children, abide in him [always remain loyal and faithful to the whole Word of God]; that when he shall appear, [speaking of Christ, when he comes], that we may have confidence, and not be ashamed before him at his coming.

If we abide in Christ (John 15), acknowledging his authority as our Head [under God the Father (1 Cor 11:3)] and keeping his Word; when he comes he will receive us with gladness and we will receive him with gladness and joy, because we are abiding in him and keeping his Word, and he is abiding in us!

Yet, if we turn from him thinking that he will overlook our sin, we shall be ashamed of ourselves and ashamed of our behavior when we see him, because he will be looking at us and saying, "You sinners, depart from me you workers of iniquity (Mat 7:23)." And then we will be filled with shame at our downfall and our disgrace.

2:29 If you know that he [God] is righteous, you know that every one that does righteousness [lives by God's Word] is born of him [is of God].

God is righteous and all who are righteous are of God. The word "righteous" is just a big word for "godly" and true righteousness is the zealous keeping of the whole Word of God.

If we do what we think is right, we are being self-righteous and if we humbly do what God says is right, then we are partakers of God's righteousness.

We are to become righteous like God is righteous, by partaking of his righteousness through living by every Word of God.

If we become like him we shall be born of him on the day that the first fruits are chosen and changed to spirit.

Today we have NOT yet been chosen, only called to God. To be among the chosen we MUST overcome sin [overcome living contrary to any part of God's Word], and we must internalize the whole nature of God by passionately keeping the whole Word of God through God the Father and Jesus Christ dwelling in us by God's Holy Spirit!

1 John 3

When we sincerely repent and stop sinning, the application of the sacrifice of Christ reconciles us to God the Father; and being espoused to Jesus Christ the Son, we can receive the gift of the Holy Spirit and are then adopted as sons of the Father.

> **Romans 8:14** For as many as are led by the Spirit of God [and follow that Spirit to keep the whole Word of God], they are the sons of God. **8:15** For ye have not received the spirit of bondage again [into sin] to fear [eternal death]; but ye have received the Spirit of adoption, whereby we cry, Abba, Father. **8:16** The Spirit itself beareth witness with our spirit, [this showing that there is a spirit in man as well as a Spirit of God] that we are the children of God:

1 John 3:1 Behold, what manner of love the Father hath bestowed upon us [the faithful zealous keepers of the Word of God]**, that we should be called the sons of God: therefore, the world knows us not, because it did not know him.**

We become the sons of God through sincere repentance and the application of the sacrificial death and resurrection of the Son of God, Jesus Christ.

In the resurrection to spirit of the faithful and chosen, we will be given spirit bodies like the spirit body that Christ had before he became flesh, and then received back again after his resurrection from the dead.

3:2 Beloved, now are we the sons of God, and it doth not yet appear what we shall be: but we know that, when he shall appear, we shall be like him; for we shall see him as he is [in his spirit body].

IF we have sincerely repented, turned from our sins, had our sins atoned for through the sacrifice of Christ, and if we commit to STOP sinning in a baptismal commitment: We may then enter into the throne room and into the presence of God the Father. We can then call him our Father and he will call us his sons.

However we have not yet been chosen to be a part of the bride and born again as spirit. It is when we are changed to spirit that we will become born fully of the spirit; and at that time we will be fully born again.

3:3 Every man that hath this hope in him purifies himself [makes and keeps himself pure from all sin], even as God is pure [without sin]. **3:4** Whosoever commits sin, transgresses also the law: for **sin is the transgression of the law.**

Sin is the breaking of any part of the Word and Will of God; and we must purify ourselves from ALL sin, repenting and turning towards obedience to every Word of God the Father just as Jesus Christ passionately obeyed God the Father setting an example that we should follow.

> **John 2:15** And when he had made a scourge of small cords, he drove them all out of the temple, and the sheep, and the oxen; and poured out the changers' money, and overthrew the tables; **2:16** And said unto them that sold doves, Take these things hence; make not my Father's house an house of merchandise.
>
> **2:17 And his disciples remembered that it was written, The zeal of thine house hath eaten me up.**

Just as Christ cleansed the physical temple, he will cleanse God's spiritual Temple and will drive every willful sinner out of God's spiritual Temple.

Brethren, Christ drove these folks OUT of the physical temple as an example and instruction for US; that we should purify ourselves from all sin, or he will DRIVE US OUT of God's spiritual Temple.

1 John 3:5 And ye know that he was manifested to take away our sins; and in him is no sin.

That is, Jesus Christ lived by every Word of God the Father WITHOUT compromise.

3:6 Whosoever abides in him sinneth not: whosoever sins; hath not seen him, neither known him.

If we abide in Jesus Christ we will keep the Word of God just like Jesus Christ did. We will not sin by willfully transgressing any part of the Word of God. We will keep the whole Word and Will of God the Father like Jesus Christ did and commanded us to do.

3:7 Little children, let no man deceive you [away from our Christ-like zeal to keep the whole Word and Will of God the Father]: he that does righteousness [obeys God] is righteous, even as God is righteous. **3:8 He that commits sin is of the devil, he that transgresses God's commandments is of the devil. For the devil sins** [rebelled against obeying God] **from the beginning. For this purpose the Son of God was made known that he might destroy the works of the devil.**

Jesus Christ works to destroy the works of the devil, which are rebellion against keeping the whole Word and Will of God the Father, to do as we decide for ourselves.

We are to judge whether we will follow anyone, judging them according to their works, their deeds (Mat 7). Did Jesus Christ tell us this for nothing, or did he say this because that is exactly how God the Father will judge each of us on our day? (Revelation 20:12)

Anyone who is conceived of God by receiving the Spirit of God, does not knowingly commit any sin. Anyone who is born of God, by being changed to spirit at the resurrection has fully internalized the very nature of God in this physical life and cannot sin willfully because willful sin has become contrary to his own very nature.

3:9 Whosoever is born of God [in the resurrection] **does not commit sin; for his** [God's seed of the Holy Spirit] **seed remains in him: and he cannot sin** [knowingly and willfully], **because he is born of God.**

That is, the Holy Spirit of God, the seed of God will remain in the person who is faithful to God and is of God.

Those who are conceived of God by the Holy Spirit [which will lead us into all truth] will be empowered to live by every Word and the Will of God the Father.

If such a person remains in God the Father and in Christ, he will be empowered to overcome sin like Christ overcame sin and he WILL be among the CHOSEN. Then when we are born of God in the resurrection of the bride; we will not sin because we have become like God who does not sin.

The godly are identified by their zeal to live by every Word and the Will of God; the ungodly are identified by their LACK of zeal to keep the whole Word and Will of God

3:10 In this the children of God are known, and the children of the devil: whosoever does not righteousness [does not live by every Word of God] **is not of God,** neither he that loveth not his brother.

Those who do not love God enough to keep his Word and Will, which is and which defines true godly love, or does not love others enough to warn them to STOP sinning; are not of God.

God and the zealous keeping of God's Word always comes FIRST, and is quickly followed by God's commandment to love other humans! Those who exalt love for man above love for God make a major mistake of wrong priorities. We cannot love God and not love others; but we can love others and not love and obey God!

If we hate our brother, if we hate other human beings, if we look down on other people, we are not of God. If we do not actively love our brother and our neighbor; we are NOT OF GOD!

Yet if we do not love and live by every Word of God as our FIRST priority we are also not of God!

This goes beyond personal relationships; if we look down on a whole race of people because they are somewhat different than us, we are sinning.

> **Matthew 22:37** Jesus said unto him, Thou shalt love the Lord thy God with all thy heart, and with all thy soul, and with all thy mind. **22:38** This is the first and great commandment.
>
> **22:39** And the second is like unto it, Thou shalt love thy neighbour as thyself. **22:40** On these two commandments hang all the law and the prophets

1 John 3:11 For this is the message that ye heard from the beginning, that we should love one another.

3:12 Not as Cain, who was of that wicked one, and slew his brother. And wherefore slew he him? Because his own works were evil, and his brother's righteous.

3:13 Marvel not, my brethren, if the world hate you.

3:14 We know that we have passed from death unto life, because we love the brethren. He that loveth not his brother abideth in death.

The obvious question that comes up here is, who is your brother? And Jesus Christ handled the same question when he was asked, "Who is my neighbor?" And he told the Parable of the Good Samaritan (Luke 10:29).

Every human being is our brother because we are all the children of Adam. We are all the creation of Jesus Christ and God the Father.

If we hate or despise any human being anywhere, we are not the spiritual children of God, this is a serious problem that many need to repent of and quickly correct themselves on.

If we are a child of a father and we hate our brother, do we not then hurt our father? What father would like to see one of his children kill another or harm another or abuse another of his children? No father likes to see that happen and God is no different.

God the Father does not like to see us hurting one another, abusing one another, and hating and killing one another. God is no different than other fathers and is not willing that any should perish. The whole Word of God defines the way that we should behave to be at peace and in harmony with God and with one another.

The law protects people. It gives them certain rights. It gives you the right to life and protection against being murdered. It gives people the right to property and protection against having it stolen and so on.

If we have a dispute over such things we are to handle it according to God's Word! Or we are to leave it in God's capable hands if we cannot settle the matter among ourselves. Each person giving way before the other, and acting in the best interests of his neighbor and not selfishly.

God's law is holy, and just, and good,

> **Romans 7:12** Wherefore **the law is holy, and the commandment holy, and just, and good.**

Those who hurt God's children [who wrongfully hurt anyone] are eventually going to be disciplined. They are going to be corrected; and if they will not change, they will be removed. The law of God defines LOVE: for:

> **Romans 13:10** Love worketh no ill to his neighbour: therefore love is the fulfilling of the law.

All those who are willing to embrace God's Word and Will to keep it faithfully, are filled with the true love of God: they will have a part at some point in entering the family of God.

Those who are adamantly insistent on doing things their own way do not have the love of God in them [no matter what they claim]: and they will have to be removed for the good of the whole family.

1 John 3:15 Whosoever hates his brother is a murderer: and you know that no murderer hath eternal life abiding in him. **3:16** Hereby perceive we the love of God, because he laid down his life for us: and **we ought to lay down our lives for the brethren.**

This means more than being willing to die for others it means living for the good of others and doing good for others.

3:17 But whoso hath this world's good[s], and sees his brother have need [or being in need], and shuts up his bowels of compassion from his brother, how dwells the love of God in him?

If we see another person hurting, or in pain, or in need and we do not have compassion and we do not try and help them; where is the love of God in us? Remember faith without works is dead. If we love God and we are filled with love from God, we would be helping our brethren; especially by telling them the truth and warning them to STOP sinning.

Why is true godliness so hard to understand for those claiming to be God's people?

3:18 My little children **let us not love in word, or in tongue; but in deed and in truth. 3:19** And hereby we know that we are of the truth, and shall assure our hearts before him. **3:20** For if our heart [if our own conscious] condemn us, [remember that] God is greater than our heart, and knows all things [knows our every sinful thought and deed]. **3:21** Beloved, if our heart [if we are faithful and zealous for God through God's Spirit in us] condemn us not, then have we confidence [if we faithfully obey God through the power of God's Spirit in us, we are acceptable to God] toward God.

If we are zealously keeping the whole Word and Will of God, we can be confident that God will accept us and therefore we can have a clean conscious before God.

3:22 and whatsoever we ask, we receive of him, because we keep his commandments.

That is one of the primary reasons why prayers are not answered; because we do not faithfully and zealously keep the whole Word and Will of God!

There is no way that we can go to a restaurant on a Sabbath or a Holy Day and pay people to serve us and cook for us for our own pleasure or commit any other willful sin; and have God answer our prayers.

There is no way, that if we work a bit late into the Sabbath or we decide to spend the Sabbath watching TV instead of spending time with God or if we neglect the things of God; that God will listen to us.

If we deceive ourselves by thinking, "Oh that's just a little thing. It is not important." Or by taking the attitude that, "Well, I am only flesh, I am weak and it doesn't matter:" Then God will NOT hear us.

If we have those kinds of evil attitudes or if we say we must believe in the Bible as interpreted by, or as explained by some man, if we have the attitude of allowing someone to come between us and God's Word; we commit idolatry of men and spiritual adultery and there is no way, brethren, that our prayers will be answered positively by God.

God answers those who live by every Word of God, not just some of those words but ALL of them. If we want positive answers to our prayers, and if we want healing or anything, we must be zealous to keep the whole Word and Will of God.

Right now, the world is full of religions calling themselves godly, who are full of idolatry.

They are full of Sabbath breaking. They are full of all manner of sins and then they wonder why their prayers are not answered and why they have many problems.

Their prayers are not answered because they do not take pleasure in the things of God: They do not hold God's Word to be precious and holy and right and good. They are doing their own thing in their own way, and every day they are getting a little bit further from God. Therefore, God is not listening to them and he will not answer their prayers.

What we need today is a revival and a wholehearted turning to the Eternal.

We need to wake up and realize how far away from God we have gotten, and we need to start turning back toward our Father in heaven, back toward God. We need to sincerely repent and embrace God to keep his Word and Will, and we need to seek God with all our hearts and all our strength, and we need to get right with our God.

3:23 And this is his commandment that we should believe [Remember that belief without the works of obedience is vain.] on the name of his Son Jesus Christ, and love one another.

We should believe, and act on that belief. We should love God enough to be zealous to keep his Word with Christ-like zeal; which IS godly love.

If we loved God then we would obey his Word and wholeheartedly work to please him.

If we keep God's Word, the Spirit of God the Father and of Jesus Christ will dwell in us: And if God's Spirit dwells in us, then we are dwelling in God. We become a branch which has been grafted into the trunk of the tree of Jesus Christ.

Jesus Christ is the trunk of the tree (John 15:1-8), and if we are grafted into the trunk of that tree, into Christ; Jesus Christ will be dwelling in us and we will be living by every Word of God the Father even as Jesus Christ lived by every Word of God the Father.

How do we know that we are godly?

Because the person who dwells in God will be zealous to live by every Word of God and by the entire Will of God!

Those persons who are not zealous to keep the whole Word and Will of God and instead follow idols of men are NOT of God, they are in a state of idolatry and sin against God!

3:24 And **he that keepeth his commandments,** [any person who keeps all of God's Word, for the commandment tells us to obey our fathers] **dwelleth in God, and God in him.** [God will dwell in that person.] **And hereby, we know that God abides in us, by the Spirit which God has given us.**

1 John 4

1 John 4:1 Beloved, **believe not every spirit, but test the spirits whether they are of God: because many false prophets have gone out into the world. 4:2 Hereby know ye the Spirit of God: Every spirit that confesses that Jesus Christ is come** [Christ will dwell in us through God's Spirit and he will do the same thing in us that he has always done; he will keep the whole Word of God and do the whole Will of God in us.] **in the flesh is of God.**

How do we know if a spirit is the Holy Spirit of Almighty God?

Every prophet and every person, who confesses that Jesus Christ is literally dwelling in us through the Holy Spirit, and is keeping the whole Word and Will of God the Father with Christ-like zeal within us; has the true Spirit of God!

Jesus Christ dwelling in us will still be keeping the whole Word and Will of God the Father like he has always done; anyone who confesses that the Spirit of God and the Spirit of Jesus Christ is dwelling literally in our flesh, empowering us to zealously live by EVERY WORD of GOD: is of God!

4:3 And every spirit that confesses not that Jesus Christ is come in the flesh, [Any man or spirit that does not teach that Jesus Christ is keeping every Word of God the Father while literally dwelling in us, anyone who says we do not need to keep every single aspect of the whole Word and Will of God in Christ-like zeal without any compromise and without any hint of turning aside: is an Antichrist.] **IS NOT OF GOD,** and this is that spirit of antichrist, whereof ye have heard that it should come; and even now already is it in the world. . . .

Any person or any spirit that comes along and says, "You cannot keep all of God's Word. The flesh is too weak; is telling a half truth: That person is an Antichrist he is against Jesus Christ and against God. He is not of God! This is the spirit of rebellion against God, the spirit of Satan!

No, we cannot please God by our own efforts: Yes we can please God through the power of the Holy Spirit dwelling in us, if we are zealous to live by every Word of God.

Of course the flesh is weak and cannot overcome on its own; which is why God gave us the Spirit of God to dwell in us to strengthen us to overcome like Christ overcame.

It is by the Spirit of Jesus Christ dwelling in us that we are empowered to learn and to live by every Word of God, and God's Spirit will lead us into a passionate love and zeal to learn and to live by every Word of God!

Does that mean we will never slip?

No, It means that we have begun a learning process and that we will never again sin intentionally, and that as soon as we find any error we will correct ourselves to come that much closer to God; and if we do make an unintentional mistake, we will quickly repent as soon as we find out about it.

We are to be like David who committed sin with Bathsheba and his eyes were blinded by his lust; yet later when the prophet Nathan came to him and when his eyes were open and he saw himself as God saw him: **He quickly repented**.

There are some who excuse their sin by pointing out that David sinned. Brethren, this ridiculous excuse is a self-serving self-justifying stench of filth in the nostrils of Almighty God; David sincerely repented of his sins! We are never to make excuses for our sins [David never did], and we are also to STOP sinning like David STOPPED sinning!

We need to quickly repent as soon as we see our error like David did.

Every person, or prophet, or spirit; that does NOT confess that Jesus Christ is living by every Word of God while dwelling in our flesh by the Spirit of

God; and claims that Christ is not keeping God's Word in us as he has always kept the Word of God the Father, such a person or spirit is an Antichrist.

. . . Whereof you have heard that antichrist should come; and even now already is in the world. **4:4** Ye are of God, little children, and have overcome antichrist [We do not overcome sin by our own strength; we overcome by the power of the Holy Spirit of obedience to God the Father and Jesus Christ dwelling in us.] because greater is he that is in you. [God the Father and Jesus Christ dwelling in us through the Holy Spirit are greater than the spirit of rebellion against God which is Antichrist.] than he that is in the world, [which is the spirit of Satan the Adversary and arch rebel against God.]

Those who compromise with God's Word are worldly and NOT of God.

4:5 They are of the world, [this Satanic society, spiritual Egypt and Babylon] therefore, speak they, the things of the world, and the world hears them. **4:6** We are of God [if we do God's will and keep his Word]: he that knows God [those who are of God] hears us [they hear the scriptures and accept the truth of the whole Word of God]; **he that is not of God** does not hear us [does not hear and live by every Word of God]

The wicked do not accept the scriptures, choosing to follow their own false ways; despising truth and running after falsehoods.

This is how to discern between the wicked and the godly:

The godly will diligently reject all error and accept the truth of the whole Word and Will of God; the wicked will reject truth for their own false traditions!

. . . . Hereby know we the spirit of truth, and the spirit of error.

We should love GOD first and then love others, just as Christ gave himself for God the Father and for all humanity. Love is defined by the whole Word of God; which Word defines how we are to behave towards God and towards humanity.

4:7 Beloved, let us love one another: for love is of God; and every one that loves is born of God, and knows God. **4:8** He that loves not knows not God; for God is love. **4:9** In this was manifested, the love of God toward us, because that God sent his only begotten Son into the world [to die for us] that we might live through him.

If we do not keep the whole Word and Will of God, we do NOT love God; and if we say that we love God and we do not do what God says, we are paying lip service and not loving with deeds: therefore our love is only a verbal pretense.

4:10 Herein is love, not that we loved God, but that he loved us, and sent his Son to be the propitiation for our sins.

God the Father gave up his only begotten Son to die for us, and Jesus Christ set us an example in giving up his Godhood to be made flesh and then dying for us in obedience to God the Father.

4:11 Beloved, if God so loved us, we are also to love one another.

> **Luke 6:46** And **why call ye me, Lord, Lord, and do not the things which I say?**
>
> **6:47 Whosoever cometh to me, and heareth my sayings, and doeth them,** I will shew you to whom he is like: **6:48** He is like a man which built an house, and digged deep, and laid the foundation on a rock: and when the flood arose, the stream beat vehemently upon that house, and could not shake it: for it was founded upon a rock.
>
> **6:49** But **he that heareth, and doeth not**, is like a man that without a foundation built an house upon the earth; against which the stream did beat vehemently, and immediately it fell; and the ruin of that house was great.

1 John 4:12 No man hath seen God at any time [God the Father]. If we love one another [according to God's definition of love], God dwells in us, and his love is perfected in us.

God's Spirit is given to those who obey him (Acts 5:32).

If we turn from our sin, sincerely repent, and commit to sin no more, the sacrifice of Jesus Christ can be applied to us and then we can have access to God the Father and he will give us his Spirit to dwell within us.

4:13 Hereby know we that we dwell in him, and he in us, because he hath given us of his Spirit.

God's Spirit empowers us to overcome sin and to internalize the very nature of God through the keeping of the Will and the whole Word of God.

4:14 And we have seen and do testify that the Father sent the Son to be the Saviour of the world.

4:15 Whosoever shall confess that Jesus is the Son of God, God dwelleth in him, and he in God. **4:16** And we have known and believed the love that God hath to us. **God is love** [therefore God's Word and Will are the definition of godly love]; **and he that** [all who live by every Word of God are filled with God's love] **dwelleth in love dwells in God, and God in him.**

4:17 Herein is our love made perfect, . . .

Godly love is made perfect in us through our zealous keeping of the Will of God and through living by EVERY WORD of GOD. In doing this we internalize in ourselves the very nature of God which is love, and if we diligently live by every Word of God we may approach God the Father with boldness and not with the knowledge of guilt for trespassing the Word of God.

. . . . that **we may have boldness in the day of judgment: because as he is, so are we** in this world.

We become like God only by doing what God does and what God tells us to do.

We are to follow the example of Jesus Christ, obeying God the Father and internalizing the nature of God through the zealous keeping of the whole Word and Will of God.

4:18 There is no fear [of God] in love [which is faithful obedience to God]; but perfect love [which is the keeping of the whole Word and Will of God, which casts out all fear of being condemned by God's judgment] cast out fear: because fear has torment. He that fears is not made perfect in love.

We love God by keeping his Word; and we love our fellowman by keeping God's Word.

If we faithfully keep God's Word, we need have no fear of God's righteous wrath against those who practice wickedness by living contrary to the Word of God.

It is when we are living contrary to God's Word that we should fear being judged, fear being condemned by God, because we are guilty.

God is a God of LOVE; God loves all of his children. He is loath to discipline his children and only does so to turn them away from hurting his other children, or as a last resort to save them when they go astray.

Many fear the coming Great Tribulation and speak of a rapture, or place of safety; to avoid this correction.

The tribulation is nothing compared to eternity! The tribulation is a merciful correction and humbling of the wicked to bring them to accept the whole Word and Will of God the Father. The purpose of the tribulation is to afflict the flesh to save the spirit unto eternal life! The way to eternal life and to avoid correction from God, is to correct ourselves and to be diligent for God's ways.

The only way to avoid God's correction is to sincerely repent and begin to accept the truth, correcting ourselves so that God does not need to correct us. This is the way to spiritual safety and eternal life.

4:19 We love him because he first loved us. 4:20 If a man say, I love God, and hateth his brother [or any other person], he is a liar: for he that loveth not his brother whom he hath seen, how can he love God whom he hath not seen? 4:21 And this commandment have we from God, that he who loveth God should love his brother also.

1 John 5

1 John 5:1 Whosoever believeth that Jesus is the Christ is born [He who believes that Jesus was resurrected to spirit by God and who also obeys God, having the same works of faith that Jesus has; if he perseveres he will be changed to spirit and will be fully born of God to spirit just as Jesus Christ is now spirit again.] of God: and every one that loveth him that begat [God the Father] loveth him also [also loves the Son] that is begotten of him.

If we love God the Father, we will also love the Son; and if we love the Son, we will love the Father. If we love the Son, we love the Father; and if we love the Father, we will love the Son.

The love of God is defined as, every Word of God.

5:2 By this we know that we love the children of God, when we love God, and **keep his commandments. For this is the love of God.**

LOVE IS: the zealous keeping of the whole Word and Will of God!

Anyone who disparages zeal for keeping the whole Word of God is disparaging God the Father and the Son; because the Word of God is the very nature of God the Father and Jesus Christ in print!

It is only by being zealous to learn and to live by every Word of God that we can internalize the very nature of God to become like God! Being like God means to believe and to live as God lives! To live by every Word of God!

Satan has infiltrated the people of God to destroy our zeal to become like God and to lead us to follow idols of men in spiritual adultery against our espoused Husband Jesus Christ; just as he inspired Balaam to entice physical Israel into adultery and idolatry!

Today we are taught to compromise with worldliness; and we are not taught how to overcome worldliness!

These wicked men lead us away from God the Father and Jesus Christ to follow false traditions and idols of men away from zealous godliness!

Godly love is to keep the whole Word and Will of Almighty God! Godly love is to keep the commandments, laws, statutes, judgments, will and precepts of God the only Holy Father!

In the New Covenant the laws of the Mosaic Covenant are NOT done away; exactly the opposite; they are written on our hearts forever by God's Holy Spirit!

Beware the false teaching that the New Covenant replaces the law with a false emotional ersatz "love;" when godly love IS the keeping of the whole Word of God and Jesus himself taught us to live by every Word of God the Father (Mat 4:4).

> **Jeremiah 31:31** Behold, the days come, saith the Lord, that I will make a new covenant with the house of Israel, and with the house of Judah:
>
> **31:32** Not according to the covenant that I made with their fathers in the day that I took them by the hand to bring them out of the land of Egypt; which my covenant they brake, although I was an husband unto them, saith the Lord:
>
> **31:33 But this shall be the covenant that I will make with the house of Israel; After those days, saith the Lord, I will put my law in their inward parts, and write it in their hearts; and will be their God, and they shall be my people.**
>
> **31:34** And they shall teach no more every man his neighbour, and every man his brother, saying, Know the Lord: for **they shall all know me, from the least of them unto the greatest of them, saith**

the Lord: for I will forgive their iniquity, and I will remember their sin no more.

1 John 5:3 **This is the love of God, that we keep his commandments: and his commandments are not grievous;** [Keeping the whole Word and Will of God is not difficult, it is Satan's attacks that make it seem burdensome.] **5:4 For whatsoever is born of God overcometh the world:** [The godly, will overcome sin and worldliness by their faith and their works of faith through the power of God dwelling in them!] **and this is the victory that overcometh the world, even our faith. 5:5 Who is he that overcometh the world, but he that believeth that Jesus is the Son of God?**

It is our faith that God the Father and Jesus Christ dwell in us through the agency of the Holy Spirit leading and empowering us; which enables us to overcome sin and live a Christ-like life.

5:6 This is he that came [dwells in us] by water [baptism] and [the sacrificial blood of Christ] blood, even Jesus Christ; not by water only, but by water and blood.

We are to be baptized in water and into the Holy Spirit just like Jesus Christ was.

And it is the Spirit [the presence of the gift of God's Spirit dwelling in us is proof of God's salvation for those who live by every Word of God] that bears witness, because the Spirit is truth. **5:7** For there are three that bear record in heaven, the Father, the Word, and the Holy Spirit: and these three are one [united in their witness].

The Word of God Father and the sacrifice and resurrection of the Son and the presence of their Holy Spirit (nature) dwelling in us, all bear the same witness that salvation is through sincere repentance, a baptismal commitment to STOP sinning, the application of the sacrificial blood of Christ and the gift of God's Spirit in us: if we STOP sinning.

This statement does NOT say that the Holy Spirit is a person and has nothing to do with any trinity.

The "three are one" does not refer to three individuals being one person at all; it refers to the witness of the presence of God's Spirit in us, along with the witness of the Word of God the Father and the truth of the sacrifice and resurrection of Jesus Christ; being united together in witnessing the same way to salvation.

This verse has nothing to do with any trinity and does NOT say that the Holy Spirit is a person at all; it speaks of God's Spirit being a witness of God within his people.

5:8 And these three that bear witness in earth, the Spirit [the presence of God's nature dwelling in us], and the water, [our baptismal commitment to live by every Word of God], and the blood, [the atoning sacrifice of Christ]: and these three agree.

If we hear and believe human witnesses, the witness of God's Holy Spirit in us is a greater witness for it is the witness of God dwelling in us.

5:9 If we receive the witness of men, the witness of God is greater: for this is the witness of God which he hath testified of his Son. **5:10** He that believeth [and responds with the works of faith; which are sincere repentance and the zealous keeping of the whole Word and Will of God] on the Son of God hath the witness in himself [receives the Holy Spirit] and he that believeth not God hath made him a liar; because he believes not the record that God gave of his Son. **5:11** And this is the record; that God hath given to us eternal life, and this life is in his Son.

The fact that the Son of God, Jesus Christ, was resurrected and given eternal life; is a witness or an example, showing us that if the Son dwells in us through the Holy Spirit, and we wholeheartedly strive to live as he lived; we can also receive the same eternal life.

5:12 He that hath the Son [if the Son dwells in us by the Holy Spirit] hath life; and he that hath not the Son of God hath not life.

If Jesus Christ is not dwelling in us through God's Spirit, and if Christ is not keeping God's Word in us through God's Spirit, we do not have eternal life.

If Jesus Christ is dwelling in us through the power and the vehicle of God's Spirit, and he is keeping every Word of God in us and through us; then we have eternal life dwelling in us because we will be keeping the whole Word and Will of God just like Jesus Christ did and does!

5:13 These things have I written unto you that believe [this is for all those who are called out and are sincerely repentant having the Spirit of God] on the name of the Son of God; that ye may [believe and know that you have eternal life dwelling in you] believe on the name of the Son of God. **5:14** And this is the confidence that we have in him, [God] that if we ask any thing **according to his will**, he heareth us.

If we are zealous to learn and to keep the whole Word of God, we can KNOW that God hears us! and if we ask ACCORDING TO GOD'S WILL we may receive it because we keep the whole Word of God and do God's Will.

If we compromise and reject any zeal to learn and keep the whole Word of God, doing our own ways and keeping the words of our idols of men instead; God will not hear us!

The key to positively answered prayer is to zealously keep the whole Word and Will of God, and to ask according to the will of God: understanding that like a child everything that we want is not always good for us.

Think of yourself as a child asking something of its parent; the good parent will note the request of the child but will do what is right and good for the child. God is the very best of father's and will do the same thing; doing what in his greater wisdom is good for us in the long term.

The things to ask for are godly wisdom and a good understanding of the Word and Will of God; and a good understanding of what God is trying to teach us by our circumstances

5:15 And if we know that he hear us, whatsoever we ask, we know that we have the petitions that we desired of him. **5:16** If any man see his brother sin a sin which is not unto death, he [if we pray on behalf of a sin being sincerely repented of (James 5:14), the supplicant] shall ask, and he [God will forgive the sincerely repentant sinner] shall give him life for them that sinneth not unto death. There is a sin which is unto death [the sin that brings eternal death is the willful sin of refusing to repent] : I do not say that you should pray for that. **5:17** All unrighteousness is sin: and there is a sin not unto death

The sin which is not unto death is the sin that is sincerely repented of.

If we sin and when we realize it, we acknowledge it and we repent of it, and we STOP doing that sin and turn away from it, that sin is forgiven and it is not unto death.

There is another sin which brings death

That is the situation whereby we sin and when we realize it, we say that we are justified in doing that sin, we are not going to repent, and we are not going to stop doing it: then we cannot be forgiven, simply because we have not turned away from it in sincere repentance.

Later if we do finally repent we can be forgiven, however if we never repent and continually refuse to stop the sin, that continual willful self-justified sin will bring eternal death.

Atonement and Justification are applied to the SINCERELY REPENTANT, who commit to stop the sin and to go and sin no more.

We can only be forgiven if we acknowledge our sin and we repent of it and we become sorry enough to turn away from it, and to stop doing it.

The sins that are not unto death are those sins that are unintentional and when discovered are sincerely repented of with a solid commitment to "go and sin no more!"

The sins that bring eternal death are those willful sins that we justify in ourselves and refuse to sincerely repent of.

The person that has sincerely repented and been begotten of God through the gift of the Holy Spirit, keeps himself pure from sin and does not commit willful sin, although he may sin inadvertently.

Those who are born of God in the resurrection to spirit cannot sin, for they are given the full nature of God and power over all evil.

5:18 We know that whosoever is born of God sinneth not; but he that is begotten of God keepeth himself, and that wicked one toucheth him not.

The sin that is not unto death is the sin that has been sincerely repented of: The sin unto death is the willful sin that is self-justified and NOT repented of.

A key to overcoming temptation is to understand the value and cherish the birthright of our calling, and to understand how destructive and loathsome sin is; and to instantly thrust aside any thought of sin. If we dwell on temptation, it will grow in us until it bears the fruit of sin.

If we follow God's Spirit and learn to abhor sin for the terrible suffering, decay and death that sin brings; we will not be tempted to do what we have learned to abhor.

5:19 And we know that we are of God, and the whole world lieth in wickedness. **5:20** And we know that the Son of God is come [to dwell in us by the Holy Spirit], and hath given us an understanding [the Holy Spirit is the Spirit of understanding and truth], that we may know him that is true [God the Father and the Son are truth, therefore their whole Word is truth], and we are in him that is true, even in his Son Jesus Christ [God the Father and the Son are truth]. This is the true God, and eternal life.

5:21 Little children, keep yourselves from idols. Amen.

Yes, we are to keep ourselves from idolatry.

What is an idol? An idol is anything that comes between us and God!

Can your church be an idol? Yes, it can.

Can our friends be idols? Yes, they can, if we value them more than we value God and God's Word. If we allow them to lead us astray, if we go along with what they are doing, even when we know it is wrong, we have valued them more than we have valued God and God's Word.

Can your minister be an idol? Yes.

Can some man be an idol? Yes! If we say, "We must understand the Scriptures as interpreted by this or that person," then that person has become our idol and we have become an idolater because we have preferred and loved someone else more than we have loved our God.

We must always put God first. Jesus Christ dwelling in us will be living by every Word of God the Father; if we refuse to live by every Word of God the Father then Jesus Christ will NOT dwell in us!

If we reject any part of zealously keeping the whole Word and Will of God; we quench God's Spirit and Jesus Christ will not long dwell within us. By compromising with God's Word we are cutting ourselves off from the trunk of the tree, Jesus Christ; cutting our branch off from the trunk and the roots of true godliness!

Remember the commandment against Idolatry and spiritual Adultery.

> **Exodus 20:5** Thou shalt not bow down thyself to them, nor serve them: for I the LORD thy God am a jealous God, visiting the iniquity of the fathers upon the children unto the third and fourth generation of them that hate me;

Second John

2 John 1

John identifies himself as an elder which simply means a person who is older in the faith, someone long experienced in the faith; who is able to help others because of his experience and the wisdom that he has learned and been taught by God. The Ekklesia [the called out brethren] collectively are being presented as the Elect Lady, a term for the assembly of the called out to God, espoused as a collective bride to Christ.

The term Elect Lady is only one of the MANY different correct names for the true people of God.

2 John 1:1 The elder [John] unto the elect lady [the spiritual Ekklesia] and her children [the individual members of the body, the Ekklesia of Christ], whom I love in the truth; and not I only, but also all they that have known the truth;

All those who have been called to God the Father through Jesus Christ and who sincerely repent, committing themselves to "go and sin no more;" are a part of the body of Christ regardless of any organizational affiliation.

There IS NO SUCH THING as a corporate "true church" of God!

All who love and zealously live by every Word of God are full of godly love; for God's Word defines godly love and teaches us how to love as God loves.

1:2 For the truth's [God's Word is truth!] sake, which dwelleth in us [if we follow the Holy Spirit to keep God's Word with Christ-like zeal], and shall be with us for ever; **1:3** grace be unto you. mercy, and peace, from God the Father, and from the Lord Jesus Christ, the Son of the Father, in truth and love.

God is love and truth therefore God's Word is love and truth.

John 17:17 Sanctify them through thy truth: thy word is truth

2 John 1:4 I rejoiced greatly that I found of thy children **walking in the truth, as we have received a commandment from the Father.**

If Jesus Christ came today; would he find our organizations and each of us walking in the truth and in a genuine love of zeal for the whole Word and Will of God? Most certainly NOT!

Both organizationally and individually, the vast majority of today's Ekklesia has no zeal to live by every Word of God, and instead follow idols of men and past false traditions, exalting them above the learning and the keeping of the whole Word and Will of Almighty God!

1:5 And now I beseech thee, lady [the brethren], not as though I wrote a new commandment unto you, but that which we had from the beginning, that we love one another.

The scriptural definition of godly love is to diligently learn and zealously live by every Word of God!

And this is love; that we walk after his commandments [True godly love is to live by every Word of God. Therefore the commandment to love God and to love our neighbor means that we are to live by every Word of God.] This is the commandment, That, as ye have heard from the beginning, you should walk [God's Word from the very beginning at creation and later through Moses is the same as today's New Covenant, we are to live by every Word of God, which is true godly love.] in it.

Today there are many false teachers even in the brotherhood who claim that Jesus Christ will not keep his Father's Word in us; that instead Christ will overlook our sins and tolerate them. That is the doctrine of Antichrist, denying the name [authority and power] of Jesus Christ and denying his mastery over Satan and sin.

Yes we are weak, but Jesus Christ is STRONG, he is MIGHTY to deliver his faithful; if we are only zealous to follow him and to live by every Word of God!

The whole experience of physical Israel in the wilderness was for our example, showing us that as long as we are faithful to follow and live by the Word of God he will go before us to deliver us; but if we turn away from our zeal to live by every Word of God we shall fail and fall into grave correction.

It is the spiritually lazy who fall away, not having enough love for God to make an effort to keep his Word and to do God's Will, and then making excuses to try and justify their lack of effort to keep the whole Word of God

Jesus Christ lived by every Word of God the Father, and if Christ dwells in us he will keep his Father's Word in us, and we will have the strength of Christ in us to live by every Word of God just like Jesus did and does.

Anyone who does not keep the whole Word and Will of God the Father and the instructions of Jesus Christ with passionate zeal and makes excuses to sin wilfully has gone astray and MUST REPENT quickly; lest Christ refuse to dwell in us any longer.

If anyone says "don't worry about doing that, God is love and will overlook it" they are teaching people to sin and leading them into severe judgment: They are LIARS and Antichrists!

1:6 And this is love, that we walk after his commandments. This is the commandment, That, as ye have heard from the beginning, ye should walk in it.

If Jesus Christ is dwelling in us, he will be keeping the Will of God the Father and he will be living by every Word of God the Father; in us.

If Christ is in our flesh through the Holy Spirit; we through his strength and his power will be living by every Word of God the Father: and if we sin in ignorance or inadvertently and we quickly sincerely repent as soon as the matter is known to us, and we stop doing it; it is a sin that is not unto death and we will be forgiven!

How do we know this? Because the sinless Jesus Christ said, "I have overcome the world." And since he overcame and he is dwelling in us, he will give us the power and the strength to overcome the world.

We do not learn or overcome all things instantly, which is why we need the lead of God's Spirit as it brings us into full compliance with God's Word. But if we sin willfully, thinking that God will overlook our sins, we make a mockery of the sacrifice of Christ; for he did not give his life so that we might continue in our sin, but so that we might be delivered from bondage to sin, Satan and death!

1:7 For many deceivers are entered into the world, who confess not that Jesus Christ is come [dwelling in us by the Holy Spirit] in the flesh [Such deceivers reject the scriptures that say that Christ will dwell in us and enable us to overcome sin by the Holy Spirit. Instead they teach tolerance for sin and justify a lack of zeal to overcome sin as Christ overcame sin.]. This is a deceiver and an antichrist.

Any spirit or any person that does not confess that we need to live by every Word of God, and that we can do so through the power of God dwelling in us; is a deceiver and an Antichrist.

1:8 Look to yourselves, that we lose not those things which we have wrought [Do not give up but continue to grow and overcome so that our spiritual growth is not lost through giving up the struggle to become like our Father in heaven.], but that we receive a full reward.

1:9 Whosoever transgresses [God's Word, knowingly willfully]**, and abides not in this doctrine of Christ,** [The doctrine that Jesus Christ is dwelling in us as the great overcomer and will liberate us from sin if we zealously follow him and keep the whole Word of God as he does.] **does not know God. He that abides in the doctrine of Christ** [The doctrine that the sinless Christ is living in us by the Holy Spirit, enabling us to also overcome sin.]**, he hath both the Father and the Son** [dwelling in us by the Holy Spirit].

The Spirit of God the Father and the Spirit of Jesus Christ, are dwelling in us if we have been called and we have sincerely repented; committing to "go and sin no more.

The Father and the Son will both dwell in us through the power of God's Spirit.

The Holy Spirit of God is the very nature of God. Do you think that the Spirit of God which is dwelling in us would tolerate sin or departure from God's Word? Then hear the Word of Almighty God!

> **1 Corinthians 3:17** If any man defile the temple of God [with self-justified sin], **him shall God destroy**; for the temple of God is holy, which temple ye are.

What? Is God's Spirit, which is the very nature of God, divided against God? or is Almighty God powerless to strengthen us to overcome sin and to become like God our Father in heaven?

Anyone who follows idols of men and corporate entities and is not zealous to keep the whole Word and Will of God, rejects the doctrine [teaching] that Christ dwelling in us through Gods Spirit strengthens us to overcome sin: **does not know God and is an Antichrist.**

We have become complacent towards keeping the Word of God, while becoming zealous for our groups and leaders; our idols of men!

We are organizationally proud; and have become idolaters, turning from any zeal to keep God's Word, towards doing whatever we are told by our idols of men.

Of course, God will keep his own Word, because the Word of God is the very nature of God; and if his Spirit is dwelling in us it will lead and empower us to keep the Father's Word; just as Jesus Christ kept the whole Word and Will of God the Father.

If the Spirit of Christ is in us, then it will empower us to keep the Father's Word like Christ does.

Just as the Being who was made flesh and become Jesus Christ killed Uzzah (2 Sam 6) when he thought to do God a service while breaking God's Word; so Jesus Christ will have no mercy on those who today think that they are doing God a service as they do what they want and refuse to do what God has commanded.

Have you not read what happened when David was filled with a righteous desire to bring the Ark of God up to Jerusalem, and did so improperly and contrary to the scriptures?

David did what he thought was right and good because of his zeal for the Eternal and Uzzah was trying to help. Yet God struck Uzzah down because they were not doing their good thing in the manner that God had commanded!

> **2 Samuel 6:6** And when they came to Nachon's threshingfloor, Uzzah put forth his hand to the ark of God, and took hold of it; for the oxen shook it. **6:7** And the anger of the Lord was kindled against Uzzah; and God smote him there for his error; and there he died by the ark of God.

Those people were bringing up the Ark with great rejoicing just as we rejoice at the Feasts of the LORD; and God did not accept them because they were not FULLY keeping the whole Word of God!

Those who teach compromise with God's Word and wilful sin, saying "God is love and will understand and God will overlook your sin," are Antichrists. We are commanded by God to have nothing to do with such persons.

> **1 Corinthians 5:11** But now I have written unto you not to keep company, if any man that is called a brother be a fornicator, or covetous, or an idolator, or a railer, or a drunkard, or an extortioner; with such an one no not to eat.

Brethren, many call the Sabbath holy and then walk all over the Sabbath and Holy Days polluting them.

According to John, we in today's Ekklesia have become an execration [a thing held in abomination and loathed] by Almighty God!

2 John 1:10 If there come any unto you, and bring not this doctrine [Have nothing to do with anyone who does not accept that we are to live by every Word of God and that Jesus Christ dwelling in us by the agency of the Holy Spirit strengthens us to live by every Word of God.], **receive him not into your house, neither bid him God speed: 1:11 For he that bids him God speed is a partaker of his evil deeds** [is in agreement with his sins].

Brethren, we are to have no time for anyone willing to compromise with any part of God's Word, or with those who deny the authority of the whole Word and Will of Almighty God and the need to zealously obey God, or who make a mockery of Christ's sacrifice by wilfully sinning! Yet how many elders teach this wickedness in today's Ekklesia?

1:12 Having many things to write unto you, I would not write with paper and ink: but I trust to come unto you, and speak face to face, that our joy may be full.

1:13 The children of thy elect sister greet thee. Amen.

The term "elect sister" refers to the particular sister congregation from which John is writing, and the term "her children" refers to the various individual brethren sending greetings to the addressed congregation.

Third John

3 John 1

This letter is addressed personally to Gaius who is living by the truth, which is the whole Word of God, and this Epistle is by extension for all the faithful who live by every Word of God. John first blesses all those faithful called out who live by every Word of God, This blessing of prosperity is first of all a blessing of spiritual growth and second a blessing of the physical necessities.

3 John 1:1 The elder unto the well-beloved Gaius, whom I love in the truth. **1:2** Beloved, I would above all things that thou mayest prosper and be in health, even as thy soul [pneuma spirit] prospers. **3:3** For I rejoice greatly, when the brethren came and testified of the [spiritual truth of the Word of God] truth that is in thee, even as thou walkest in the truth.

God's Word is truth and this Epistle is for all the faithful who live by every Word of God.

1:4 I have no greater joy than to hear that my children walk in the truth,

The term "my children" refers to the brethren in the faith. John's chief joy lies in knowing that others also live by every Word of God.

Gaius was faithful to God's Word and was a generous man, helping and furthering the brethren in their travels.

1:5 Beloved, thou doest faithfully whatsoever thou doest to the brethren, and to strangers; **1:6** which have borne witness of thy charity, thy generosity before the church [brethren of the Ekklesia]: whom if thou bring forward on their journey after a godly sort, thou shall do well:

It appears that Gaius allowed traveling brethren including messengers from John to rest and be refreshed in his home on their journeys.

1:7 Because that for his name's [to teach Christ and the Word of God] sake they went forth [these traveling brethren are traveling for the sake of the gospel and Gaius is setting an example for all], taking nothing of the Gentiles.

We ought to help the true laborers in the faith. Even if we have nothing to give, we can provide a bed or a place to sleep on the couch for God's servants.

1:8 We, therefore, ought to receive such [faithful workers of the Word of God], that we [that each one of us may help forward the preaching of the gospel by our prayers and hospitality] might be fellow helpers to the truth.

Even in John's time there were false elders and teachers in the Ekklesia who maligned any zeal for the truth of God; trying to deceive the brethren into following themselves and even casting the zealous for the whole Word of God out of the assemblies as is done in the Ekklesia today.

Today the assemblies are full of such false men and Jesus Christ will cast them out into a great correction of tribulation in the hope that by afflicting the flesh he might save the spirit (Rev 3:14-22).

1:9 I wrote unto the church: **but Diotrephes, who loveth to have the preeminence among them, receive us not. 1:10** Wherefore, if I come, I will remember **his deeds which he does, prating against us with malicious words: and not content therewith, neither doth he receive the brethren, and forbids them that would, and cast them out of the church.**

Sometimes certain men become known as elders, or prophets, or apostles (Rev 2:2); who are not worthy of that distinction. Diotrephes was not filled with the love of God and was self-willed, desiring pre-eminence and neglecting the Word of God; like very many elders today.

Many teachers and elders today do not teach any zeal for the whole Word and Will of God and reject all those who are zealous for God's Word, while teaching men to idolatrously follow themselves and their false traditions: From such false teachers turn away.

It is a great heartbreak that very many in today's called out Ekklesia are like Diotrephes, compromising with God's Word and rejecting those who are zealous; labeling them Pharisaic and self-righteous; and mocking and pressuring them to also compromise with the Father's Word or be cast out of their group.

1:11 Beloved, follow not that which is evil, but that which is good [Always be consistent with and zealous for God's Word and Will: For only God is good.]. He that doeth good [all those who keep the Word and Will of God] is of God: but he that doeth evil [Those who live contrary to any part of God's Word or Will and are not zealously living by every Word and the Will of God; are evil and not of God.] has not seen God.

1:12 Demetrius has a good report of all men, and of the truth itself: yea, and we also bear record; and ye know that our record is true,

John's information was that Demetrius was a godly person of good reputation, and the brethren should support him and those like him then and today. Do NOT support those who exalt themselves above all that is called god as supposed moral authorities in place of God's Word; like Diotrephes did.

1:13 I had many things to write, but I will not with ink and pen write unto thee: **1:14** But I trust I shall shortly see thee, and we shall speak face to face. Peace be to thee. Our friends salute thee. Greet the friends by name.

John encourages and exhorts those people who are godly to do good and to help the faithful on their journeys to preach the gospel and visit the brethren, because they are journeying for the sake of God in Christ.

John writes in so many words; "You have demonstrated your faith by your works and you have demonstrated your love by your actions, thus revealing that God is dwelling in you."

If we are of God and God is dwelling in us by the Holy Spirit, we will engage in godly behavior. We will love God and we will live by every Word of God; we will be living like Jesus Christ lives!

When we blindly follow corporate idols and idols of men to keep their words without proving them by the whole Word of God and we follow them instead of zealously keeping the whole Word and Will of God, we are being disloyal to God: We have become idolaters!

If such deceitful men say "we are God's servants and you must follow us" they LIE! For a man is the servant of those he obeys; and if any person does not obey God, they are NOT God's servants!

> **John 8:34** Jesus answered them, Verily, verily, I say unto you, Whosoever committeth sin is the servant of sin.

> **Romans 6:16** Know ye not, that to whom ye yield yourselves servants to obey, his servants ye are to whom ye obey; whether of sin unto death, or of obedience unto righteousness?

Brethren, obeying anyone contrary to God the Father and Jesus Christ is spiritual idolatry against God our Father and against Jesus Christ: It is allowing persons or things to come between us and our God.

How many of us will run along with our friends and compromise on any zeal for God's Word.

How many of us do things that we know are not right just because we want to keep our friends, or we want to be part of some group, or we want to enjoy social club religion, [which is what many congregations have become]; while we have no zeal to seriously study into the whole Word of God or to question what we are told, and we are afraid to keep God's Word with zeal lest we stand out?

That is wrong, brethren; We must sincerely repent of our idolatry and our lack of zeal for God and start putting the whole Word and the Will of God first: Relying on God's Word regardless of what anybody else says or does.

It is because we have gotten so far from our God and we have quenched his Spirit by not putting God and zeal for God's Word first, that our prayers are not answered and we are not being healed and there are so many divisions and so much confusion and frustration and competition in the assemblies.

We lack the love of God [lacking any zeal to learn and to live by every Word of God] and we lack the Spirit of God. We have quenched the Spirit of God because we are not proving all things and zealously keeping the whole Word and Will of God, and we are allowing idols of men and corporate idols to come between us and God.

> **Matthew 15:9** Ye hypocrites, well did Esaias prophesy of you, saying,

> **15:8 This people draweth nigh unto me with their mouth, and honoureth me with their lips; but their heart is far from me.**

15:9 But in vain they do worship me, teaching for doctrines the commandments of men.

When we call the Sabbaths of God holy and then we openly pollute God's Sabbaths and Holy Days we become an appalling abomination before Almighty God. Today we even feel justified in observing our own High Days on our own dates for our own supposed convenience, and in our own ways; as counterfeits of God's true Holy Days!

It is time that we started looking at ourselves in the mirror of God's Word and it is time we started understanding what God thinks of us.

It is very natural and worldly to want to think the best about ourselves, but it is really time that we woke up and started examining ourselves in the mirror of God's Word and we started realizing what God really thinks of us. It is time to wake up and straighten up and sincerely repent and turn to God with a whole heart; before he gets out the rod of HIS correction.

Jesus Christ has told us plainly through John that if we do not keep the whole Word and Will of God the Father like Jesus Christ did and does; if we do not follow the example of Jesus Christ and live as he lived, by every Word of God: WE ARE NOT OF GOD!

Let us turn back to God our Father with deep respect, to love him just as Christ loved him; loving God the Father enough to keep His Word; and then to go that extra mile and wholeheartedly seek to please our revered Father and to do all His Will with passionate enthusiastic zeal!.

Luke 17:9 Doth he thank that servant because he did the things that were commanded him? I trow not.

17:10 So likewise ye, when ye shall have done all those things which are commanded you, say, We are unprofitable servants: we have done that which was our duty to do.

If we keep the commandments with zeal and we are still unprofitable servants; what is the end of those who willfully compromise with and rebel against any zeal for keeping the whole Word of God?

Matthew 25:30 And cast ye the unprofitable servant into outer darkness: there shall be weeping and gnashing of teeth.

It is past time that we turned to our espoused Husband Jesus Christ, with the passion of a new bride for her bridegroom, to exalt him in our eyes and to hold him in great esteem above any other man, or organization; to give ourselves FULLY to him, as he gave his very life for us.

We are to not only keep the whole Word of God with passionate love and zeal; we are to go far beyond that and do all in our power to PLEASE and assist our Espoused Husband and our beloved Father God in the fulfillment of their will in ALL things.

When we start out on this path we may make mistakes and inadvertently or ignorantly sin, being a child growing in godliness; but if we quickly repent and diligently follow God's Spirit, wholeheartedly desiring to do the will of God; then we will be led into more and more truth and we will grow in maturity in the keeping of the Word and the doing of the will of God.

However, when we begin to compromise with God's Word and to justify spiritual laxity; we are burying our talent and quenching the Holy Spirit.

The Parable of the Talents

> **Matthew 25:14** For the kingdom of heaven is as a man travelling into a far country, who called his own servants, and delivered unto them his goods. **25:15** And unto one he gave five talents, to another two, and to another one; to every man according to his several ability; and straightway took his journey.
>
> **25:16** Then he that had received the five talents went and traded with the same, and made them other five talents. **25:17** And likewise he that had received two, he also gained other two. **25:18** But he that had received one went and digged in the earth, and hid his lord's money.
>
> **25:19** After a long time the lord of those servants cometh, and reckoneth with them.
>
> **25:20** And so he that had received five talents came and brought other five talents, saying, Lord, thou deliveredst unto me five talents: behold, I have gained beside them five talents more. **25:21** His lord said unto him, Well done, thou good and faithful servant: thou hast been faithful over a few things, I will make thee ruler over many things: enter thou into the joy of thy lord.
>
> **25:22** He also that had received two talents came and said, Lord, thou deliveredst unto me two talents: behold, I have gained two other talents beside them. 23 His lord said unto him, Well done, good and faithful servant; thou hast been faithful over a few things, I

will make thee ruler over many things: enter thou into the joy of thy lord.

25:24 Then he which had received the one talent came and said, Lord, I knew thee that thou art an hard man, reaping where thou hast not sown, and gathering where thou hast not strawed: **25:25** And I was afraid, and went and hid thy talent in the earth: lo, there thou hast that is thine.

25:26 His lord answered and said unto him, Thou wicked and slothful servant, thou knewest that I reap where I sowed not, and gather where I have not strawed: **25:27** Thou oughtest therefore to have put my money to the exchangers, and then at my coming I should have received mine own with usury.

25:28 Take therefore the talent from him, and give it unto him which hath ten talents.

25:29 For unto every one that hath shall be given, and he shall have abundance: but from him that hath not shall be taken away even that which he hath. **25:30** And cast ye the unprofitable servant into outer darkness: there shall be weeping and gnashing of teeth.

Brethren, we have been deceived and distracted into doing a business model work to bring in new folks our own way; instead of preaching a Gospel of Warning and Repentance so that God could use that message to call men to himself.

We have destroyed the quality of our message to reap a harvest of tares into our organizations who understand little and are willing to DO less. We are calling people TO US, instead of being a means for God to call people to HIMSELF!

This has resulted in a watered down, sin tolerating, man exalting system of idolatry and physical focus; which had quenched the oil of God's Spirit in us, so that our light is flickering out.

We are to diligently consider the law of God day and night and to always be focused on God and his whole Word. We are to FOLLOW God's Spirit as it leads us into further understanding, and we are to diligently seek more spiritual understanding through study and the active DOING of the Word of God.

We are NOT to get into a "I know it all spiritually and have need of nothing" attitude that is Laodicea (Rev 3:14-22): We are to grow through the use of the measure of the Holy Spirit and the talents [gifts of the Spirit] that God has given us.

Burying Our Talent

25:31 When the Son of man shall come in his glory, and all the holy angels with him, then shall he sit upon the throne of his glory: **25:32** And before him shall be gathered all nations: and he shall separate them one from another, as a shepherd divideth his sheep from the goats: **25:33** And he shall set the sheep on his right hand, but the goats on the left.

When Christ comes he shall judge between those who are faithful and productive servants and those who are complacent and self-satisfied, relying on their own false traditions and idols of men, having no zeal to live by every Word of God.

Jesus Christ will require an accounting from every person as to what they did with the measure of God's Spirit that was given to each of us.

A blessing on the faithful and zealous for God and his Word

25:34 Then shall the King say unto them on his right hand, Come, ye blessed of my Father, inherit the kingdom prepared for you from the foundation of the world [God's plan was made before the world was formed]: **25:35** For I was an hungred, and ye gave me meat: I was thirsty, and ye gave me drink: I was a stranger, and ye took me in: **25:36** Naked, and ye clothed me: I was sick, and ye visited me: I was in prison, and ye came unto me.

25:37 Then shall the righteous answer him, saying, Lord, when saw we thee an hungred, and fed thee? or thirsty, and gave thee drink? **25:38** When saw we thee a stranger, and took thee in? or naked, and clothed thee? **25:39** Or when saw we thee sick, or in prison, and came unto thee?

25:40 And the King [the Messiah the Christ] shall answer and say unto them, Verily I say unto you, **Inasmuch as ye have done it unto one of the least of these my brethren, ye have done it unto me.**

This is speaking in metaphors and is talking about BOTH physical and spiritual service to God the Father, Jesus Christ and the flock of God.

You elders, Do you feed the flock with the spiritual meat of sound doctrine in due season? Do you teach the way to peace, harmony and unity with God? Do you teach the way INTO God's Kingdom and eternal life?

Or do you keep the sheep OUT of the Kingdom by teaching them to commit idolatry and put men first? Do you teach men to tolerate sin? Or teach people to allow and actually teach to compromise with God's Word? Do you keep people OUT of God's Kingdom by teaching rejection of parts of scripture, spiritual complacency and lukewarmness for God's Word?

Do you teach repentance and rebuke sin, or do you tolerate sin to play politics to be popular and look like a nice guy?

If you rebuke sin, you may offend some, yet you may also save a life if the sinner repents! Which is more important to God?

When he comes; Jesus who many falsely claim will tolerate sin, will reject these wicked men, today's religious leaders, elders and brethren who persecute those zealous to live by every Word of God: and Jesus Christ will cast the wicked into damnation unless they sincerely repent.

25:41 Then shall he say also unto them on the left hand, Depart from me, ye cursed, into everlasting fire, prepared for the devil and his angels: **25:42** For I was an hungred, and ye gave me no meat: I was thirsty, and ye gave me no drink: **25:43** I was a stranger, and ye took me not in: naked, and ye clothed me not: sick, and in prison, and ye visited me not.

25:44 Then shall they also answer him, saying, Lord, when saw we thee an hungred, or athirst, or a stranger, or naked, or sick, or in prison, and did not minister unto thee? **25:45** Then shall he answer them, saying, Verily I say unto you, Inasmuch as ye did it not to one of the least of these, ye did it not to me.

25:46 And these [the unrepentant wicked who are not zealous to learn and to live by every Word of God] shall go away into everlasting punishment: but the righteous into life eternal.

Jude

Jude 1

Jude 1:1 Jude, the servant of Jesus Christ, and brother of James [the younger brother of Jesus], to them that are sanctified by God the Father, and preserved in Jesus Christ, and called:

Jude is directly addressing the Sanctified, the Set Apart Called Out of the New Covenant!

This Jude is the brother of James and both are the brothers of Jesus. Jude, James and Joses were the physical sons of Mary (Mat 13:55) and knew and were closer to Jesus Christ than any others.

1:2 Mercy unto you, and peace, and love, be multiplied.

1:3 Beloved, when I gave all diligence to write unto you of the common salvation, **it was needful for me to write unto you, and exhort you that ye should earnestly contend for the faith** [we are to fight for the truth of the sound doctrine of every Word of God] **which was once delivered unto the saints** [in the Holy Scriptures].

Jude tells us that we must earnestly contend for, and to VIGOROUSLY FIGHT FOR, the sound doctrine of Holy Scripture; especially in this latter day when love of the truth has grown cold.

Our faith and salvation are under very strong and subtle attack.

We need to remember Satan's subtlety in the garden where sin was made so desirable in appearance and the logic to partake of it seemed so reasonable, that Eve was tempted to obey Satan [to believe and trust Satan], instead of obeying and having faith and trusting in God.

Those who do not please God by putting God first in all things and who are not diligent to learn and to LIVE BY EVERY WORD of GOD: are demonstrating by their actions that they love worldliness more than they love godliness, and they will be judged by their works.

Our faith in God and the Word of Almighty God the Father is under attack!

Our faith and zeal to live by every Word of God is being attacked through the temptation to take the easy way; through the temptation to sit back and let others work out our salvation for us; through the temptation to just sit back, blindly follow and depend on the institution, or the leader; instead of making a personal effort to grow in knowledge, understanding and godliness by diligently studying and faithfully living by every Word of God.

We are being tempted to follow someone or some organization instead of being diligently faithful to our God. "Just do what the elder says and you have it made" is the mantra of the day. Personal responsibility has been replaced with relying on men instead of relying on the God of Our Salvation and our personal relationship with him.

We have been warned of this TEST from ancient times; which test is intended to see if we are fit for the resurrection to eternal life!

1:4 For there are **certain men crept in unawares, who were before of old ordained** to this condemnation, ungodly men, turning the grace [Turning the mercy of God for the sincerely repentant into a license to continue in sin.] of our God into lasciviousness [license or permission to tolerate sin] and denying the only Lord God [Denying the authority of the Word of God, by justifying sin.], and our Lord Jesus Christ.

It was ordained from the beginning that God would allow wicked men to enter into the congregations to TEST his people. Ungodly wicked men who would pervert the grace of God into a license to continue in sin. Men who would say that "God is love and he will forgive us if we fudge on what we do on the Sabbath or compromise with God's Word; for he understands and loves us." Who teach: "Yes keep the commandments, but tolerate sin as well." Who teach the lie that once baptized we enter a state of grace where willful sins are tolerated.

Yes, God is love; therefore he will NOT excuse or tolerate continued sin.

Yes, God is love and he will rejoice at every sinner who truly repents and CHANGES his ways, becoming zealously diligent to live by every Word of God.

God loves the sinner and that is precisely why he will NOT tolerate sin; because sin destroys the sinner whom God loves.

The Eternal is sifting his people!

Jesus Christ wants to know who he can trust to enthusiastically obey him and God the Father; regardless of all temptations to do otherwise. God is watching us and selecting those who HE wants to be a part of a faithful, loving, cooperative, supportive, and yes obedient wife, for Jesus Christ.

God the Father and the Son want to know if they can trust us: Will we love and cherish them beyond all else, and above anyone and anything else?

The Pearl of Great Price is well worth fighting against wickedness and contending for, sacrificing for, and even suffering for! We are to be like Daniel's friends who said: Our God can save us; and if he chooses not to save us physically; we shall gladly die serving him and we will serve NO other (Dan 3:16)!

1:5 I will therefore put you in remembrance, though ye once knew this, how that **the Lord, having saved the people out of the land of Egypt, afterward destroyed them that believed not.**

We have forgotten God's Great Power and his Mighty Strength, and we make excuses for our sins instead of relying on that Great Power to deliver us from bondage to sin.

It seems to be easier for us to make excuses for our sins than it is to have FAITH in the power of the "Mighty One Who Inhabits Eternity!"

We have been focusing on our troubles and on the men and organizations that we adore as our idols and we have lost sight of our Great God! We have been zealous for corporate idols, and we have not been focusing on the Eternal!

We have obeyed our corporate leaders as if they were speaking with God's mouth; and we have lost sight of God. We have allowed men and corporations to come between us and God the Father, the Mighty King of the Universe and so we have lost our faith in him.

These men have used the word "God" to get brethren to focus on themselves and to aggrandize and enrich themselves; or to teach their own words and ways in place of God's sound doctrine! They have not focused the brethren on the Eternal: Therefore we have lost our faith in God and our faith is in others.

We buy food and drink on Sabbath because some man said this sin was alright. Is man God that we should obey men and not the Holy Scriptures? Will some man judge us in place of Almighty God who judges us out of God's Word?

> **Acts 4:19** But Peter and John answered and said unto them, Whether it be right in the sight of God to hearken unto you more than unto God, judge ye.

Jude 1:6 And the angels which kept not their first estate, but left their own habitation, he hath reserved in everlasting chains under darkness unto the judgment of the great day.

1:7 Even as Sodom and Gomorrha, and the cities about them in like manner, giving themselves over to fornication [pornea includes all disloyalty including spiritual disloyalty against God the Father and our espoused Husband, Jesus Christ], and going after strange flesh [Following after the false traditions of men and not following the whole Word of God the Father and our espoused Husband, Jesus Christ.], are set forth for an example, suffering the vengeance of eternal fire.

These physical sins are a type of our spiritual adulteries against our LORD by following others and tolerating false ways!

1:8 Likewise also these filthy dreamers defile the flesh [defiling ourselves, the spiritual Temple of God, with sins], despise dominion [we despise God's Word by rejecting large portions of it to go our own ways], and speak evil of dignities.

Speaking evil of dignities refers to attacking godly persons for their zeal to learn and keep the whole Word of God.

They lie saying that "we obey God not because we have to, but because WE want to;" making us sovereign and God subject to our whims; thereby deceiving the brethren away from any zeal to live by God's Word; when the Word of God is Absolutely BINDING. God's Word is absolutely binding and if we go contrary to any part of God's Word we shall surely perish.

These Antichrist liars are leading the brethren to destruction while falsely claiming to be ministers of God!

These deceitful workers try to lead us into compromising with God's Word and into all manner of sin beginning with the IDOLATRY of exalting themselves. These wicked persons pay lip service to God while despising the dominion [authority] of God the Father and speaking evil of those who are diligent in serving the ALMIGHTY ONE!

1:9 Yet Michael the archangel, when contending with the devil he disputed about the body of Moses, durst not bring against him a railing accusation, but said, The Lord rebuke thee.

1:10 But these speak evil of those things which they know not [attacking the sound doctrine of the truth of God]: but what they know naturally, as brute beasts [they corrupt themselves by following the false and ignorant doctrines of men], in those things they corrupt themselves.

1:11 Woe unto them! for they have gone in the way of Cain, and ran greedily after the error of Balaam for reward, and perished in the gainsaying of Core.

These three things are examples of self-seeking and a willingness to pervert the truth for personal gain. Today how many elders remain where they are and tolerate evil for the sake of their pay cheques and positions?

These wicked false teachers would destroy the righteous, those who are zealous for God's Word; just like Cain killed righteous Abel.

They would lust after reward, seeking personal gain in wealth and power; as did Balaam.

They would rebel against the Mediator of the New Covenant just as Korah rebelled against the mediator of the Mosaic Covenant; seeking to exalt themselves as mediators of the New Covenant to come between the people and God in place of our High Priest Jesus Christ.

1:12 These are spots [of sinfulness] in your feasts of charity, when they feast with you, feeding themselves without fear: clouds they are without water [Appearing godly but not having the substance of true godliness, not having the Holy Spirit, and without any true godliness. They are high pressure salesmen and con men; who steal your means and your crown.], carried about of winds; trees whose fruit withereth, without fruit, twice dead, plucked up by the roots;

1:13 Raging waves of the sea [they rise up and they will fall back to be gone forever, like the waves of the sea (if they do not wholeheartedly repent)], foaming out their own shame; wandering stars, to whom is reserved the blackness of darkness for ever.

These deceivers appear as one of us, while they attempt to subvert us. They eat with us and observe Feasts with us, fearlessly fellowshiping with us; and they are seen as leaders among us, yet they are sons of wickedness sent by Satan to deceive us and allowed by God to TEST us.

God is TESTING US NOW! To see if we will follow charismatic false teachers or if we will be loyal to HIM!

> **Deuteronomy 13:1** If there arise among you a prophet, or a dreamer of dreams, and giveth thee a sign or a wonder,
>
> **13:2** And the sign or the wonder come to pass, whereof he spake unto thee, saying, **Let us go after other gods, which thou hast not known, and let us serve them;**
>
> **13:3 Thou shalt not hearken unto the words of that prophet, or that dreamer of dreams: for the Lord your God proveth you, to know whether ye love the Lord your God with all your heart and with all your soul.**

This is the Word of God which was prophesied for this latter day

Satan has brought in wicked men that deceitfully appear as angels of light.

With their "love, love" tolerate sin approach, they seduce the weak into a perverted view of Christ saying "he will surely overlook our willful sins and forgive us because God's Word is impossible for us to obey so we need not be over righteous or zealous for God's Word."

This is a damnable lie of Antichrist for we can overcome through the Holy Spirit of God dwelling in us. God will surely correct those who tolerate and justify any sin and if they fail to repent, God will destroy such wicked men.

Jude 1:14 And Enoch also, the seventh from Adam, prophesied of these, saying, Behold, the Lord cometh with ten thousands of his saints, **1:15 To execute judgment upon all, and to convince all that are ungodly among them of all their ungodly deeds which they have ungodly committed,**

and of all their hard speeches [deceitful words] which ungodly sinners have spoken against him.

The words of these men are against the Word of God.

1:16 These [wicked deceivers] are murmurers, complainers [Complaining against the Word of God, saying it is too hard for us to be zealous to obey God, and they pervert the Word of God for their own false ways.], walking after their own lusts; and their mouth speaketh great swelling words, having men's persons in admiration because of advantage [they are flatterers of men and not followers of God].

People have become respecters of persons rather than respecters of God, seeking personal advantage; full of pride in themselves or their group, or leader; rather than full of devotion for the Eternal.

They are self-willed and murmur against God's Word saying that "it is impossible to keep, so God will not judge us for failing to do so," thus encouraging the brethren to remain in sin.

1:17 But, beloved, remember ye the words which were spoken before of the apostles of our Lord Jesus Christ;

Jude reveals that he is writing directly to us, in these latter days.

1:18 How that they told you there should be mockers **in the last time**, who should walk after their own ungodly lusts.

In today's latter day spiritual Ekklesia many mock those who seek to diligently live by every Word of God.

11:9 These be they who separate themselves [from the truth of sound doctrine], sensual [worldly], having not the Spirit .

They have a spirit, but it is NOT the Spirit of God, it is the spirit of Antichrist.

Men who reject any zeal to live by every Word of God in favor of their own false traditions, whether they call themselves Pope's, Evangelists, Apostles, Prophets, Elders or Leaders, or by whatever title; are just sons of wickedness, slipped in by Satan to lead astray the unwary and TEST God's people. They are sensual [carnal and not subject to God]; playing power politics and seeking personal advantage, authority, wealth and power.

They mock the zealous and condemn those faithful to live by every Word of God.

They consider people who are loyal to God to be a threat, and they condemn the faithful for obeying Almighty God and for not following the false traditions of men.

Jude's instructions to the godly

1:20 But ye, beloved, building up yourselves on your most holy faith [We are to build our lives on the solid foundation of the whole Word of God.], praying in the Holy Ghost,

1:21 Keep yourselves in the love of God [we must love God enough to passionately live by every Word of God], looking for the mercy of our Lord Jesus Christ unto eternal life.

> **I John 2:3** And **hereby we do know that we know him, if we keep his commandments.**
>
> **2:4** **He that saith, I know him, and keepeth not his commandments, is a liar, and the truth is not in him.**
>
> **2:5** **But whoso keepeth his word, in him verily is the love of God perfected:** hereby know we that we are in him.
>
> **2:6** He that saith he abideth in him ought himself also so to walk [live], even as he walked [lived, lives].

Jude 1:22 And of some [The faithful are to have compassion for the sincerely repentant.] have compassion, making a difference:

We can make a difference through teaching all people to live by every Word of God in the hope that they might be saved.

1:23 And others save with fear, pulling them out of the fire [saving people by teaching the entire Word of God and strongly rebuking sin and rebellion against God's Word]; hating even the garment spotted by the flesh.

We are to be filled with the faith of God and we are to be full of the Holy Spirit that empowers us to overcome Satan and sin. We are to have compassion on others by teaching the truth of every Word of God and rejoicing with those that sincerely repent.

We are to loath sin to the point where we would despise even a cloth that appeared to have a connection to any sin or spiritual uncleanness. We are to work to save our brethren; warning them of the perils of sin and delivering them through zealously warning and exhorting them to passionate faithfulness to God.

1:24 Now unto him that is able to keep you from falling, and to present you faultless before the presence of his glory with exceeding joy,

It is the power of God's Spirit which strengthens us and keeps us from falling; that Spirit is given to those who are faithful to live by every Word of God (Acts 5:32).

Let no man deceive you, neither God the Father nor Jesus Christ will tolerate any sin.

> **Ezekiel 18:20** The Soul that sinneth, it SHALL die.
>
> **1 Corinthians 3:17 If any man defile the temple of God** [justify committing sin], **him shall God destroy; for the temple of God is holy, which temple ye are.**

Visit Our Website

theshininglight.info

www.ingramcontent.com/pod-product-compliance
Lightning Source LLC
Chambersburg PA
CBHW081348230426
43667CB00017B/2761